Between Femininity and Feminism

Between Femininity and Feminism

Colonial and Postcolonial Perspectives on Care

Kanchana Mahadevan

with a Foreword by
Veena Poonacha

Indian Council of Philosophical Research
New Delhi

PRINTWORLD
Publishers of Indian Traditions

Cataloging in Publication Data — DK
[Courtesy: D.K. Agencies (P) Ltd. <docinfo@dkagencies.com>]

Kanchana Mahadevan, 1964-
Between femininity and feminism : colonial and postcolonial perspectives on care / Kanchana Mahadevan.
p. cm.
Includes bibliographical references (p.) and index.
ISBN 13: 9788124607305

1. Caring — Moral and ethical aspects — History. 2. Feminism Moral and ethical aspects — History. 3. Feminist theory — India — History. 4. Feminist theory — England — History. 5. Ramabai Sarasvati, Pandita, 1858-1922. 6. Wollstonecraft, Mary, 1759-1797. I. Title.

DDC 155.3330954 23

ISBN 13: 978-81-246-0730-5

First published in India, 2014 Print run : 550 copies

Published by:
INDIAN COUNCIL OF PHILOSOPHICAL RESEARCH
Darshan Bhawan, 36 Tughlakabad Institutional Area
Mehrauli Badarpur Road, New Delhi - 110 062

and

D.K. PRINTWORLD (P) LTD.
Regd. Office: "Vedaśrī", F-395, Sudarshan Park
(Metro Station: Ramesh Nagar), New Delhi – 110 015
Phones: (011) 2545 3975, 2546 6019; *Fax*: (011) 2546 5926
e-mail: indology@dkprintworld.com
Website: www.dkprintworld.com

Printed by : D.K. Printworld (P) Ltd. New Delhi

In memory of
my parents

Foreword

THIS volume, *Between Femininity and Feminism: Colonial and Postcolonial Perspectives on Care*, is an important addition to the growing body of feminist interrogation of mainstream disciplines. Located at the boundaries of Western and Indian philosophical traditions, the volume provides fresh insights into a fundamental dilemma of feminist moral philosophy on the gendering of human identity and the ethics of care. The positing of this dilemma in feminist philosophical traditions can be traced to the rise of feminist activism in the 1970s. Feminist philosophies grew out of the twin compulsions of understanding women's subordination and determining political strategies.

Challenging some of the foundational assumptions of the dominant paradigms that have informed mainstream disciplines, feminist philosophies have sought to interject women's experiences within these theories. By the 1980s these tentative attempts to delineate women's lived experiences within the existing theoretical paradigms soon gave way to criticism of the epistemological traditions of thinking in hierarchical–binary opposition, in terms of the mind–body, nature–culture, reason–feeling and private–public divide (Jaggar and Bordo 1992: 1-10). These epistemological questions challenged the seeming divide in philosophical traditions between the inner self and the external world. They critiqued the tools of articulation, interpretation and analysis that substantiated male standpoint as the norm (Friedman 2000: 205-24). To overcome some of the limits to the traditional mind-centred approach to knowledge, feminist theories became increasingly self-reflexive.

This criticism of mainstream theories does not indicate that feminism is not without its own tensions. Like all complex schools of philosophy, feminism too encapsulates diverse viewpoints. Thus, a concern for women's autonomy and independence may lead to the conceptualization of theories in terms that do not recognize human interdependence. Conversely, a concern to stress the capacities of women for caring and empathy with others may lead to the conceptualization of such capacities in terms that offer women little space to meet the needs of the individual self (Grimshaw 1986: 10-15). As Friedman (2000) argues, despite the evidence of a dilemma between moral autonomy and the ethics of care there are certain key principles in feminist ethics. Feminist ethics (as other branches of feminist theoretical engagements) is grounded in a commitment to end oppression, subordination and exploitation of women. Therefore, it has focused on restrictive silhouettes of women's lives (such as marriage and motherhood, as well as discrimination in employment and entitlements) — precisely those areas neglected by traditional debates on ethics.

The Theoretical Frames of the Book

The theoretical frames of *Between Femininity and Feminism: Colonial and Postcolonial Perspectives* are located within these debates in feminist moral philosophy. The broad contours of the debate are triggered by Carol Gilligan's empirical studies on the correlation between gender and ethics. Gilligan suggests that men are characteristically concerned with substantive moral matters of justice, rights, autonomy and individuation, while women are concerned with care and personal relationships. The difference in moral reasoning of men and women implies that men focus on abstract and universalist principles, whereas women are concerned with the immediate and the particular. Gilligan's ideas contributed significantly to the conceptualization of women's selfhood within the ethics of care. Along with many other feminists, defined as radical–cultural feminists, her work emphasized that women's distinct traits and moral reasoning were not necessarily inferior to those of men. The real problem is that society has failed to appreciate women's ethics of care. These revolutionary concepts challenged the prevailing utilitarian and Kantian frames in the 1970s and triggered a search for alternative theory of care ethics, highlighting the moral importance of caring practices. Despite the revolutionary potential for development of an alternative paradigm on the ethics of care, there were voices of protest against such a conceptualization of women's ethics: for an ethics of care based on women's experiences as a primary caregiver in the family could reify prevailing differences of gender.

The argument is that women's orientation to care and personal relationships reflected their existing stereotypes. It was, therefore, morally problematic; apart from restricting women's lives to their traditional roles, it supported compulsory heterosexuality and justified the denial of women's search for autonomy and selfhood. Gilligan's study has also been faulted for the limitations of the sampling. It is argued that since the sample was restricted to white, middle-class women, the findings have limited applicability. The study does not reflect either the class or the ethnic differences in women's lives. Counterpoised to this ethics of care is the notion of moral autonomy. The latter is the extent to which an individual is able to behave and live in accordance with the values and commitments that she or he considers as his or her own. Yet moral autonomy (which requires a high level of understanding and decision-making power) is also not without limitations: for it does not necessarily recognize the nature of human interconnectedness and the context in which choices are exercised.

Mahadevan adds a new dimension to the debate by specifically asking whether philosophical concepts are gendered, and if so, is there a distinct feminist mode of moral reasoning? To find answers, the book examines the works of philosophers such as Mary Wollstonecraft, Simone de Beauvoir and Susan Moller Okin who have located their arguments within the liberal and existential philosophies. Subsequently, juxtaposing these arguments, with the alternative paradigm proposed by Gilligan, the book examines the possibility of a synthesis between the feminine ethics of care and the ideals of moral autonomy. Some of the questions Mahadevan raises are centred on whether ethics has a gender dimension. They specifically articulate the following dimension of the debate: can the "feminine" be defined? And if so, to what extent would the definition of the "feminine" become essentialist? Finally, can there be a fusion of the feminine and feminist within moral philosophy between care and the ideas of justice?

The important dimension that Mahadevan introduces into this debate is that of locating the question within colonial and postcolonial contexts in which these ideas have emerged. She argues that despite differences in their historical locations, there is a comparable concern for a women's moral autonomy comparable with the male ideals of autonomy. To substantiate this argument, she turns to the writings of Pandita Ramabai (in nineteenth- and early twentieth-century India — a colonized country) and Mary Wollstonecraft (in the eighteenth-century colonizing England). Subsequently, the discussion shifts to the twentieth-century postcolonial context and contemporary feminist discourse. In this discussion by drawing upon Maria Mies's writings, she interjects the exploitative postcolonial relationship between the first world and Indian feminists. Apart from the economic exploitation that exists between the first world and the developing nations, Mies has also critiqued de Beauvoir's concept of autonomy. She has argued that this highly individualist concept of autonomy is exploitative of Indian women.

The importance of this book is Mahadevan's expertise in Western and non-Western philosophical traditions; it also grows out of her commitment to an interdisciplinary philosophical enquiry. This attempt to analyse philosophical questions within a specific historical, cultural and socio-economic context reveals Mahadevan's feminist consciousness — a consciousness that remains a refreshing alternative to the overarching truth claims of many dominant philosophical traditions. Additionally, by bringing together Western and non-Western feminist voices, the book creates an inclusive space for philosophical engagements in a changing global context. The usefulness of this book to disciplines of philosophy, social sciences and women's studies cannot be underestimated. It opens doors for a broad-based philosophical enquiry into the theory and praxis of women's struggles against all forms of discriminations.

Veena Poonacha
Professor and Director
Research Centre for Women's Studies
SNDT Women's University, Mumbai

Preface

THE steady and diverse feminist intervention in the philosophical canon has posed provocative questions regarding the status of philosophical concepts and language. Can gender-neutral concepts convey women's experiences? Should they, instead, be replaced by a womancentric vocabulary? Is the use of male pronouns as indicative of all human beings responsible for the discriminatory treatment of women? What is the relation between language and thought? Following Moira Gatens, classification, feminist philosophers such as Mary Wollstonecraft, Susan Moller Okin and Simone de Beauvoir have intervened in the male philosophical tradition of Jean Jacques Rousseau, Thomas Paine, John Rawls and Jean Paul Sartre, from the point of view of women's experiences (Gatens 1991: 90). However, they saw feminist philosophy as accommodating women's themes within the existing philosophical vocabulary of reason, rights, freedom and justice. Indeed, Wollstonecraft and de Beauvoir even used the mainstream male-specific language as a universal referent while writing about women. Alternatively, philosophers such as Carol Gilligan argued for a distinct feminist philosophical vocabulary based on feminine embodiment, feeling, family and relationships, emerging from women's lives. Difference, according to this view, is the only way to remedy the patriarchal bias of concepts. This book engages with the contribution of these feminist thinkers to examine their transformation of the activity of philosophy itself in the course of its contact with the feminine. It does so by exploring the tension between their feminist ideals and feminine virtues. It also endeavours to show how feminist philosophy brings about a greater awareness of philosophy's relation to history, culture and other disciplines. Consequently, feminist philosophy cannot but help be an interdisciplinary activity inscribed within the social dimension. Further, its interdisciplinarity also opens up an intersectionality, where Western and non-Western philosophical debates and responses overlap. Hence, this book also interrogates the relevance of Western feminist thought to non-Western contexts.

The struggle between femininity and feminism in the philosophical corpus of feminist thinkers such as Ramabai, Wollstonecraft, Gilligan, Okin and de Beauvoir is examined with reference to the concept of care. This book takes pioneering feminism during the colonial period as its starting point, and moves to its second wave during the postcolonial period to examine the trajectory of the concept of care. There are several reasons for choosing these periods to discuss feminist philosophy. Feminist consciousness itself is reflected through women writing critically about patriarchy and politics, during these periods. Further, the intersection between Western feminism and non-Western contexts can be explicitly discerned during the periods of pioneering feminism and the second wave. The former with its overlap between life and writing, and the latter's overtly theoretical concerns are diverse ways of engaging with philosophy from the perspective of "lived experience".[1] By inserting their activist autobiographies in philosophical reflection, pioneering feminists opened the possibility of theorizing the concept "woman". Although second wave feminists do not adopt an explicitly activist or autobiographical mode, by adopting the term "woman" in their theorization, they subscribe to intersection between the personal and the philosophical. The latter intersection is

---

[1] This phrase is derived from Moi (2005: 63).

explicitly theoretical, although it emerges from years of activism. Since the domain of lived experience is heterogeneous, both pioneering and second wave feminist thought have contemporary relevance.

Women, whether Western or non-Western, do not form a homogeneous category. Hence, this book explores the extent to which Ramabai, Wollstonecraft, Gilligan, Okin and de Beauvoir can dialogue with contemporary women. The relationship between these thinkers and their arguments, which is not viewed from a chronological point of view, is conceptually connected. Hence, although de Beauvoir initiated the second wave in the late 1940s, this book engages with her writing towards the conclusion. This is because there has been a proliferation of scholarship on de Beauvoir in recent years, subsequent to the lessons that have been learnt from Gilligan and Okin (Moi 2005; Deutscher 2008). This scholarship also suggests that de Beauvoir, despite her avowals, does not merely apply Sartre's philosophical concepts to women. Moreover, some of the problems with de Beauvoir's position have been attributed to the inadequate translation of her *Second Sex* by H.M. Parshley in 1953, which consisted of several deletions from and misinterpretations of the original French text (Moi 2002; Glazer 2004). The much awaited new translation by Constance Borde and Sheila Malovany-Chevallier that was published in 2009, opens the possibility of reading de Beauvoir's views on feminine care in ways that could integrate them with autonomy and freedom.[2]

---

[2] Parshley was a zoologist who did not do justice to the philosophical aspects of de Beauvoir's work. Malovany-Chevallier and Borde have brought back the philosophical nuances in de Beauvoir's text (2012a). Interestingly, they have four cook books to their credit, revealing against the grain that the feminine is not an obstacle to philosophy. On the contrary, Malovany-Chevallier and Borde have rightly observed that →

In the course of exploring the arguments of key women philosophers, this book addresses questions such as: What is meant by femininity? Can one define the feminine at all? Can an appeal to the feminine be a feminist gesture? How does the feminist feminine differ from the patriarchal feminine? Can male philosophical frameworks be employed in feminist directions? Can the feminist appropriation of the feminine be reconciled with moral and political values that have been traditionally perceived as masculine, such as justice and autonomy? What is the place of Western feminism in global contexts?

While grappling with the above set of questions, this book investigates the shifts from colonial to postcolonial periods in the feminist approaches to care. Thus, it argues that despite the diversity of their locations the pioneering feminists, Ramabai in the nineteenth-century colonized India, and Wollstonecraft in the colonizing England of the eighteenth century, denounced femininity and care, in spite of which they invoked it in their arguments for gender equality. This is because they responded to the elaborate construction of the feminine as domestic, in which the British empire's interpretation of care as sympathy and an antagonistic Indian nationalism had their stake during the colonial period. Hence, at the incipient stage of the movement, feminists distanced themselves from care and its related meanings given the patronizing undertones that it carried in terms of empire and nationalism. In contrast, the postcolonial shift towards theory in the twentieth century saw feminine care being introduced by Gilligan as a critical concept, against the lacunae in traditional moral philosophy. The articulation of care through Gilligan's feminist lens differs from care in Ramabai's and

→ occupations such as cooking, traditionally associated with women in the domestic space, tend to get masculinized in the public domain (2012b).

Wollstonecraft's prefeminist phases or in their feminist defence of motherhood. Gilligan advocates the feminine virtue of care in a non-patriarchal and postcolonial context, unlike the patriarchal and colonial inflections that were later critiqued by Ramabai and Wollstonecraft during their feminist periods.

This book also investigates the possibility of integrating Gilligan's feminine care with the political concepts of justice and autonomy following Okin. Further, since Okin does not adequately dwell on the central concept of freedom, this book returns to de Beauvoir in a postcolonial context to explore the extent to which her notion of autonomy and freedom can accommodate care. This return is also an endeavour to address the theoretical relationship between Western and Indian feminism, in the light of the criticism made by Maria Mies that the bourgeois Western context of de Beauvoir's autonomy, makes it exploitative of Indian women. Thus, this book explores the debate on care and autonomy both from the perspective of feminism's internal debate and from the international point of view of privilege among women in a globalized world.

This book adopts an added task of intervening in the conceptual categories of Western feminism in an attempt to blur the strict binary between Indian and Western traditions. It argues that such a binary is not feasible in the Indian context because feminist consciousness was explicitly articulated through Ramabai at the interface of Indian nationalism and British colonization, introducing Western concepts to Indian feminism. Moreover, in recent times Mies's critique has opened up the debate regarding Western feminism's hierarchical relation with local feminisms such as those in India. Through an examination of the conceptual schemes of Western feminism in the Indian context, this book hopes to democratize the theoretical terrain of feminist philosophy.

There is a large body of Indian scholarship on gender and feminism in the disciplines of literature and social sciences. Economic, literary, legal and sociological debates on feminist themes continue to increase. However, philosophical treatments of feminism in the Indian context are few and far between, though this context provides a rich field for philosophizing gender. Philosophy can step in to foreground the analytic, hermeneutic, critical and normative issues raised by introducing gender, since much of the work done on gender in the empirical fields are of a descriptive nature. On her visit to India in the 1990s, Martha Nussbaum noted:

> . . . that women in India do extremely well in the academy, better than in any other nation I know, in terms of occupying top positions in a variety of fields. On the other hand, philosophy is an underdeveloped and low-prestige field, and none of my feminist contacts was a philosopher.
>
> —1998: 785, n. 51

However, this statement overlooks the rich debates in colonial and postcolonial Indian philosophy in its harsh verdict on the state of philosophy in India.[3] Moreover, Nussbaum's first person empiricist cognition of feminist philosophers hastily overlooks Roop Rekha Verma's contribution to both activism and philosophy. Verma's significant essay on personhood and feminism (1995) is published in the anthology that Nussbaum has edited herself. The growth of feminist interest in the Indian academy is evidenced by the publication of two major insightful books on feminist philosophy in India, since

---

[3] Kapur has a similar critique of Nussbaum's neglect of postcolonial feminist theorizing in India (2012: 260-65). Interestingly, Nussbaum in the context of her critique of Butler's post-structuralism gestures in the direction of the irrelevance of theory for Indian feminism, which in her view has only practical focus (1999). As Kapur observes, Nussbaum tends to be oversimplistic in the Indian context (2012).

Nussbaum made her remark. Shefali Moitra's book *Feminist Thought: Androcentrism, Communication and Objectivity* (2002) examines the theme of objectivity in knowledge from the point of view of the feminist challenge. Meena Kelkar's and Deepti Gangavane's anthology, *Feminism in Search of an Identity: The Indian Context* (2003) is a much-needed critical and deconstructive study of the Indian philosophical tradition from a feminist point of view.[4] The following work on care, from colonial and postcolonial philosophical perspectives, hopes to be an additional voice on feminist moral philosophy from the intersections between Indian and Western thought, society and politics.

This book is divided into two parts, which are preceded by an introduction and followed by an afterword. The first part is on the emergence of the care debate in the colonial context in India and England. It comprises two chapters. The second part that has three chapters, examines care as a critical theoretical concept during the postcolonial period. The introduction, chapters and afterword, address the paradox of the tension between the feminine and feminist moments of the care debate. Each chapter foregrounds a specific feminist thinker, to examine her relation to the feminine virtue of care in the course of articulating a feminist position. However, the thinkers are situated in the context of the debate on care, rather than in chronological histories or as compartmentalized individuals. Thus, this book does not endeavour to bring out the epochal history of feminist theory and practice in Western and Indian contexts. Rather, it moves in and out of these contexts to explore the relationship between feminist aspirations and feminine care. The relevance of the care debate to the Indian context is delineated in each of these chapters. The thinkers have been selected from colonial and postcolonial

[4] Contributions from feminist perspectives also inform Indian philosophy journals.

Indian and Western perspectives to follow the trajectory of the feminist espousal of freedom and its critique from the feminine perspective of care.

The introduction, "Philosophizing as Women", discusses the motivations, context and scope for entering into the debate on feminist ethics of care. It shows how the negligible presence of women in traditional philosophy and feminist criticism mandates a discussion of women and philosophy. This discussion also explores the implications of feminist philosophy in terms of interdisciplinarity and intersectionality. It outlines the main issues that would form the focus of the chapters that follow.

The first chapter, "Pandita Ramabai and Feminism in Colonial India: Tradition, Modernity and Domestic Nurture", examines the conflict between the feminine and feminist points of view, through the historical context, life and writings of Pandita Ramabai (1858–1922). This chapter elaborates the explicit emergence of mainstream Indian feminine identity as the domestic nurturer in a complex vortex of tradition and modernity, through dialogue with colonial history. It argues that the tropes of both Indian and Western philosophy and politics frame debates regarding culture and language in the colonial context, paving the way for raising the woman's question. It proceeds to sketch the simultaneous rise of feminist consciousness in the struggle with the feminine, by locating Ramabai within women's philosophical history.

The second chapter, "Feminine/Feminist Gestures in Colonial England: Mary Wollstonecraft", overviews Mary Wollstonecraft's (1759–1797) philosophy and its overlaps with Ramabai's activism. It explores the development of her feminist argument through a struggle with femininity, in the context of her critique of the British empire and engagement with radicalism. The discussion concludes by locating her within the legacy of women philosophers such as Hypatia and St. Teresa.

The third chapter, "The Ethics of Care: Carol Gilligan", shifts to the theoretical concept of feminine care in Carol Gilligan's (1936) feminist ethics. It also examines this concept from the point of view of postcolonial India. Gilligan responds to the traditional exclusion of women's experience from ethical theory by bringing in the feminine dimension. The discussion explores the extent to which feminine cultural traits such as interdependence, community and nurture under the rubric of "care" are transformed when they are upheld with a feminist sensitivity following Gilligan. The conclusion argues for extending Gilligan's insight by informing care with justice.

The fourth chapter, "Integrating Justice and Care: Susan Okin", addresses Susan Okin's (1946–2004) attempt to develop the ethical insight of care by expanding it in the direction of justice, freedom and state. Hence, it explores her feminist critique and revision of Rawls's account of justice, in the course of integrating Gilligan's care ethics with the concepts of freedom and justice. In the light of some of Okin's suggestions for state intervention for a caring and just family, this chapter also examines the relationship between the family and the state from a gendered point of view, both in the West and in postcolonial India. It suggests that Okin's notion of individual autonomy should be re-thought in a non-individualistic way in the light of the conclusions that emerge from Gilligan's care perspective.

The fifth chapter entitled, "Rethinking Freedom and Care: Simone de Beauvoir", endeavours to fill the lacuna in Okin's integration of care and freedom with a suggestion for a non-individualist notion of freedom or autonomy, by turning to Simone de Beauvoir (1908-86). It also attempts to examine the debate between feminine care and feminist freedom to examine the relevance of Western feminism in the postcolonial global context. Hence, this chapter addresses the eco-feminist Maria Mies's suggestion that the notion of autonomy, advocated by

Western feminists such as de Beauvoir, be abandoned as a Western individualist ideal by women who are located in Bangladesh or India. Mies defends the feminine virtue of care from the perspective of the community as appropriate for non-Western feminism. This chapter argues that Mies overlooks de Beauvoir's phenomenological conception of the body as a situation, to which the feminine is contingently related, and the resources it provides for rethinking freedom in non-individualist ways relevant to non-Western women, as well.

The afterword, "Towards Global Feminisms", discusses the possibility of reading Western feminist thought from other locations, both critically and in a spirit of solidarity with global feminisms. Following Angela Davis, Chandra Talpade Mohanty and Gayatri Spivak, it argues that the problem of privilege among women has to be central to such a reading, so that the possibility of reading feminist philosophical texts in dialogue with contemporary global concerns is opened.

Contents

Foreword – Veena Poonacha vii

Preface xiii

Acknowledgement xxv

Introduction: Philosophizing as Women 1

Part 1
Colonial Perspectives

1. **Pandita Ramabai and Feminism in Colonial India: Tradition, Modernity and Domestic Nurture** 33

   The Construction of Indian Womanhood 34

   Ramabai's Feminist Voice 51

   Women in Indian Philosophy 63

2. **Feminine/Feminist Gestures in Colonial England: Mary Wollstonecraft** 73

   British Radicalism, Critique of Empire and Female Manners 74

   Intersecting Spaces: "Entangled" and "Embattled" 83

   Female Ancestry 92

Part 2
Postcolonial Contexts, Perspectives

3. **The Ethics of Care: Carol Gilligan** 105

Critique of Mainstream Ethics 107

The Perspective of Care 118

Care in Patriarchal and Colonial Contexts 123

4. Integrating Justice and Care: Susan Okin 142

Justice and Family: Critique of Rawls 143

A Feminist Reinterpretation of Rawls 147

Gender Justice: Liberalism and the Family 153

5. Rethinking Freedom and Care: Simone de Beauvoir 180

The Disquietitudes of Individualist Freedom 182

Relational Freedom, Embodied Situation and Ambiguity 192

Reproductive Freedom in Global Contexts 212

Afterword: *Towards Global Feminisms* 223

Bibliography 242

Index 264

Acknowledgement

WHILE working on this manuscript I have been fortunate to receive support, feedback and counsel, both at the institutional and individual levels. At the outset, I wish to put on record my gratitude to the Indian Council of Philosophical Research (ICPR), New Delhi for awarding me a research project on feminist philosophy from July 2008 to March 2011, on which this book is based. Many thanks are due to Mrinal Miri, Chairperson of ICPR and his team for supporting the publication of this research project. I thank ICPR officers, Mercy Helen and Arun Mishra, for their constant advice, assistance and patience in this endeavour. I acknowledge Godabarish Misra and Nirmalaya Chakraborti for their kind help during their respective tenures as Member Secretaries, ICPR.

I am obliged to the Indian Institute of Advanced Study, Shimla for providing a congenial work environment during a study visit. I am grateful to the staff of libraries at the Research Centre for Women's Studies, S.N.D.T.; the Asiatic Society; the Max Müller Bhavan and the University of Mumbai (Kalina and Fort Campuses) for providing access to their wide range of books and journals on women's studies and philosophy. Let me also place on record my sincere appreciation to the administrative staff at the Department of Philosophy, University of Mumbai for their kind assistance. Many thanks are due to Susheel K. Mittal and the editorial team at D.K. Printworld for their valuable assistance in copy-editing the text thoroughly.

In the course of writing this book, I have benefitted from conversations with Sharad Deshpande, Mary Fifield, Pradeep Gokhale, Biraj Mehta, Markar Melkonian and Kanchana Natarajan. Their contributions are whole-heartedly appreciated and acknowledged. I am grateful to Meera Mahadevan and Markar Melkonian for painstakingly reading the proof and making helpful suggestions, despite punishing schedules. My thanks to Prajakti Pai, Ashish Upadhyaya and Mahesh Ursekar for their timely help. I am grateful to my family for its unstinting care, while working on this project.

Needless to say, all the shortcomings in this book are entirely mine.

Introduction
Philosophizing as Women

ALTHOUGH feminist philosophers have situated philosophical concepts in contexts of gendered history for several decades now, this relation has not received enough attention to make it a part of the mainstream philosophical corpus. Across continua of epistemology, metaphysics, ethics and the like, those with an inclination to canonical philosophy treat the gendered roots of concepts as debatable and for most part as a non-issue.[1] Arguing that philosophical concepts are historical and gender-neutral, they envisage the traditional task of philosophy as one of either a non-sensuous contemplation of an ultimate reality, or of a sensuous apprehension of facts, both of which emphasize vision.[2] These preoccupations explain

1 The term "canon" is used to signify traditional philosophical texts that are routinely studied as a part of a history of philosophy curriculum. Such textbook philosophy spans several periods, the ancient, the modern and the contemporary. It also cuts across the Indo–Western divide. Thus, the writings of Plato, Aristotle, Rene Descartes, John Locke, Kauṭilya, Vivekananda, A.J. Ayer and Martin Heidegger (amongst others) can be classified as the canon. Among contemporary philosophers gender neutrality is upheld by those who follow the tradition like Susan Haack. Yet there have been arguments against gendered thinking from the non-canonical perspective as well, as the instance of Richard Rorty demonstrates. See Mahadevan (2008).

2 See for example Plato 1987d: 516b; Descartes 1951b: 180; Locke 1997: 326. For an overview of the supremacy of the ocular in Western philosophy, see Jay 1994: 21-82. Luce Irigaray →

why a cursory glance at some of the positions in ancient and modern philosophy would reveal the absence of any relation between women and philosophy. Vision as a foundation of objective distance (between the knower and the known) and clarity are commonly affirmed as central to knowledge in both Western and Indian philosophy.[3] Despite their epochal differences, Plato's ancient Greek perspective and Rene Descartes's modern approach are united in upholding attributes that depend on embodied and changing sense-perceptions to be misleading; they treat as essential, qualities that are accessible to the mind's eye.[4] In keeping with this approach, Plato for instance claims:

> . . . the body is the grave of the soul which may be thought to be buried in our present life, or again the index of the soul, because the soul gives indications to the body . . . the soul is suffering the punishment of sin, and that the body is an

→ critiques Plato's use of the visual metaphor in his allegory of the cave in his *Republic* as testimony to how a philosopher comes of age by passing from ignorance to knowledge from a feminist perspective (Irigaray 1985a: 245-364). For Irigaray, the cave in this analogy represents the womb, a web of embodiment and relationships, which can be accessed through touch. Hence, Plato's allegory is for her a metaphor of men leaving behind the domestic domain of women to attain the supremacy of knowledge.

3 Western and Indian traditions do not exhaust the canvas of philosophy as is well known. Afro–Asian philosophies have their own traditions and reconstructions. So do Latin American ones. However, given the constraints of space the present research work is confined to Western and Indian perspectives.

4 See Plato 1987d: 510-11; Descartes 1951a: 86-89; Locke 1997: 109-360. The atomists in ancient Greek philosophy also maintained a similar view by distinguishing between the inherent attributes of atoms such as shape, size and so forth, and their illusory combination based on human perception (Kirk and Raven 1957: 400-26).

> enclosure or prison in which the soul is incarcerated or kept safe . . . until the penalty is paid. — 1987c, 400c[5]

Descartes differs from Plato in not disparaging the body as sin and takes it as an ontologically relevant category in the spirit of modern science. He takes the body seriously but only as an extended substance — *res extensa* — that can be measured and thus he intellectualizes it (Descartes 1951a: 88). For Descartes the philosopher who cultivates a calm mind that is not clouded by passions or emotions can see the essential properties of both soul and body clearly and distinctly with a rational eye (ibid.: 81-82). The Indian tradition analogously terms the classical systems of philosophy as *darśana* (Joshi 2004: 1; Kelkar 2003: 101), which " . . . not only implies knowledge but direct experience of reality" but is also separated from the body (Kelkar 2003: 103).[6]

The celebration of vision, admonition of bodily change and immortality of the soul are recurrent themes that provide the foundation for traditional conceptions of moral philosophy.[7] Thus, Plato's ethics delineates the virtues of courage, temperance, wisdom, justice and piety as unified by their genus good (1987b: 329d, 330ab). For him, virtues comprise performance of one's function in accordance with

---

5 Plato also maintains that "Of the men who came into the world, those who were cowards or led unrighteous lives may with reason be supposed to have changed into the nature of women in the second generation" (1987e: 91a). See Kamtekar (2002) and Mahadevan (2010) for a detailed discussion of the gendered dimension.

6 Since the focus of this discussion is in the context of the Western conceptual framework, the few references to Indian philosophy are only by way of hinting at affinities. A detailed debate in the context of the Indian canon is available in Kelkar and Gangavane (2003).

7 As Plato implies in the *Timaeus* the body can only be a recreation topic for philosophers (1987e: 17a, 20c).

the three parts of the soul (the appetites, the spirits and reason), where the body has no role to play. It is through virtuous activity — of the soul — that an individual from the empirical world can attain the good, which is the *telos* of human activity in the world of forms (1987d: 353). Plato's dialogue *Charmides* discusses wisdom and temperance as virtues of the soul (1987a: 175e), while his *Republic* treats justice, as a disembodied activity that is valuable for its own sake and for its end in the good (1987d: 358). Thus, justice for him also has the task of preserving the order of the soul (upon which the world is modelled) and attaining the good. Plato's good is a goal in the world of forms, outside the domain of empirical experience and the body. Amongst the moderns, Immanuel Kant upheld the singular individual's freedom from bodily passions or what he terms as the "material" conditions of sensory "feeling" as the condition for the pursuit of duty (Kant 1956, §3). In a similar vein, in the context of Indian traditions such as Buddhism, Jainism and Yoga, moral action results when there is separation from bodily attachment.[8] One could keep adding to these examples which found morality on the metaphysics of disembodiment and epistemology of vision.

Moral philosophy is connected to the normative assumptions of epistemology and metaphysics. A key metaphysical assumption, of the insignificance of the body based on the epistemological disrepute of transitory senses, affirms the normative worth of the soul. This has led to an ethics of disembodiment, which accords prime position to detachment. Contrary to received opinion, each of these concepts is historically laden and feminist philosophers have

---

8 See Bhelke and Gokhale (2002) for an overview of Indian moral philosophy.

unearthed their patriarchal undertones.[9] This is because the body is symbolized as feminine in most cultures and women's work is rarely individualistic. However, this diagnosis should guard against simplistic conclusions of attributing such male bias to most philosophers being men or their misogynistic views about women (Grimshaw 1988: 36-37).[10] Rather patriarchy, in the sense of privileging male experiences at the expense of women, can be discerned in the philosophical omission of women's work and experience, which occur in the disembodied space of domesticity (ibid.: 37-38). Women's work in the feminine mode of care is based on the "sexual division of labour". As feminist scholars have pointed out, this division is one where women work in the domestic sphere and men in the public. Domestic labour is the unacknowledged basis for public work and is not compensated as it is seen as inconsequential and inferior (Chodorow 1994; Connell 1994). The subordination of women's interests is established through what Connell terms as "gender regimes" (1994: 30) where there is an organization of activities along sexual lines with set ideological stereotypes of masculinity and femininity or a

---

9 The recent edition of de Beauvoir's *The Second Sex* (2010) begins with a quote from Pythagoras as follows:

"There is a good principle which created order, light and man, and an evil principle which created chaos, darkness and woman."

The notions of disembodiment and individualism are also laden with class, caste and race. The Western philosophical tradition abounds with feminist critique as the writings of Wollstonecraft, de Beauvoir, Gilligan, Irigaray and Okin, among several others convey. In the Indian philosophical context, though critiques are few and far between, Ramabai (Kosambi 2000), Kelkar and Gangavane (2003) are significant for their engagement with Indian philosophical categories.

10 Such a view also overlooks how women philosophers such as Hannah Arendt have themselves shown signs of patriarchy.

"gender order" (ibid.: 30).[11] Such "regimes" and "orders" can be observed in politics, schools, workplaces, families and so forth in formal and informal ways. These "regimes" are not imposed by a dictator with a written code of conduct; rather they come alive through practices in the social, political and linguistic spheres.[12] Women for the most part are culturally associated with the body; history reveals that for most part privileged men have women labour for them by tending to their bodily functions so that they are free to contemplate.[13] Yet, in their contemplative flights, male philosophers valorize the world of pure ideas and are either indifferent or contemptuous towards the bodily activities that serve them. In the dichotomy between form and matter, the former is masculine and the latter feminine. Contemplation as the non-sensuous vision of the soul, opposes itself to the labouring activity of the body.[14] The subject of thought emerges by

11 Connell's expressions "gender regimes" and "gender orders" will henceforth be used with quotation marks.

12 Recent high court judgements in Mumbai pertaining to divorce portray such "gender regimes" where they blame the increasing rates of divorce on educated women and their inability to adjust to domesticity (Sequeira 2012b). When a woman did not want to join her husband who got posted in a far-off place, one of the judges tried to persuade her asking "When Sītā could join Rāma in *vanvāsa*, then why can't you go?" (ibid.: 2012a). Sītā is a mythological character in the epic *Rāmāyaṇa* who is venerated for her wifely devotion. In another case, the husband filed for divorce claiming that his wife deserted him. The judge advised the wife to work on her relationship with her husband since she was actually out all day getting computer skills, "Leave computer training aside. This training is more important" (ibid.: 2012c).

13 Plato for instance in his "Timaeus" regards matter, ". . . the receptacle and in a manner the nurse of all generation" (1987e: 49a-b), which receives the masculine form to make creation possible.

14 Labouring activity includes slaves and animals as well.

transcending the body or defining it as alien to thought; thus, the philosopher is a "... 'man' whose sex is unspecified, circumvents sexual difference to affirm himself as a thinker." (Irigaray 1985b: 247)[15]

It is in this context that feminist philosophers such as Alison Jaggar diagnose Western ethical theories from Plato, Kant and Hegel to their contemporary *avatāras* in Kohlberg and Rawls, as overestimating masculine cultural traits such as autonomy, separation, reason, culture, transcendence, war and death (Jaggar 2000). This is because they focus on the disembodied individual and privatize women's experiences to the domestic sphere to eradicate them from epistemology and morality. As Jaggar argues, this is linked to a devaluation of feminine cultural traits such as interdependence, community, emotions, nature and immanence (ibid.). Consequently, traditional ethics advocates a masculine mode of reasoning comprised rules,

---

15 Kelkar has similarly pointed to the patriarchal strands in the Indian philosophical tradition. She identifies three modes of understanding man–woman relationships in metaphysical frames in the Indian tradition (Kelkar and Gangavane 2003: 101-20) and *darśana* is central to these. Within the *brahma-māyā* paradigm where the former is reality while the latter is appearance, women are relegated to appearance and do not enjoy an independent status (ibid.: 118). The *puruṣa–prakṛti* model is one where the former is an eternally conscious knowledge while the latter is an inert non-conscious action. Women are identified with the latter and have an independent existence (ibid.: 108-11). The Śiva–Śakti model does not look down upon Śakti but makes her integral to pure consciousness or Śiva as pure energy (ibid.: 111-12). However, in Kāśmīr Śaivism's interpretation of this model there is no equality between the sexes since Śiva is independent and Śakti is active and both are related like the sun and its rays. But Śākta and Tantra philosophies interpret the Śiva–Śakti relation as harmony between the inactive perceptual force and active energy (ibid.: 113). The world is, hence, grounded in the play between Śiva-Śakti.

universality and impartiality, overruling feminine reasoning, based on relationships and particularity.

In engaging with the tradition of moral/political philosophy feminists have taken embodiment and women's care-oriented domestic work into account to correct the imbalance between the masculine and the feminine. However, the relation between feminism and philosophy since the time of Wollstonecraft's publication of her *Vindication of the Rights of Woman* in 1792 has a complex route.[16] Some feminists have distanced themselves from philosophy, claiming that feminism aims at practical change and has no theoretical basis (Gatens 1991: 86).[17] Yet this line of thinking is problematic, as practical change requires theoretical direction; conversely philosophical concepts, as argued above, are rooted in historical practice. Hence, such an approach leaves intact the oblivion to which women whose association with embodiment and domesticity are condemned within the framework of disembodied individualist reason and morality. Thus, as Irigaray notes, women as matter and domesticity need to enter into the hitherto "prohibited" discursive domain of philosophy to disrupt taken-for-granted assumptions of knowledge and morality (Irigaray 1985b: 157). Hence, rather than separate themselves, a large number of feminists have intervened and engaged with the philosophical tradition — albeit, in different ways. Thinkers such as Ramabai, Wollstonecraft, Okin and de Beauvoir have argued from the women's point of view within the structure of the male canon.[18] Indeed, they retain the latter to problematize women's difference and consequently, include them as equals within the canon. Their argument is that gender

---

[16] This discussion is influenced by Gatens (1991: 85-99).

[17] Gatens cites Solanas, Daly and Spender as diverse versions of such "theoretical separatism" (1991: 86-89).

[18] Indeed Okin appreciates Plato's abolition of the family and private property in his *Republic* and its consequent →

neutrality cannot be assumed as given. Rather, it is an achievement that is the outcome of recognizing and eradicating hierarchical difference between the sexes. Alternatively, feminists such as Gilligan critique canonical philosophy as male-biased and argue for a distinct women centric philosophical terminology; for in their view women cannot be accommodated within the categories of male philosophical concepts.

With the emergence of heterogeneous feminist philosophies, the relation between gender and philosophical concepts has become vexatious, both amongst feminists and between feminists and mainstream philosophy.[19] Yet with a few exceptions gender subordination, what de Beauvoir has termed an "irritating subject", has been raised by women themselves within the discipline of philosophy (de Beauvoir 2010: 3, 5).. This is because, as she argues, "masculine" and "feminine" are not symmetrical terms, sharing a formal equality. Rather, their differences have been imposed on the woman where she is made aware of her anatomy as "wrong" (ibid.: 5). The male body is understood without reference to the female, while it is quite the opposite in the case of the woman's body (ibid.: 6). The issue regarding whether concepts are gender-neutral or gendered is related to whether the gender of the thinker affects the concepts advocated. de

---

→ emancipation of female guardians (Okin 1991). She contrasts this position with his later defence of family and private property without female guardians in his laws. However, in her appreciation and critique of Plato, Okin overlooks Plato's neglect of women's work in the domestic sphere and the masculine undertones of his seemingly androgynous model of leadership. This emerges from her failure to interrogate Plato's epistemological and moral categories.

19 See Haack (1999), Pinnick (1994) for a defence of gender-neutral perspectives against feminist interventions in philosophy.

Beauvoir's point in explicitly writing as a woman is to introduce the dimension of subjectivity and lived experience in philosophical diction (Moi 2005: 207-08). Thus, she ". . . discovers a way of doing philosophy in which the personal and the philosophical are intrinsically linked" (ibid.: 207).

Most of the canonical philosophers do not introduce their gender into the philosophical texts they write. As Moi observes, Sartre does not do so (ibid.: 208).[20] Kant's antipathy to the feminine not withstanding,[21] one could follow his Copernican revolution,[22] which claims that one cannot hold on to observer-independent concepts without falling into the trap of the correspondence theory of truth. Thus, the thinker and concept are correlated, wherein concepts are rooted in the thinker. However, this invocation of Kant requires

---

20 The equation between de Beauvoir and Sartre on the basis of her own proclamations to this effect overlooks important differences between them.

21 As argued above, his ethics banishes the feminine by keeping sensuous desires at bay. But in his *Anthropology from a Pragmatic Point of View,* Kant declares that "Feminine traits are called weaknesses" (1996: 303). See Kant (ibid.: 303-11) for his views on the feminine as a tool to culture and masculinity. Kant also precluded women from active citizenship because they were neither independent nor full-fledged members who contributed to the creation of the commonwealth (Kant 1985: 314-15, §46). Despite noting that the very notion of a passive citizen contradicts the very idea of citizenship, he goes on to list "an apprentice of a merchant or an artisan, a servant; a minor; all women; and generally any one who must depend for his support not on his own industry, but on arrangements by others (with the exception of the state) . . . " as passive citizens (ibid.: 315, §46). The latter in his view " . . . lack civil personality, and their existence is only a mode of inherence" (ibid.). Also see Kneller (1993) and Gangavane (2004) for feminist critiques of Kant's disparaging views on femininity.

22 See Kant (1965: xvi).

qualification. The thinker is not an a priori noumenal subject, but is situated within history, geography, culture and the like; the thinker is, rather, an embodied being within historical space and time.[23] Further, the seemingly neutral term "subject" is not so neutral. As feminists have argued, the universality in philosophical arguments such as "All men are . . . " is based on the eradication of the sexual difference between men and women (Irigaray 1985b: 74). The subject in philosophy is the individual male thinker who has an unacknowledged, exploitative and privileged relationship to the domain of women's care-giving domestic work. Given such interaction, one cannot merely describe differences between sexes in value neutral ways for it is a difference marked by patriarchal exploitation (Benhabib 1986: 405-06). Consequently, as Seyla Benhabib observes, the interaction between philosophy and feminism has led to an expansion of the notion of individual identity as an embodied lived experience of the symbolic, psychic and the social within the ambit of sex and gender (ibid.: 406).

Yet the subject enters the philosophical discourse because of the force of language (Irigaray 1985b: 74, 149-50). Language reinforces the social acceptability in speaking a sexually or as a male, but not as a woman (ibid.: 148-49). By homogenizing all speakers in masculine or gender-neutral gestures, it plays a vital role in the way human beings see themselves and the world. Language makes the world available as an embodied socio-cultural practice that is inextricably simultaneous, continuous and entangled with thought and concept. Language is, thus, a form of life or an activity where words acquire meaning through being learnt and put to use in social contexts, following Ludwig Wittgenstein's later work (1958: §23). As a form of life, language is never complete, words are added, deleted, improvized making it a heterogeneous activity that

23 Kant also has an abstract conception of space and time.

is in progress.[24] Words do not have absolute meaning or reference; one does not learn the use of words but rather uses them in socio-cultural contexts (ibid.: §9). As Wittgenstein says, " . . . the meaning of a word is its use in language" (ibid.: §43). Yet given that language cannot be separated from the natural, social, metaphysical or any other domain which it articulates as a mere representative tool, it does not have any pre-given order or form.[25] Thus, human beings are linguistic in that they "require language in order to be . . . " (Butler 1997: 1-2). Extending this insight to gender, patriarchal language signifies a patriarchal way of life. Yet, it is not inexorable on the contrary the fact that words do not have a necessary relation to an idea or a thing also opens the possibility of change. For such contingency between words and things implies that language is inherently incomplete. Thus, language has a capacity to shape human life and this capacity precedes the individual human subject (ibid.: 2). Language is the condition for the possibility of human existence.[26] Hence, linguistic agents who "do things with words",[27] act under conditions that are far from egalitarian, exercising their agency under such conditions that are far from ideal and not of their making. Considering that it is a daily social activity, language determines, and is in turn determined by the hierarchies that prevail in the society. Thus,

---

[24] Wittgenstein compares language to a town or an ancient city: it has an identity without exactitude (1958: §18).

[25] The account of language as primarily a representation has been questioned since de Saussure's *Course in General Linguistics* (1966) and Wittgenstein's *Philosophical Investigations* (1958). For a discussion of Austin's ordinary language philosophy and de Beauvoir's feminism, see Moi (2005: 207-26).

[26] It is a transcendental condition in the Kantian sense without his apriorism.

[27] This is derived from J.L. Austin's book of the same name, *How to Do Things with Words* (1962).

the power relation between men and women is expressed in language. This is evident in the way the generic usage of masculine pronouns is socially accepted. Early English grammarians prescribed that the noun "man" and the pronoun "he" should be used not only to refer to men but also for general reference to all persons.[28] In fact, in 1590 Wilson decreed ". . . in speaking at the leaste, let us keep a natural order, and set the man before the woman for manners sake".[29] In 1850 this so-called grammatical rule of correct usage became a parliamentary compulsion. A male-specific usage and cognitive model was taken as the paradigm, whereby male-specific roles are learnt first and transmitted to women. Hence, generic usage does not contain generic meaning. For many do not think of people when the word "man" is mentioned; think of men and then of human beings in general. As a result, the figure of the woman becomes cognitively invisible, as the history of philosophy reveals.

However, language also makes women visible with words that stereotype their roles and meticulously conveys their deviation from such words. Language is far from being gender-neutral and has contributed to the masculine aspect of philosophical concepts by identifying men as thinkers and women as embodied. Consider the following examples: *mother–working mother, mother–single mother, prostitute–male prostitute, nurse–male nurse, doctor–lady doctor, secretary–male secretary,* among others (Goddard and Mean 2000: 61). In addition, the female form acquires a derived and imitative status by adding "ette as actor–actress or manager–manageress demonstrate" (ibid.). The pronoun "she" is used, when women are given a context-specific reference. In such references, women are depicted in a subordinate way — as the wife or secretary of

---

28 This is derived from Eckert and McConnell-Ginet (2003).

29 This quotation is derived from ibid., 34.

the man. There is an imposition in such terms of roles and emotions of a specific subordinate kind upon women. Thus, sex specific references appeal to a binary opposition between men and women. For example: hysterical women/rational men. Further, almost all languages contain expletives that target women.[30] Again, a term such as "care" has the connotation of being secondary, while "freedom" carries a sense of significance. This is because the former is associated with feminine domestic work, while the latter with the masculine public domain.

As Moi observes, the phrase "intellectual man" is not used commonly because a patriarchal society associates men with the intellect in a self-evident way (Moi 2005: 295). Conversely, "intellectual woman" is a normalized term. The word "hysteria", for instance, is rarely associated with men and its association with women is justified on the basis of their biological constitution. Hysteria–hysterical originate from Greek *husterikos* (of the womb), but there is no absolute relation between the signifier "hysteria"/*husterikos* and the signified, namely the concept "womb". Their relation is arbitrary.[31] Since biological concepts are themselves linguistically mediated, language cannot be justified by appealing to biology. Yet the contingency between word and concept, or in the spirit of de Saussure, signifier and signified also open the space for the critical capacity of language.

It is because of the struggle over meanings of words and their values that feminist philosophers speak from the position of being women. Thus, de Beauvoir, for instance, in her *Second Sex* wants women to "... gain access to the universal as *women*, not as fake men nor as some impossibly gendered beings" (ibid.: 205). Feminist philosophy foregrounds femininity in its

30 For a discussion of curse words targeting women see Mahadevan (2007).

31 This is derived from de Saussure's linguistics.

quest for language and thought in which men and women can participate. It does so by inscribing the philosopher's gender in its activity of reading, writing and speaking (ibid.: 207-08). Hence, feminist philosophy pays heed to how the feminine subject is constructed through language in socio-historical, economic and psychical contexts. But it does so in order to critique it, renounce it or appropriate it in liberating ways.[32] Thus, to philosophize from a feminist point of view is to struggle over words and concepts such as "woman", "care", "freedom". This struggle is about rewriting them in ways that are sensitive to the woman's situation, which has been ignored so far. It does not advocate a deterministic relation between being female and feminine on one hand and being feminist on the other. Consequently, feminist philosophy aims at overcoming what Moi characterizes as the patriarchal choice between being imprisoned in one's femininity and renouncing it completely (ibid.: 205-06).

The problem of women being what de Beauvoir termed "the second sex" is not so much about the exclusion of women, but about their inclusion as stereotypes of the "feminine magic".[33] Women's invisibility and exclusion are sustained by

---

[32] Feminist philosophers of language critique the male bias in the vocabulary of ordinary language (Saul 2010). But they also argue that such a bias is an outcome of the individualist and intentionalist assumptions in language. They diagnose the ahistorical and asocial approach of language philosophers as the source of this problem. But, like their moral/political philosophy counterparts, feminist language philosophers are divided over whether the woman's question should be accommodated in the existing philosophy of language, or whether a specifically woman's language should replace male individualism or whether there can be sharing between the different linguistic patterns of the sexes (see Hornsby 2000; Irigaray 2004; Saul 2010 for extended discussions).

[33] de Beauvoir's expression for stereotyped feminine characteristics (2010: 193).

their visibility in standardized oppressive roles in which they do tasks of nurture that are regarded as subordinate from a cultural and socio-economic point of view. Such tasks, which are defined as feminine, form the constant point of reference, which is simultaneously excluded and included. The feminine foregrounds women in a patriarchal culture where they are rendered invisible; yet with its restrictions, the feminine also encourages the invisibility of women through their visibility. Thus, the feminine is the ground for engaging with women in philosophy and gendering concepts, as the increasing corpus of feminist philosophy in recent years conveys. However, there is no unilateral agreement among feminists on the normative status of the feminine; feminists have both critiqued, as well as, appropriated and reconstructed the feminine.

As Moi observes, "feminism" is a political position that exposes and critiques patriarchy in the course of aspiring for an equality between women and men, this critique and aspiration is upheld by the women's movement as well (Moi 1997: 104-05).[34] Rather than just another theoretical perspective, feminist philosophy is committed to critiquing and ending the "gender regime" and "gender order" of patriarchy. It differs from both the "feminine" as culturally defined gendered norms and "female" as the biological dimension of sex, since "feminism" stands in a critical relation to both. Further, one cannot collapse the feminine into female for "patriarchal oppression consists of imposing certain social standards of femininity on all biological women, in order to precisely make us believe that the chosen standards of "femininity" are *natural*. Thus, a woman who refuses to conform can be labelled both *"unfeminine* and *unnatural*'" (ibid.: 108).

---

[34] The women's movement like feminist philosophy is heterogeneous marked by debates, differences and self-criticism.

As Moi observes, the distinction between these terms is crucial to working out the theoretical and practical issues entailed by feminism (ibid.: 104). Rather, following de Beauvoir, biological facts have to be comprehended through the lens of ideology and culture, which play a role in articulating these facts. This is precisely why all writings by women are not necessarily anti-patriarchal. Further there are several instances of female writers who have written in a non-feminist mode.[35] Conversely, men too have written in defence of feminism.[36] Thus, rather than bind gendered concepts to female or biological origins, philosophical sensitivity to women would allow for appropriating concepts with origin in the male canon to be appropriated for feminist purposes (ibid.: 105).

Since the feminist, feminine and female aspects are neither independent of each other, nor determined by each other, there is a need to explore the relationship between feminine nurture and female nature.[37] One has to approach both gender and sex critically, by situating them in a historical context. The relation between sex as a set of biological characteristics and gender as socially defined expectations has been extensively debated by feminists. This debate has oscillated between a "scientistic understanding of sex and an idealist understanding of gender" (Moi 2005: 113). As Moi observes in the 1960s and 1970s, there was a tendency to think of the two in terms of biological determinism, where sex was the basis of gender. One can see traces of this in the writings of Gayle Rubin (1997). With the advent of post-structuralists such as Judith Butler, only gender remains as performance, obliterating the concept of sex as biologism (Butler 2007). Yet

---

35 Haack (1999) is a case in point.

36 Engels and Mill are well-known instances of men supporting women's issues.

37 Following Moi, " . . . 'feminine' represents nurture, and 'female' nature in this usage" (1997: 108).

one needs to work out this relationship without taking recourse to either treating sex/body/nature as an absolute given or denying it completely.[38] Moreover, despite their critical relationship to the feminine as evidenced in Ramabai and Wollstonecraft, feminists have also appropriated the feminine perspective of care, as Gilligan and Mies have done. Thus, since the matrices of feminism, femininity and female are not isomorphic, there are significant debates within feminism regarding their relationship.

Feminist moral and political philosophers such as Gilligan, Okin, Mies and de Beauvoir have negotiated the relationship between feminism and femininity in diverse theoretical ways. They do so by either critiquing or appropriating the feminine. However, despite their differences, both approaches are united in their feminist moment of disentangling the feminine from biological determinism of the female body and avoiding its socio-cultural essentialization. Thus, feminism perceives feminine nurture as contingently related to both biology and society. Yet, feminists approach feminine nurture in diverse ways depending on their relation to the traditional philosophical corpus. de Beauvoir adopted existentialist insights of the free human being to critique the socio-cultural stereotyping of women into the feminine subject position of care. Gilligan, in contrast, renounces the autonomous individual as a patriarchal residue that ignores the web of relationships (so characteristic of women's lives), which are largely committed to practices of care. Okin combines Gilligan's insights of care with Rawls' account of impartial justice, to explore the possibility of a notion of justice interwoven with feminine nurture. Their contrast notwithstanding, both

---

[38] The implication of this stance for moral philosophy grounded in freedom will be explored in Chapter 5 which discusses de Beauvoir.

de Beauvoir and Gilligan take feminine difference manifested in care as the basis of feminist moral philosophy.

Although de Beauvoir is committed to the normative view that women and men are equal, she critically turns to the feminine as the distinctive mark of women to locate its patriarchal assumption as the basis of women's inequality. For Gilligan, the feminine is not reducible to the patriarchal and has its own unique position in women's lives as the repository of peace and nurture to etch out a different voice of women.[39] In the context of the opposing views of de Beauvoir and Gilligan on feminine care, the feminine emerges as either equivalent to patriarchal cultural norms or as an anti-patriarchal position. Despite their differences, both de Beauvoir and Gilligan root the fate of feminism in femininity. Femininity, in the sense of being the binary other of masculinity, is a cultural construct that determines women's conduct and virtue. However, they differ in their approaches to the male philosophical tradition. For de Beauvoir it can be redeemed when it resolves women's problems, while for Gilligan one has to change the very vocabulary or paradigm of traditional philosophy to make room for women philosophers.

In patriarchal societies, as de Beauvoir observes, men mythologize women into a feminine ideal that reflects their own fears and desires (de Beauvoir 2010: 221-74).[40] In a myth,

---

39 Others include Helene Cioux and Irigaray (see Moi 1997).

40 The myths that de Beauvoir cites are derived from literature: Montherlant's disorderly women, Lawrence's erotic women, Claudel's divine servant, Breton's muse and Stendhal's flesh-and-blood women (2010: 221-74). de Beauvoir is aware of the eternal feminine in non-Western contexts (see for example 2010: 91- 92 for her citation of the laws of Manu). Verma provides an interesting analysis of Hindu Brāhmanical femininity (1995: 434-39). See Leslie (1995) for similar myths in the Indian context centering around the "perfect wife". Women are "fantasized" (Žižek 1993: 108) through the

the subject ties together both hopes and fears whereby the feminine assumes several contradictory features all at once.

> She is an idol, a servant, a source of life, power of darkness; she is the elementary silence of truth, she is the artifice, gossip and lies; she is the medicine woman and witch; she is man's prey; she is his downfall, she is everything he is not and wants to have, his negation and his *raison d'être*.
>
> — ibid.: 166

Moreover, the feminine is often defended on biological grounds of having a female body, which is problematic given that it ignores the variety of ways in which the feminine is constructed in different cultures. As Moi observes:

> Patriarchy has developed a whole series of feminine characteristics (sweetness, modesty, subservience, humility, etc.). — Moi 1997: 109

Further, it also assumes that all women experience their bodies — in the sense of undergoing reproductive motherhood and nurture — in the same way. Thus, the female or biology is taken as a natural given that determines the path of feminine behaviour. Yet, such a premise overlooks that biology is not an intractable given or a "destiny".[41] Rather biology too intersects with society and culture so that it is not immutable. Hence, extending Moi's suggestion to a feminist moral philosophy, instead of a blanket affirmation of the feminine, would dissolve the feminine/masculine binary (ibid.: 113). Moreover, it would also question the notion of the "female" as a solid determinate entity. Thus, a feminist moral philosophy would take all three terms, female, feminine and feminist, as

---

oppressive features of femininity in a variety of historical contexts. All of which go to show as Žižek aptly observes, "By opposing "patriarchal domina-tion", woman simultaneously undermines the fantasy support of her own "feminine identity" (ibid.).

41 See de Beauvoir (2010: 21-49).

entry points into biology, culture and politics, where none of them is intractable and each of which can be transformed. As Moi asks:

> Should feminists then really try to develop another set of "feminine" virtues, however desirable? —ibid.: 109

This is because patriarchy has always trapped women in feminine roles that have been preset. Hence, any feminine gesture from the feminist point of view will have distinguished itself from patriarchy very explicitly. In addition, one needs to investigate the manner in which the feminist feminine differs from the patriarchal feminine. Alternatively, from the perspective of thinkers such as Wollstonecraft, Okin and de Beauvoir who take the male canon as their starting point a different set of questions emerge: Is the retention of male philosophical frameworks by Wollstonecraft and de Beauvoir equivalent to women endorsing patriarchy as Gatens suggests (1991: 6-7)? Can the feminist appropriation of the feminine be reconciled with moral and political values that have been traditionally perceived as masculine such as justice and autonomy? How does the feminist approach to justice differ from masculine versions of the same? Thus, the relationship between the two strands of thinking amongst feminists, namely, those who adopt the feminine and those who critique it is at stake. What is also at stake is the respective difference between patriarchal versions of their positions. In the course of asking these questions and debating with feminist philosophers against patriarchy, one needs to interrogate how feminist interventions change patriarchal notions of feminine care, as well as, masculine justice and autonomy.

To address these theoretical questions, one needs to examine the relation between the feminine and feminist perspectives at the intersection of practical philosophy, of moral and political thought within feminist philosophy. In doing this, one should also attempt to define the framework of a heterogeneous feminist philosophy. Although feminist philosophy itself emerged as an academic discipline because of the women's movement, it cannot be reduced to applied philosophy. In the latter, one merely applies traditional philosophical concepts of ethics and politics to a gendered context. Yet the concept of gender is not a mere add on to traditional canonical arguments in ethics and politics. Applied philosophy does not probe into the cultural and normative evolution or implications of its conceptual repertoire. It perceives philosophical concepts as unchanging and sees its task as one of connecting these to practise at various given points in time. In contrast, feminist philosophy as a theoretical/ practical task becomes possible only by overcoming the conceptual bind of application. The very point of introducing gender in the philosophical corpus is to transform existing concepts and show their historical overtones. Feminist philosophy's theoretical task also has a practical import in that it aims at an egalitarian relation between the sexes.

Though philosophy is a theoretical discipline, it does not take place in a vacuum, but has empirical reality as its backdrop. Both gendered oppression and activism against it are integral to the latter. It is motivated by the impact of transformatory theory on practice. Yet gendered philosophy, as observed above, also comprises responses to decades of activism. Thus, there is a mutual relation between theory and practice, where each simultaneously and reciprocally impacts the other. Hence, feminist philosophy is interdisciplinary whereby it integrates the contribution of activism and data from the social sciences (and even natural sciences) with the argumentative tradition of philosophy. From the feminist point of view, philosophy can no longer aspire to be the ultimate judge of knowledge, but can only aspire to be "a stand in and interpreter" (Habermas 1990: 1-20). It would have to take the research in other disciplines into account while raising feminist questions. Thus, science and philosophy do not have a "cut-and-dried division of labour" (ibid.: 14). Feminist philosophy inserts the category of gender as a "genuinely philosophical idea like a detonator into a particular context of research" (ibid.: 15); it is like Marxism, psychoanalysis and Habermas's reconstructive sciences in this respect. Drawing upon everyday practice, activism, as well as, literary and scientific accounts of gender, feminist philosophy functions as a "mediating interpreter" (ibid.: 19) that brings together heterogeneous communities in dialogue, rather than as an ultimate arbitration of experts who offer absolute solutions.

A large part of philosophy has confined itself to textual studies and neglected the dimension of the lived world. It has placed the notions of thought and experience in a vacuum and celebrated the abstract thinker. Yet one cannot overlook the extra-textual conditions of race, caste, gender and colony that implicitly (and sometimes explicitly) frame philosophical texts. As has been mentioned above, feminist research has repeatedly reminded us that the abstract rational thinker is a man and that gender-neutrality is a cover for androcentrism. Feminist interventions in philosophy transform the very activity of philosophy by challenging its territorial preserve as pure thought. They reveal that philosophy can no longer be viewed as a purely textual or intellectual activity, but is unavoidably interdisciplinary. It is by taking feminist research in science, psychology, history and politics into account that gender-related questions can be raised within the discipline of philosophy. For example, feminist philosophers who focus on embodiment (rather than thought) and question traditional definitions of morality as rights oriented, do so on the basis of empirical research in natural science, history, psychology and sociology. Conversely, philosophical insights into gendered embodiment and critical interpretation provide perspective into empirical research. In the Indian context, this work straddles the boundaries of tradition and modernity, both from the colonial and global perspectives. It believes that a theoretical approach to gender is especially significant in the Indian context, where it has been neglected.

With respect to the Western world, as Irigaray notes, philosophy is a "master discourse" (Irigaray 1985b: 74). Its concepts do not only reflect or describe science, culture, society and politics, but also set the terms and conditions to legitimize these latter discourses (ibid.: 159-60). Thus, philosophical abstraction has an active relation with science, language, literature and culture. This holds true even in the Indian context, where despite not being Irigaray's "master discourse", philosophical assumptions of disembodied thought and pejorative domesticity have a hold on academic, institutional and cultural life. However, philosophy is not just a critical undertaking that questions accepted schools of thought; rather it is also a reconstructive one. Hence from the feminist point of view, if a certain way of doing philosophy, namely emphasizing contemplation, becomes conducive to a patriarchal society; one would have to do philosophy in ways that are conducive to a non-patriarchal, democratic and egalitarian society. To rectify the exclusions in human life, it is also important to reinterpret the tasks of philosophy, given its bearing and reciprocal relation with other aspects of life. This is indeed the case, both in the West and in India, where philosophy occupies different positions. In the West, as well as in India social change requires reflection and therefore, philosophy. Thus, to transform the hierarchical dimension of "gender regimes", one requires a feminist philosophy sensitive to practice. It is not enough to document the innumerable and increasing cases of women's oppression. Activism does not just stare at unjust facts, but attempts to change them. This in turn mandates that practice towards a sustained change requires a conceptual framework. For instance, if gender roles are understood to be naturally given then it would be difficult to initiate change.[42] On the other hand, if gender roles are viewed as socially constructed there is room for change. Feminist philosophy uses gender as a historically embedded concept, which problematizes the differences between the masculine and the feminine. The concept of gender does not just document or provide statistics of the many instances of exclusion and oppression of women in specific histories and topographies, even though it is rooted in such documentations and statistics. Rather, as a philosophical concept, gender is both a descriptive and a normative structural category. Its existing obstructions are studied to examine avenues for growth. Feminist philosophy thus, works *in tandem* with practice. In fact, it would not have been possible to philosophize gender without decades of activist struggle.

Extending Habermas's insight, the feminist philosopher is not a judge or an arbiter of the ultimate order of things, be it biology or culture (Habermas 1990: 14-15). Rather, she does reflect, somewhat abstractly, on issues of gender, but in dialogue with other disciplines such as history, sociology, literature and the like. An investigation of a concrete practice or phenomenon opens up the conceptual and the abstract assumptions that underlie it. For instance, while examining the concrete instance of the exclusion of women in language

---

[42] Academic research in the nineteenth-century West adhered to such a hierarchical naturalism. Moi gives the example of Patrick Geddes and J. Arthur Thomson who write "We have seen a deep difference in constitution expresses itself in the distinction between male and female, whether these be physical or mental. . . . What was decided among the prehistoric Protozoa cannot be annulled by Act of Parliament . . . " (quoted in Moi 2005: 18). Popular culture continues to propagate such a natural difference with theses such as "men are from mars and women are from venus".

one is drawn to philosophy. One examines a concrete phenomenon of say the allergy to women's speech in everyday discourse. If one proceeds further to read philosophical literature one finds that it is a discourse that is founded on the masculine "subject" represented by words such as "human being" (Irigaray 1985b: 74, 149-50). Thus, one gets enmeshed in philosophy while proceeding from concrete practice to concept. As the instances of androcentrism in philosophy discussed above reveal, academic philosophy does not present unproblematic answers to the travails of ordinary speech; on the contrary, like ordinary speech it rests upon the feminine and yet disavows it. Further, both ordinary language and philosophical discourse have the critical potential to expose such paradoxes. Thus, the feminist engagement with academic philosophy is also an attempt to disrupt its patriarchal assumptions (ibid.: 68, 78).

The Indian context is especially significant in that the critique of the patriarchal assumptions of philosophy from a feminist perspective has not been adequately theorized from within the discipline of philosophy. Given the contributions of other disciplines to gender, philosophy can step in to pay attention to the normative issues raised by introducing gender as much of the work done on gender in the empirical fields is of a descriptive nature. Descriptions of gendered practice require an analysis of human identity as concrete and gendered in terms of masculine and feminine, as well as those who are not able to fit into either of these categories. Gender, thus, becomes a category of philosophical analysis which depends upon science and culture. Yet, gender is not a value-neutral category of analysis, its philosophical use presupposes a normative commitment to feminism. Thus, the cluster of terms female/feminine/feminist carry with them descriptive, analytical and critical/normative dimensions. They also convey tensions between descriptions of the female/feminine aspects and the normative feminist perspective. Further, the point of raising the question of gender from a theoretical perspective is not merely to make women visible as feminine entities. Rather, it is about showing some of the limitations that underlie canonical accounts of the feminine. Thus, the feminist perspective interrogates the feminine and brings in the critical attitude. This in turn raises normative issues regarding the validity of research in domains such as ethics and politics.[43] As Benhabib remarks feminist theory has the task of not just diagnosing the various ways in which patriarchal oppression takes place but also that of a Utopian critique (Benhabib 1986: 405). Since feminist philosophy is a theoretical enterprise — with its share of tensions — which is nevertheless closely related to practice.

Theoretical feminist interventions in the Indian academy have to confront the dogma of Eurocentrism, where Western theory is quoted lock, stock and barrel, despite being irrelevant or even antithetical to the Indian context. Susie Tharu and K. Lalita have observed that those such as Elaine Showalter who employ notions of recovery, release, authentic experience and a hidden female nature found them in a separate individual self typical of Western modern discourses (Tharu and Lalita 1991). Even though this self is a woman, it requires the supplement of those it exploits — its others, namely those without privilege often from the non-white world (ibid.: 35). As Chandra Talpade Mohanty notes, many Western feminists subject non-Western women to their imperialist gaze by branding them as tradition bound (Mohanty 1984). Since the arrival of Tharu's and Lalita's pioneering two-volume anthology — *Women Writing in India* (1991) — it has become apparent that much of Western feminist theory — especially the second wave — neglected the presence of non-Western

43 There could be other areas such as science and aesthetics as well.

women. Spivak exposes how the search for an authentic self, defined against other women, in the French feminist Julia Kristeva's work is premised upon unexamined assumptions about Chinese women (Spivak 1987: 136-40). This line of thought is shared even by Western feminists such as Moi who observe that black/lesbian feminism and "third world" feminism pose theoretical questions for Anglo-American feminism (Moi 1985).

All concepts have corruptible roots in history and culture, yet Indian (and non-Western) feminists face the challenge of reconstructing them in egalitarian ways, rather than forsaking them. In a globalized world these differences are not innocuous, since they reflect relations of privilege. Thus, Indian women in export processing special economic zones could be labouring away for their privileged Western and Indian counterparts, whereby the cultural meanings attached to their bodies contribute to their exploitation (Mahadevan 2001). All women do not share the same location; gender is fragmented by caste, race, nationality and class. Indian feminists have the task of working towards theoretical positions that take the inevitability of "otherness" or the foreign element in identity, labour as a theoretical category, embodiment, ways of integrating an ethics of care with that of freedom without falling into the trap of individualism. All of this no doubt involves translating some of the categories of the philosophical canon in ways that overturn their sexism; but, as importantly, it also involves the possibility of translating Western philosophical concepts in non-Eurocentric critical ways after which they can be abandoned, retained or reconstructed. Such a process of translation process is also a creative one. Theory in this instance cannot be speculative, but would have to be dialogical and grounded in lived practices of women's lives. Thus, thought need not necessarily repeat the violence of speculative logic; there are other ways of thinking which maintain a close relation with the body and its labouring activities. Moreover, instead of searching for pure identities of gender, it would have to appreciate the degree to which the foreign or otherness is inherent to identity.

Hence, feminist philosophy in the Indian context cannot adopt the revivalist path of perceiving the past as having all the answers to contemporary problems. This path attempts to discover a uniquely Indian "identity", often traditional, religious or spiritual. The problem with most of the traditional sources (which exclude others) to which revivalists turn in their quest for an Indian identity is that they are not only gender-neutral, but also inimical to women. For instance, proponents of Indian ethics defend the *puruṣārtha*s against the alleged Western emphasis on rights. Yet feminist philosophers such as Belsare, who have critiqued this tradition, argue that the very term *puruṣārtha* is problematic — after all what is it but a reduction of the purpose of life to that of the man (*puruṣa*) (Belsare 2003). Again, in societies such as India with plural histories, fixed identities become absolutist and antithetical to feminism despite paying token homage to women.

Feminist research and practice in India have challenged both imperialism and revivalism in knowledge through its commitment to a more democratic and pluralistic world. Such philosophical writing in India has also steered clear of unreflectively regurgitating Western concepts or Indian traditional ones. Thus, the search for gendered roots of concepts shows that there are no ready-made paradigms available. Further, application of set philosophical systems and theories, whether Western or Indian, is counter-productive in the gendered context. As it has been discussed above, the language user is often assumed to be a masculine individual, who is also at the centre of academic philosophy that rests upon the feminine and yet excludes it. Conversely, gender is a philosophical concept that is rooted but not restricted to women's oppression in specific histories and topographies. As a descriptive and normative concept, gender has a reciprocal relation with activism as well. Hence, philosophy, in the Western academic world where it is privileged, as well as in India where it is not, is both critical and reconstructive. This interface between theory and practice can be seen in the moment of Ramabai's pioneering feminism in colonial India.

Part 1
Colonial Perspectives

1

Pandita Ramabai and Feminism in Colonial India

Tradition, Modernity and Domestic Nurture

> Pandita Ramabai alone, amongst all the nineteenth-century writers . . . understood the phenomenon of male domination and provided the most sustained critique of women's oppression during her day. — Chakravarti and Gill 2001: 4

THE forging of a somewhat homogeneous Indian femininity that construed domestic care as women's natural vocation, took place between the poles of tradition and modernity during the colonial period (Chakravarti 1989). Yet the critique of this femininity was also pioneered during the same period, paving way for an explicit theory and practice of feminism in India. The sources of the tension between femininity and feminism in modern India are rooted in both Indian and Western discourses. Although it foregrounds their modern spirit,[1] this chapter also hints at latent residues of ancient and medieval thought in these debates. Contemporary Indian philosophy emerged at the intersection of tradition and colonial

---

[1] The term "modern" is used in a philosophical way to characterize the history of thought from the late sixteenth century to the present. "Ancient" and "medieval" philosophies are similarly utilized in a philosophical–epochal manner.

Western modernity. Feminist activism and consciousness in India since the nineteeth century contributed to such philosophizing. The modern feminist activism initiated by Ramabai develops a contemporary idiom of philosophy through a critique of both tradition and colonization.[2] By shaping Indian philosophy, which reconstructed aspects of tradition in ways compatible with modernity, Ramabai paved the route to a feminist philosophy that cut across national boundaries. This is especially because in the course of her travels abroad she came into contact with the Western feminist movement, pioneered by philosophers such as Wollstonecraft.

An exploration of Ramabai's feminist contribution reveals that feminine identity as care was articulated and contested in the "entangled space"[3] of modernity and tradition in nineteenth-century colonial India. The tension between femininity and feminism was also played out in the same space. Hence, an examination of Ramabai's evolution as a feminist requires an investigation of the emergence of the woman's question in the nineteenth-century Indian context and its roots in women saints of ancient and medieval India.

The Construction of Indian Womanhood

The constitution of an ideal femininity as domesticated Hindu-Indian womanhood and its contestation took place in a society that retained many of its traditional problems despite undergoing major changes. As Tharu and Lalita put it:

> . . . all the grand abstractions of the times — empire, human nature, ethical responsibility, tradition, nationalism, Indianness, masculinity, each with important stakes in the woman's question. . . . — 1991: 153

2 Ramabai did not write theoretical philosophy; yet an attempt is made to make her work "philosophically available" to use Mrinal Miri's description from an informal conversation.

3 This expression is derived from Sangari (1994: 40) and will henceforth be used in quotation marks to indicate the same.

The woman's question was articulated during the nineteenth century through both "multiple patriarchies"[4] and incipient feminism. The multiple "gender regimes" were comprised British and Indian patterns of thought into which women were schooled (Sangari 1994: 57). Conflicting economic and social formations carved out a "middle-class private sphere" in which ". . . the domestic economy was left intact structurally but modified outwardly both by the state and by middle-class reformers" (Chakravarti 2006: 200-01). Consequently, an Indian patriarchy of social reform also emerged by challenging tradition (ibid.: 200). The female world tended to be limited to the domestic sphere of reproduction, labour and kinship relations (ibid.), within which feminine identity was cast. There were several economic, legal, historical, cultural and philosophical conjunctures between modernity and tradition in nineteenth-century India that contributed to the tension between femininity and feminism.

Following Habermas (1987: 5, 7), modernity is both an epochal and a normative term. The renaissance, reformation and scientific spirit were some of the benchmarks in the separation between the middle and modern ages since the sixteenth and seventeenth centuries (ibid.: 5). Secularism, constitutional government and capitalism became political characteristics of the modern world. Modernity does not take normative criteria from another epoch, but rather builds them out of itself (ibid.). It prioritizes the autonomous individual through a break with tradition and roots institutions of knowledge, morality and culture in the free person, rather than tradition. Instead of inheritance and esoteric intuition, modernity stresses the process of critical reflection and examined evidence. The Western world professed to have instituted these normative commitments by the nineteenth

[4] This expression is from Sangari 1995 who uses it in another context.

century, by outlining three distinct spheres of human experience founded on freedom, namely, science, morality and art (ibid.: 19).

Since the late fifteenth century or so, European modernity questioned the authority of tradition to encourage the growth of experimental sciences, philosophy, literature, economics and politics, with human freedom as its foundation. These ideals were rooted in the materiality of an economic order based on the accumulation of wealth and market contracts, rather than inheritance. They also gave rise to a democratic secular polity founded on principles of free choice of citizens to which the rule of law was committed. A civil society of freedom to form associations emerged between a capitalist economy and polity. By the nineteenth century the Western world stabilized its internal foray into modernity.[5] However, the non-Western world's transition to the modern was not as consistent, since it preserved many premodern forms of life, as well. Its transition to modernity was effected through an external process of colonization by Western countries. Struggle was a part of both internal and external modernity, in the former case against despotic landlords and monarchs, while the latter had the added task of resisting colonial power. "The dynamic concepts" that expressed the "modern age" since the eighteenth century were "revolution, progress, emancipation, development, crisis and *Zeitgeist*" (ibid.: 7). Yet, these concepts entered India through the external route of British colonization, whereby instead of ushering non-traditional forms of institutions it introduced policies that were "Janus faced, both breaking into and working with traditional social hierarchies" (Chakravarti 2006: 62).

The ideology of domesticity emerged with a selective colonial modernization of the economy whereby women were

5 The distinction between "internal" and "external" modernity is derived from Winfield 2001.

structurally rendered to do domestic work.[6] Though the colonial state was thoroughly industrialized, it did not engage in a reorganization of Indian society as a whole. It allied with the "martial", high-caste, aristocratic, landowning sections of India for its own profit (Sangari 1994: 36).[7] Policies meant to serve colonial powers unintentionally created openings for the colonized. They released the possibility of social mobility at one level, leaving intact the traditional hierarchies of caste and gender at another. Thus, unlike nineteenth-century England where women migrated to urban areas and entered factories, India witnessed a greater incarceration of women within the domestic sphere.[8] This was because of the

---

6 This domestication continues more than sixty years after Indian independence. The structural adjustment programmes in India since 1992 under the aegis of the World Bank and International Monetary Fund (IMF) appreciate women's domestic status (Sangari 1999: 288). Further, women were a part of the domestic economy even during premodern times. For instance, Horner has thrown light on the woman worker under primitive Buddhism (2001: 86-91). During this period, poorer women worked outside their home: in paddy and cotton fields, on cremation grounds, as acrobats, as domestic slaves, musicians, dancers and courtesans. These are instances of their ability to rely upon themselves from an economic point of view without being a part of the "domestic space" of the family (ibid.: 6). However, since these occupations extend to the public space what women have traditionally done in the private they too are "domestic". They relied upon the sexual division of labour. Further, these occupations are premodern instances of the Indian feminine, as well.

7 But profit alone was not the motive; as Sangari observes, such an affiliation was also connected to the resurgence of aristocratic values in England because of the pastoral nostalgia due to the industrial revolution (1994: 36). She also observes that British rule had a martial–mercantile character.

8 The discussion that follows is based on Banerjee (1989). Colonial India also reveals how women contributed to the industry by working in their households. See Sen (1999).

modernization of their traditional occupations, which was taken over by men (Banerjee 1989: 271).[9] Colonizers selectively modernized the Indian economy to acquire raw materials and manufacture commodities for import. This process did not offer women mass participation in the industrial workforce, but encouraged them to participate in the domestic service sector (ibid.).[10] Further, the overhauling of village economies shifted women from non-agrarian to agricultural occupations. Women participated in traditional low-capital labour-intensive work like superior craft for the market. They also worked in caste-based occupations like pottery, sweeping and washing, sowing, and cultivation of seeds. Women were also engaged in sbsistence craft making, animal husbandry, processing forest produce and the like. These occupations did not require special skills and were derived from local material. "In their own perception, women saw these tasks not only as part of their daily drudgery but also as a backdrop to their life cycle, their longings and their celebrations" (ibid.: 284-85). However, men started replacing women to make such daily commodities because of their mobility, migration and mechanization. Consequently, women could neither continue with their traditional skills nor enter the mechanized workforce because of traditional restrictions on their mobility. They increasingly started providing domestic service such as cooking in other families to sustain themselves.[11] These services were open to

9 There was a spurt in the construction of roadways and buses during colonization. However, the growth of mechanized transport led to the decline of premodern water- and road-based transport (Banerjee 1989: 276).

10 In Bengal about 70 per cent of women in 1911 were in domestic service (Banerjee 1989: 278). Banerjee's account is confined to Bengal.

11 Some impoverished women started working in mills and factories. See Sen 1999, for an account of women's domestic labour to jute production during the colonial period.

women from all caste groups.[12] Women who migrated to cities were often destitute and supplemented their income with prostitution. The men on the other hand had their wives and children in the rural area to whom they sent their savings.[13] The gendered divide between the public workplace of factories and the private one of domesticity was heightened with the advent of modernity.[14] Indeed, in the Indian context there was little conflict between public and private patriarchy (Banerjee 1999: 330). Patriarchs within the household determined women's entry into the labour market by using them as "flexible resources" (ibid.: 230) for family income. Women's productive labour adapted to changes in the economy, with family destiny and political change. Yet ". . . there is to be found a remarkable degree of uniformity over time in ideas of familial controls over women's sexuality and reproductive capacities . . ." (ibid.: 330-31).[15]

Besides the economic, the projection of domesticity as a normative domain for women emerged in bureaucratic, legal and historical contexts as well. Although England adhered to free trade, the East India Company subjected India to rigid forms of bureaucracy (Sangari 1994: 34). In order to elicit the co-operation of the new recruits into bureaucracy, colonial rule kept intact and even codified India's patriarchal,

12 "Even brāhmaṇa women could work as cooks in other families" (Banerjee 1989: 291). Yet women did not form a homogeneous category and their domestic labour in India needs to be contextualized by factors of caste and class.

13 Banerjee observes that workers in the Mumbai mills did take their families along (1989: 293). Also see Sen (1999).

14 The private is here defined as the domain that is restricted to the home. Thus, in this context the economy is public.

15 "In Britain, because of the strength of women's pressure in the public arena through the feminist struggles of the last hundred years or so, the state can no longer safely collude with domestic patriarchy on most matters (witness the recent law against rape in marriage); but in India there is as yet no equivalent . . .. " (Banerjee 1999: 332).

hierarchical past. "The contradictory character of colonial rule produced divided readings of India as the barbaric subject of reform and as the 'civilized' repository of usable 'feudal' modes" (ibid.: 38).[16] The state and secular law governed civil, criminal and business matters in the public sphere, while the family and personal law governed the private sphere. The public sphere came under the aegis of modernity and the private under tradition. Thus, a divide was established between a common civil and a multiple religion-based personal law, where the former governed civil and criminal disputes, while the latter applied to domestic ones.[17] Such acts of renewal were connected to the colonial political economy (ibid.: 34).[18] To quote Sangari:

> . . . the traditions they invented were extrapolated from and engrafted on existing and emerging structures of inequality.
>
> — ibid.: 38

The renewal of premodern culture and practice in colonial India was confined to upper caste elites in order to produce surplus value for the British (ibid.). This renewal often conflated religion with law (ibid.: 41).[19] The continuity of cultural and group identities was maintained through the "antiquity of religious texts" (ibid.: 39). Patriarchal distinctions

---

16 Since they also took over political power from Muslim rulers, the British projected them as aggressive in contrast to the image of Hindus as needy of British benevolence (Sangari 1994: 39).

17 See Agnes (2008) and Shramjivikanchi Ekta Samiti (1995) for overviews.

18 Rather it applied itself to retaining much of what was termed as feudal due to economic, political and ideological rationale (Sangari 1994: 34).

19 " . . . religion (Koran and Śāstras) is to Indians what the Constitution is to the British." (Sangari 1994: 41).

played a central role in establishing such continuity, which for most part was Sanskritized (ibid.).[20]

One could extend Habermas's remarks about ancient or classical natural law to the traditional Indian world-view. The latter, also known as *dharma*, was governed by a metaphysical order and occupied the same position as Western natural law. *Dharma* prescribed a "catalogue of duties in the material order of life, whether of a city or of a social class" (Habermas 1974: 84).[21] This prescription was made so that the citizens could develop their good life. *The Laws of Manu* contains a code of conduct of duties (*dharma*) that are universal (*sāmānya dharma*) and specific (*sva-dharma*). The common duties include non-violence, truth-telling, not-stealing, purification and the suppression of sensory abilities (Doniger and Smith 1991: 10.63). Members of underprivileged castes and women have the primary task of service; thus,

> the Lord assigned only one activity to a servant: serving these (other) classes without resentment. — ibid.: 1.88-91

Manu's laws uphold that women "are not fit for independence" (ibid.: 9.3) and have to therefore be protected by men to

---

20 It was during the British rule that tradition came to be defined in terms of rigid textual interpretations of *Manusmṛti*.

21 There are important differences between the premodern and modern politics. According to the former, politics is the continuation of ethics, it's a doctrine of the good and just life (Habermas 1974: 42). Human nature is an innate essence and the human being depends upon the city for its realization. While thinkers of modernity root the ethical conduct of the individual in an inner life, which differs from legality and politics discerned in external action. Ancient politics depended on pedagogy and not technique. It is praxis oriented to the formation of the individual's character. Finally, classical politics is about a *phronesis* or a prudential understanding of a situation while modern politics is about apodictic episteme where we know an object to the extent that we can make it.

whom they have duties (*strīdharma*). The latter comprises of domestic and purificatory tasks (ibid.: 9.11). Manu's code also excludes women from reciting Vedic verses (ibid.: 9.18). Women are regarded as impure in their postnatal condition so that ritual purity is maintained through "a closed structure to preserve land, women and ritual quality within it" (Chakravarti and Gill 2002: 204). Such *strīdharma* is largely directed towards the privileged-caste woman so that she can produce sons. Yet *Manusmṛti* also prescribes specific duties for the members of underprivileged castes to which women from those castes adhered.

In contrast to laws such as those of Manu, modern natural law — enshrined in the Indian constitution — prescribes formal rights as rights of freedom to allow for a sphere of personal choice in which every individual can maximize his or her own needs. Habermas's remark that "The old politics has become alien to all of us . . ." (Habermas 1974: 41) is applicable to the Western context. The forces of colonization in the non-Western world mingled the disparate world-views of the ancient and the modern through imperial domination and nationalist resistance, as well as by modern reform on the basis of the central premise of Hindu-Indian womanhood (Sangari 1994: 39). The colonial powers preserved the past both to please their elite allies in India and to demonstrate the need for reforming India. This made the woman visible as the domesticated feminine who had to be the recipient of philanthropy too (ibid.: 39). For the colonizing forces, "the history of patriarchal practices coagulates into the spurious assertion of a 'Hindu' male unity. Forms of patriarchal oppression (illiteracy, seclusion, widow immolation) are interpreted as forms of protection for women" (ibid.: 95). The law itself coalesced differences of caste and community to speak in terms of Hindu law and identity (Chakravarti and Roy 2006: 188). Women were identified under a unified Hindu law, whether they were widows who fought for their share of their spouse's property or wives (ibid.). Hence, modern bourgeois forms of essentialization of women coexisted with indigenous ones of *strīdharma* (Sangari 1994: 57).

Evangelical and utilitarian charity defined the colonial state as altruistically holding the key to both preservation of an ancient hierarchy and the initiation of reform (ibid.: 40). British orientalists[22] and utilitarians,[23] as well as, Indian nationalists[24] essentialized Indian women to reform them or restore their lost glory.[25] Thus, as Sangari notes, they engaged in ". . . a double reading of women as naturally libidinous . . . and . . . as naturally chaste . . ." (ibid.: 54).[26] Although they tended to

---

22 Orientalists such as Max Müller and William Jones glorified a Vedic past where women were extolled as goddesses on the basis of Brāhmanical Sanskrit texts (Chakravarti 1989). As Sangari observes, orientalism also became an extension of the knowledge mission of the enlightened West in teaching and learning Indian philosophy, literature, religion and language (1994: 41-42). Antiquity, chronology, common origins of language, mythology and race were all a part of this activity which became the foundational history of the West (ibid.: 41). See Said (1978) for a detailed account of this phenomenon.

23 The utilitarians were involved in British policy making. James Mill maintained that the level of a civilization is to be judged by the position of its women (Sangari 1994: 97-98).

24 See Altekar (2001).

25 This discussion in the paragraphs that follow is derived from Chakravarti (1989; Roy 2006) and Sangari (1994).

26 Sangari observes that the orientalist project reveals a tension between essentializing antiquity and employing modern rational methods to arrive at knowledge about archaic times (1994: 42). She also notes that with a couple of exceptions (Ram Kamal Sen, Mritunjaya Vidyalankar) Indians were not a part of the colonial orientalist project. Further, native interpreters, namely the *paṇḍits* in this case, often provided the raw material of manuscripts to the Westerner without authoring any interpretation.

distrust them as sexually licentious, the English simultaneously projected Indian women as epitomes of chastity to be emulated by Western women.[27] Thus, they construed ". . . the colonial state as the 'masculine' agent of a 'benevolent' patriarchy" (ibid.). Further since women did not have access to either the texts of antiquity or the philosophical aspects of Hinduism, they became objects to be surveyed by "text and custom" or "into the expressive medium" (ibid.: 55). Thus, women became "contradictory subjects of reform" (ibid.: 56).

Orientalists upheld the view that India had a magnificent past in which women were celebrated. Utilitarians such as James Mill presented an opposite picture of the Indian past as a barbaric society that encouraged cruel practices such as *satī* towards women.[28] Thus, the British empire had the onus of saving Indian women from their perceived inadequacy of Indian men. When Hindu patriarchal practices conflicted with the British domestic ideology of motherhood and wives as companionate wives, they were seen as needing reform (ibid.: 55). Yet European modernity was patriarchal in treating only men as free citizens. Rather than subjects, women were the objects or property of men: they neither had the right to vote nor associate freely in the public space of civil society. In this denial of citizenship and rights they were restricted to the private space of domestic life ordained as their natural condition.[29]

---

27 James Mill for instance believed that there was an inconsistency in Hinduism between libidinousness and chastity (Sangari 1994: 55).

28 See Chakravarti (1989) for this point.

29 The utilitarian position of reform was influenced by the struggle for emancipation of women waged by nineteenth-century English philosophers such as Harriet Taylor and John Stuart Mill (Gatens 1991: 27-47; Mill 1996). They favoured the

→

Nationalists such as Raja Rammohun Roy, Swami Dayanand Saraswati and Vivekananda responded by taking up the task of interpreting traditional texts in a changing situation.[30] They argued that there was no Vedic support for *satī* (self-immolation of the widows) and advocated widow remarriage. They also called for an abolition of child marriage. In addition, they believed that women can achieve *mokṣa*. Nationalists were analogous to the orientalists in their worry that Indian women had to be saved, not from so-called effeminate Indian men, but from the British empire. In this endeavour they affirmed India's past as one where women were venerated; they prescribed a renewal of such a past whereby women could embrace motherhood and produce sons to save the nation.[31]

→ education of women and even argued for their suffrage to improve British civilization. These philosophers articulated the problem of discrimination against women. Their writings spurred a series of gender reforms, which initiated the woman's question, but were problematic for their underlying patriarchal assumptions — not unlike the approach of utilitarian philosophers to the woman's question. They believed that women require education and voting rights to become better companions for men. Thus, women were confined to the domestic sphere as the natural realm, but had the right to cultivate their talents. In addition, they spoke on behalf of the middle-class European woman who could keep maids, and universalized her problems. In this they overlooked the "others" who served her within the nation. In a similar vein, Victorian feminists who thought themselves as liberated in the modern Western context perceived Indian women as "white women's burden" (Narayan 1995: 403).

30 See for example Roy (2001: 25-29) and Chakravarti (1989) for overviews of nationalists.

31 Responding to Dayananda Saraswati's claim that Indian women require wet-nurses to look after their children, Chakravarti (1989) foregrounds the Vedic *dāsī* (wet-nurse) in problematizing privilege among women. See Mahadevan (2002) for a detailed discussion of this problem.

As the above discussion shows "... preexisting British patriarchal attitudes enter significantly into the negotiation of Indian patriarchal forms mediated by the political economy of the colonial state and the nostalgia for 'organic' agrarian societies (ibid.: 97). Colonization splintered the British ruling class into landed gentry and the new middle class, but it also united them in holding on to the empire as their common interest (ibid.). It invested women with moral power and also sustained the divide between the public and private sphere. Family ideology and the preserving of the morality of woman became inscribed into the nation and empire (ibid.: 106). Colonialism and its excesses required the home, while the home itself could exist because of colonialism. Thus, women in England, both upper and middle-class, became symbols of superiority and cultural difference in relation to colonies (ibid.: 98). Unlike Indian middle-class women who did not have a voice to articulate their point of view, English middle-class women had already articulated a sense of agency — albeit in the domestic space (ibid.: 97). Again, they differed from Indian women in not being victims of extreme misogyny and therefore not requiring reform (ibid.: 106). "... They are also read along the same continuum of value as Hindu women-chaste, self-sacrificing, egoless, secluded (afresh) in the home, repositories of custom and religion" (ibid.). In fact, English women were asked to emulate these traits from their Hindu counterparts. It is through an affirmation of their position within the family itself that English women became such symbols of domestic bliss (ibid.: 98). Rather than denial of education, they were prescribed a specific form of education, namely, genteel curiosity, non-instrumental knowledge of learning not to know and intuitive knowledge (ibid.: 100).[32] Such a "willed ignorance" became the foundation of "inscrutability" and "the

[32] Aggressive curiosity and instrumental will to know more was cultivated by males for their colonies (Sangari 1994: 100).

capacity to instruct" (ibid.: 100); this type of knowledge is "expressive" in that it manifests itself in conduct rather than in any literary work.[33] Consequently, with what Sangari terms as the reprimanding power of female moral autonomy, male agency is encouraged to colonize with greater vigour (ibid.: 101).

> Altruism, a colonial model of dominance, is not only internalized as female attribute, but also becomes a local as well as imperial construction of female "desire".
>
> — ibid.: 104, 107

Thus, care as sympathy for the underprivileged was based on the normative role given to women in the private sphere, both in Britain and India.

The need to reform the position of women came from "diffuse" perspectives in nineteenth-century India (Kosambi 1995: 46). The British themselves wanted to reform the Hindu male, who was supposedly patriarchal in his home, through the education of Hindu women (Sangari 1994: 53). This required teaching women the virtues of care and nurture in the domestic space so that they could humanize their own husbands. Consequently, from the British point of view, education for Hindu-Indian women was seldom linked to learning the arts and literature, but to their performance in the domestic space (ibid.: 82). British women too supported education for Indian women who were seen as victims of inhuman practices such

---

33 Sangari citing Hannah More (1994: 102). Sarah Ellis who wrote the manual, *Women of England,* addresses the middle class rather than the gentry whose task remains the development of their natural altruism (Sangari 1994: 102-03). Their "moral power is the sum of narrow domesticity and a desexualized, egoless, anti-intellectual femininity" (ibid.: 104). Their domestic situation makes it practical for them to exercise such power.

as *satī*.[34] Indian nationalists, who in response, wanted to protect Hindu-Indian women from colonial slavery, were divided into progressive reformers like Gopal Ganesh Agarkar and Jotirao Phule, as well as, conservatives like Lokmanya Tilak (Kosambi 1995: 46).[35] Both sides wanted to end the oppression of women, but the conservatives in particular did not want to disrupt their subordinate domestic position. With the exception of Phule, male reformers for most part placed emphasis on negative freedom or "emancipation from" practices such as tonsuring of widows, their seclusion and early consummation of child marriages (ibid.). Further, much of the education for women favoured by reformers rendered them more compliant within the domestic sphere.[36] The purpose of women's education was often to make them worthwhile companions of men,[37] nurturing mothers and socializers (Chakravarti and Roy 2006: 203). Thus, unwittingly the nationalists too advocated a domestic role for women through education like the British. The last fifteen years of the nineteenth century turned to training women professionally, for the health and education of other women. None of this changed the traditional

---

34 See Midgley (2007: 65-91) for a detailed overview of the British imperial women's interest in the Indian women's reform and the political character of "sympathy" for the colonized.

35 Kosambi (1995: 139-40) describes Ramabai's friendship with Justice Ranade and his wife Ramabai Ranade in the latter's words. Yet Chakravarti and Roy (2006: 215-24) cite Justice Ranade's remarriage to a eleven-year-old girl, as an instance to show how social reformers too subscribed to the patriarchal image of the woman as the ideal wife and mother.

36 Sangari has shown how even many supporters of *satī* did not oppose women's education for precisely this reason (1994: 85-88).

37 But besides reproduction, young wives were also educated in art and literature to become "companionate wives" (Chakravarti and Roy 2006: 206-10).

roles of women drastically as the reasons for educating women differed from those for men. The private sphere of the home was separated from the public sphere. Education "for the reformers . . . was also the tool by which women could be converted into moral beings for a changed social order, a new means by which their *strī-svabhāva* could be transformed into a suitable variant of the traditional conception of *strīdharma*" (ibid.: 204).

Women's worlds centred around their homes, and the latter became a moral and affective component, rather than just a reproductive space. The responsibility for such an affective unit resided with the new domestic Indian woman. Thus, women began to acquire a limited type of agency, becoming "social actors for a specific purpose" (ibid.). Through their nurturing function they produced potential good wives out of girls and boys who were fit to work in the new bureaucratic order and participate in nationalism (either British or Indian). Women had to undertake education in the "domestic economy" where they learnt health care, sanitation, childcare and the like (ibid.: 205). Thus, "The militant protest against injustices of women ends in a reaffirmation of the patriarchal ideal" (Kosambi 1995: 28).[38]

The colonizers and reformers had introduced several legal changes with respect to women in the later part of the nineteenth century, all of which retained women's position in the household. Hence, "The household remained an embattled space between men, between women, and between men and women" (Chakravarti 2006: 238). Three major reforms introduced with the advent of the British were, the Abolition of Sati (1829), Widow Remarriage Act (1856) and the Age of Consummation of Marriage (1891). Each of these saw a

[38] But there were two exceptions to this, namely, Phule and Agarkar who advocated the equality of sexes.

struggle between "multiple patriarchies", while pioneering feminism did make its contribution to debates regarding age of consent. However, these changes could not materialize without the acquiescence of the female population to propagate them and convert new generations to them.

> The schooling of women thus was a major platform of middle-class reform. — Chakravarti 2006: 201

Modern patriarchy became more visible and also endeavoured to make them more controllable (ibid.: 237). Pre-modern patriarchy also made women "governable" by teaching them how to become "good wives". For instance, the *strīdharma-paddhati* prescribed a code for women so that they became good wives (Leslie 1995). Its account of virtue assured prestige, earthly happiness and heavenly life (Chakravarti 2006: 202). The code regarded women as inherently disorderly, a threat to the domestic sphere they occupied. Given that this sphere is connected with the public one its orderliness was maintained through the "feminization of evil" (ibid.: 202). However, premodern patriarchy, unlike its modern forms, was "invisible within the general framework of religion, custom and family tradition" (ibid.: 237).

The forging of Indian femininity took place under conditions where women could not just be devoted wives and mothers, but also had to be courageous nationalists who defended their homeland. As a result, "Indian women almost built superwomen: a combination of the spiritual Maitreyī, the learned Gārgī, the suffering Sītā, the faithful Sāvitrī and the heroic Lakshmibai" (Chakravarti 1989: 79). The concomitance of the diverse paradigms of tradition and modernity in Indian society, makes Habermas's question regarding retaining the normative aspect of classicism with the scientific rigour of modernity, relevant in the Indian context (Habermas 1974: 44). In the process of addressing this question, the pioneering feminist Ramabai contested the feminine from a feminist point of view by taking into account the overlaps between tradition, modernity and colonization.

Ramabai's Feminist Voice

As the above discussion reveals, the domestic ideology constituting Indian femininity was produced in the "entangled space" of colonizers and social reformers (Sangari 1994: 40).[39] However this entanglement also gave rise to feminist voices that challenged the feminine space of seclusion both in India and in England. In India Ramabai was ". . . the one to lay the foundation for a movement of woman's liberation in India".[40] Unlike her non-feminist nationalist contemporaries, Ramabai defined women as a social category and for most part focused on liberating them from the perspective of gender equality, rather than benefits to the home or nation (Kosambi 2000: 7). Despite the colonizers and nationalists pitching for a divide between Indian women and their Western counterparts, her philosophical outlook and efforts were directed towards solidarity between women across national boundaries. Her critique of gendered oppression[41] went beyond the nationalist questioning of British colonization in becoming a catalyst in the formation of an international movement of solidarity for women.[42]

Kosambi observes that Rambai's life story has ". . . a modern late twentieth-century ring" (1995: 55). She was

---

39 Sangari also adds indigenous litterateurs to this list.

40 A.B. Shah as quoted by Tharu and Lalita (1991: 243).

41 Kosambi points out that Ramabai's expose of the condition of women was often viewed as anti-national (2000: 23).

42 Ramabai's conversion to Christianity which was motivated by the subordinate position of women in Hinduism, was also an anti-colonial stance (Chakravarti 2006: 379).

educated in traditional Hindu texts,[43] exposed to Western education, married by choice to a person from a different linguistic and caste community, a participant in public life, a leader who addressed rallies and ran organizations. She exposed the contradictions in Hinduism through her textual scholarship, subsequently converted to Christianity as her "self-chosen"[44] religion and went on to question its orthodoxy. Hence, she ". . . seemed always to be outside the system of which she was ostensibly a part" (Viswanathan 2007: 249). Besides Ramabai travelled extensively both within India and abroad (to Japan, England and U.S.A.) and was, consequently, exposed to Western education and activism.

> The final "modern" touch in Ramabai's life was her capacity to manage "the woman's two roles": family life and work outside the family as a mother and a social reformer.
>
> — Kosambi 1995: 56

Ramabai did not start out as a feminist. Rather on a nationalist conservative/reformist tone in her early work *Strī Dharma Nīti* (1882).[45] She forayed into public debates on gender "as a surrogate male social reformer" (Kosambi 2000: 16),[46] to detail a code of conduct so that women could adapt to conjugality and nurture in the domestic sphere of the home (Chakravarti and Roy 2006: 391). She contributed to "schooling" women into the new colonial/reformist patriarchy within the domestic sphere. In this text, Ramabai also urged women to follow

---

43 Thus, she enjoyed gender parity in education.

44 Viswanathan (2007: 261).

45 See Kosambi (2000) for this text.

46 This work prompted Tilak's newspaper *Kesari* to applaud her as a champion of women's cause, which has so far been the "lot of men" (quoted in Kosambi 2000: 17). But this appreciation was only during her pre-feminist phase. Tilak became a staunch opponent of Ramabai when she converted to feminism and Christianity.

mythological paradigms of womanhood (Kosambi 2000: 16). Thus, there is a tension in *Strī Dharma Nīti* between her "castigation of women as culpable for their own subjection and her simultaneous exoneration of them as victims conditioned to internalize their subjection" (ibid.: 17).[47]

However, with her *The Cry of Indian Women* and *The High Caste Brahmin Woman*, Ramabai shifted to an unequivocal feminist stance.[48] She supported the non-seclusion of widows who remain single all their lives and get constrained within the domestic space (ibid.: 22). She cited the 1881 census that mentions 20,930,626 widows from diverse age and caste groups from which 669,100 were under nineteen years of age (ibid.: 175). Ramabai argued that to prevent their economic and sexual exploitation widows needed institutions for shelter and education. This would allow them to comfortably do their daily chores and acquire skills for financial independence (ibid.: 177). She lamented the lack of institutional support for women in nineteenth-century India (ibid.: 175).

Building upon the legacy of Savithribai Phule, Ramabai argued for women's education, maintaining that despite their commitment to the women's cause, male reformers did not give adequate attention to it. She made a case for young women to be instructed in vocational skills, as well as in science and teaching. Ramabai believed that as doctors and teachers they could contribute to women's health and education. Thus, she went beyond the standard view of merely imparting vocational training to women. Ramabai suggested availing the services of the best American and Indian teachers for a "combined advantage of Eastern and Western civilization and education" (ibid.: 177). She upheld that educational institutions and shelters for women acquire library collections that covered

---

47 In this work, she indicts women for being complicit in their own oppression, as well as that of the nation.

48 Both works are in Kosambi (2000).

topics on social sciences, natural sciences, humanities, literature and religion. In addition, Ramabai recommended lectures to expose female students to arts, sciences and travel. She also worked towards rehabilitating deserted wives, famine victims from underprivileged castes and sexually oppressed women through institutionalization (ibid.: 16, 22).

Ramabai broke new ground by entering the public sphere to give speeches and generate debate. Thus, she inducted women as agents who debate and dialogue about reforms such as the Age of Consent Bill, rather than as objects of debate and reform (ibid.: 23). Hence, Ramabai had crossed "the threshold of the home, to which all women and especially widows were confined, and stepped into the public space reserved for men" (Chakravarti 2006: 229).

But she did not renounce the domestic; on the contrary, she attempted to critique and transform the domestic space from such a public sphere. But this was not all. Ramabai expanded Ramabai Ranade's organization for women, namely, the Arya Mahila Samaj, to encourage women to develop skills of public speaking.[49] Further, she also urged women to participate in political life; she herself trained women delegates for the National Congress in erstwhile Bombay in 1889. Ramabai simultaneously communicated with traditional women through Purāṇa recitals (Kosambi 1995: 54). All of this reveals that Ramabai believed that women should voice their own experiences and reflections publicly so that their condition is transformed.

By focusing on the plight of the "upper-caste Hindu women", Ramabai maintained against nationalists that Hindu-Indian women did not ever enjoy a past glory, but always had to contend with three unhappy phases of childhood, married

49 She put down the clause that men could attend the sessions only if they were accompanied by women (Kosambi 1995: 55).

life and widowhood to contend.[50] Her critique was directed to the principles of rebirth, oppressive social custom and caste violence in the British codified Manu's Dharmaśāstras (Kosambi 2000: 131-35). She pointed out that girls were seen as unwanted, sinful and restricted to reproduction (Kosambi 1995: 33; 2000: 106). The prevalence of female infanticide made Indian women's entry into childhood an achievement.[51] During this period, girls were often not given the same attentive education as boys (Kosambi 2000: 107). Education was regarded as impairment of their feminine tasks in the domestic sphere. Girls were married off as children without consent, often to men who were much older than them. They were ill-treated and humiliated in their matrimonial homes.[52] Further, they were not allowed any education after marriage, since married life was meant to be spent in the drudgery of household chores and gaining approval of the spouse. Yet many a time women remained strangers to their spouses. Finally, most girls entered widowhood very early considering that they were married off to men who were significantly older than them.[53] Widowhood, "the most dreaded period in the high-caste woman's life"[54] was perceived as a retribution for either disloyalty to or murder of the husband in the past life. Widows were considered inauspicious, ostracized

---

50 The discussion that follows is derived from Ramabai's "The Upper Caste Indian Woman" in Kosambi (2000).

51 This condition is unfortunately still rampant both in India and parts of its diaspora.

52 Ramabai observes that despite all of this, the bride was frequently subject to ill-treatment that was often much worse than the prescriptions of the laws of Manu.

53 Most of this discussion is derived from Kosambi (2000: 159-69). Since the practice of *satī* was abolished in the year 1829, the problem of widowhood intensified (ibid.: 164). Ramabai argues following Max Müller that there is no scriptural justification for *satī*, as even Manu's scriptures do not endorse it.

54 Ramabai quoted in Kosambi (1995: 34).

and exploited for domestic labour (ibid.: 109). Condemned to austerity, they were humiliated with tonsured hair and vulnerable to sexual exploitation (ibid.: 110).[55] This was done to contain their sexuality since they had to occupy the domestic space with other women who were wives. The premise underlying Ramabai's critique of the plight of the upper caste woman was that she had never known freedom (Kosambi 1995: 33) to the extent that she could not even recognize the absence of bondage in her life.

According to Ramabai, women's condition in nineteenth-century India had not changed since ancient times. In the past, they were tied to the household by their husbands' power and community's strictures, while their mobility was proscribed through legal control such as Manu's laws during the colonial period (ibid.: 33-34). In both instances, the idea of a domestic feminine was justified by Hindu scriptures,[56] which perceived womanhood as a punishment for past *karma* (ibid.: 34). To acquire liberation women would have to wait for metaphysical salvation to be born as high-caste men for which they had to mandatorily worship their husbands. From Ramabai's perspective, both colonialists and nationalists contributed to plural patriarchies through bonds of feminine seclusion.

As commentators have observed, her expose of the flaws underlying British colonialism had not received much attention (Viswanathan 2007: 253). In the course of her spiritual journey she converted to Christianity. Yet, Ramabai also critiqued its mixing of human and divine attributes, and the sectarianism of the Anglican Church. Her affirmation of Christianity was independent of the British church thereby belying the complicity between colonial loyalty (or anti-nationalism) and

---

55 Ramabai observed that hair removal was linked to superstition, while sexual exploitation led to more crimes like female infanticide (Kosambi 2000: 109-10).

56 These include the Dharmaśāstras, the Purāṇas and the epics.

conversion. She did not endorse the homogenization between religious faith and national identity in one of her Christian mentor's equation of Christian kingdom to British nation. Ramabai had critiqued British colonialism as complicit with Hindu orthodoxy in the control of the woman as an exploitative and misogynistic force, even prior to her conversion to Christianity (Kosambi 2000: 22). In her prefeminist work *Strī Dharma Nīti*, Ramabai disapproved of the British for subjugating millions of Indians (ibid.). However, her conversion to Christianity sharpened this critique. Later on, in her feminist work, *The High Caste Hindu Woman*, she argued:

> We cannot blame the English government for not defending a helpless woman; it is only fulfilling its agreement made with the male population of India . . .. — ibid.: 158

She maintained that its support of "ancient institutions" (ibid.) in India was meant to increase its profit at the expense of Indian women. Ramabai demanded financial assistance from the British as a right in return for the exploitation of India (ibid.: 22). The 1897 plague in Pune prompted her to raise the question of women's health in the colonial context. In the course of her relief work, she observed in a letter to the *Bombay Guardian* that Indian women patients were being badly treated by male doctors.

> The shameful way in which women were made to submit to treatment by male doctors goes to prove that English authorities in general do not believe that Indian women are modest and need special consideration . . ..[57]

Ramabai upheld that the British government could not take care of the health of Indian women. She compared the colonial attitude to Indian women with the ancients who made them enter the funeral pyre (ibid.: 22). Again, Ramabai launched a

57 Ramabai quoted in Tharu and Lalita (1991: 246).

subtle critique of the British measures for women's education in India that ignored the specificities of the Indian situation (ibid.: 175-76). At the outset, she appreciated the efforts made by Mary Carpenter in setting up schools for training women teachers in India with the help of the British government. There were about six "normal schools" in India (ibid.: 176). However, despite the scholarships that were provided with the patronage of Carpenter and others, Ramabai discerned many problems in these schools. For one, they did not adhere to caste norms.[58] For another, many could not attend them because widows often did not get educational support from their relatives. In the case of being rendered homeless, the financial sustenance provided by these scholarships was paltry. Further, they could get financial support only after passing examinations which were beyond the reach of illiterate widows in India. Women hesitated in joining missionary schools because they had to forsake their faith to do so.

Ramabai did not turn to either Indian nationalists or the British government to support her project for women's institutions. Instead, she wrote her feminist treatise to draw attention to and get support for her widow's home from Western women (Kosambi 1995: 57). Ramabai appealed to the people of America about the condition of *The High Caste Hindu Woman*, with its publication in 1887. With her publication funds, she opened a home for widows, called Sharada Sadan, which functioned for ten years. By appealing to bonds between women that cut across national lines, Ramabai provided a global perspective to feminism. Yet there were limits to her acts of solidarity for she did not establish a women's movement on a mass scale within India that cut across caste lines. Besides, Ramabai did not succeed in establishing ties with British women for the cause of Indian women, although

[58] This is problematic from the perspective of caste equality. It also runs counter to Ramabai's critique of Hinduism as propagating the inequality of caste and gender.

she did so with the Americans.[59] She went to Britain in 1883 to become a medical doctor after converting to Christianity in the same year. She could not complete her studies because of several obstacles and in the meantime she renounced the Church's women communities of which she was a part from the religious and educational point of view.

One can trace Ramabai's failure in this respect to the ideology of British colonialism, which looked down upon Indian women as English women's burden, to be reformed through their civilizing mission. Her correspondence with the women in the Anglican clergy and between them ". . . provide first-hand evidence of how imperial power relations intruded on personal relationship and, more specifically, how the exigencies of an imperial Christianity intervened to prevent (or at least to imperil) the possibility of international sisterhood" (Burton 1995: 33).

Being one of the first to work out a feminist statement in India, Ramabai both espoused femininity, but also contested it through her juxtaposition between tradition and modernity. In a manner reminiscent of some of the male reformers, she argued for womens issues from the perspective of the equality of sexes.

> Since men and women are indissolubly united by providence as members of the same body of human society, each must suffer when their fellow-members suffer . . ..
>
> — Kosambi 2000: 170

Yet, she also reproduced the idealized feminine image of Indian women with a natural vocation as mothers, in claiming that women needed to be reformed because of their influence on children, right from the prenatal stage. Her argument for women's education maintained that their incarceration in a

---

59 This is derived from Burton (1995).

domestic set-up could not allow mothers to bring healthy children into the world (ibid.). She argued further that it created bigotry amongst women who were thereby prevented from discharging their maternal duties such as encouraging their sons to be educated or inculcating health and hygiene (ibid.: 170-71). Ramabai believed that a weak generation could weaken the nation as a whole as the colonization of India demonstrated. Thus, she upheld that women ought to become strong mothers to produce strong sons for the nation. This argument coincides with the imperial and nationalist idealization of the feminine virtue of care in the conventional view of motherhood.

However, Ramabai also had a strong feminist perspective in dissonance with the feminine. This is evident in her claim ". . . that the chief needs of high-caste Hindu women are: first, self-reliance; second, education; and third, native women teachers" (ibid.: 171). This ideal of autonomy to be attained by women through the process of acquiring and imparting education is one of the first explicit statements of feminism in India. It reveals the need for women's agency rather than being objects of reform under a colonial administration and its nationalist opponents. She argued that since women could not merely depend upon men, mere legalization of widow remarriage was inadequate. Ramabai saw that there was a social resistance to the implementation of the latter (ibid.: 168). Further, men who practised widow remarriage had to undergo immense suffering in the face of social stigma. Hence, she proclaimed:

> Remarriage, therefore, is not available, nor would it be at all times desirable, as a mitigation of the sufferer's lot.
>
> — ibid.: 169

Again, remarriage would intern the woman within her domestic situation where her lack of autonomy and isolation would be replayed. Hence, rather than depend upon entering the domestic space through marriage, women should learn to become self-reliant through education (ibid.: 171-74).[60] Ramabai believed that women should go beyond domesticity and find a place in institutions by exercising their rights to education, health and public homes as widows. She advocated institutions as sources of practical and emotional support, as well as training spaces for economic independence and self-improvement so that they became "teachers, governesses, nurses and housekeepers" (ibid.: 177). This suggests that Ramabai's reformative and transformative attitude of questioning femininity laid the foundation for feminism.

Ramabai's work on the "upper-caste Indian woman" was the outcome of her appreciation of feminist activism in the Western world (ibid.: 18).[61] Her understanding of Indian society was mediated by "the American critique of contemporary Western society and her general exposure to the women's movement in USA" . . . (ibid.: 28). Ramabai approvingly mentions the period from 1789–1809 as the "preface to the history of women's education", while discussing this struggle in the US till 1878 (ibid.: 201-02). She argued that women's education in the West provides evidence that it will not disrupt their participation in housework or arrest their health or beauty (ibid.: 202-03, 206-07). Against conservative opinion that, despite their inability for education, women infiltrate male territory in their bid to acquire it (ibid.: 203),

---

60 Ramabai testified before the Hunter Commission in 1882 that she was the "child of a man who had to suffer a great deal on account of advocating female education and who was compelled to discuss the subject and carry out his own views amidst great opposition" (Kosambi 1995: 35).

61 Her association of Christianity with gender egalitarianism was less significant than her solidarity with Western feminism (Kosambi 2000: 18).

Ramabai gave the example of Alice Freeman who balanced her home with an education and a job. All of this testifies to Ramabai's attempts to integrate feminist ideals with those of patriarchal femininity. She also exposed Western women to the Indian situation. Her own works were written for Western readers to motivate them to provide funds for her Widows Home (Sharada Sadan). Ramabai was ". . . an Indian straddling Western culture with equal facility and a social reformer aiming to alter societal core of caste and custom" (ibid.: 22). The utilitarians who critiqued Indian culture as inimical to women relied upon the history of feminist consciousness in their own country; however, their imperialist motive hindered them from taking this critique seriously. In contrast with her critique of imperialism, Ramabai extended the insights of the Western feminist movement in the Indian context.

Ramabai could engage in a feminist critique of domesticity to carve a public space for women through their struggle between femininity and feminism, but she was enabled by a strong "female ancestry" in her endeavour (Irigaray 1994: 91). A key figure in this respect was Savithribai Phule, the first modern feminist social reformer and educationist of nineteenth-century Maharashtra (1831-97).[62] Phule introduced the concept of education for girls and Dalits by starting a school. Besides, she questioned the patriarchal, Brāhmanical and casteist forces prevalent in Maharashtra. She also campaigned for the rights of widows to a normal life. In 1852 she founded the first women's association, called the Mahila Seva Mandal, and discerned the layers of oppression that Dalit women underwent on account of both gender and caste. Phule also pioneered the notion of institutional care for abandoned women and children by opening a home. (Indeed, she often

62 The account that follows is derived from Mani and Sardar (this publication does not have a date). Also see Tharu and Lalita (1991: 211-14).

gave shelter to the underprivileged in her own home.) The wife of one of the founding figures of modern Maharashtra Jotirao Phule,[63] she was also a poet and writer who published her own speeches, as well as, those of her husband. Phule was critical of Hinduism and saw several merits in Christianity. She contributed to the upliftment of society from disease, but died by contracting plague in the course of nursing people who were suffering from it. Clearly, Phule's openings made it possible for Ramabai to chart her feminist path.[64] However, as the following discussion shows these openings were not confined to modern India, but had roots in the contribution of women from pre-modern India as well.

Women in Indian Philosophy

Ramabai crystallized her ideas in relation to the history and philosophy of modernity. Yet the tension between the feminine and feminist dimensions in her life and works is not radically new, but consonant with some of the aspirations of women in premodern tradition. Thus:

> Ramabai's feminism was evident in her description of Mīrābāī, the sixteenth-century saint poet.
>
> — Tharu and Lalita 1991: 244

The Buddhist *theri* nuns, Gārgī, Maitreyī and the medieval saint Mīrābāī are some, among others, who have paved the way for the modern feminism of Ramabai. Since many of the

---

63 See Deshpande (2009). Following his nomenclature it will be apt to add Savithribai Phule to the list of those who founded modern Maharashtra (Deshpande names Phule, Bhave and Savarkar in his book).

64 Constraints of space prevent a more detailed discussion of Savitribai Phule's remarkable contribution to the women's question. The same constraints prevent a discussion of Muktabai and Tarabai Shinde.

women from the premodern period are spiritual seekers, they resonate with Irigaray's remark that mysticism ". . . is the only place . . . in which woman speaks and acts so publicly" (1985: 191). With its emphasis on indeterminacy, mysticism creates the space for questioning stereotypical identities such as the domestic feminine one of care.

The earliest traceable sources of women's philosophy in India are the *therigāthās* from the sixth century BCE.[65] They were written by Buddhist senior nuns or *theris*. Women from different walks of life, peasants, artisans, business communities, aristocrats and courtesans joined the Buddhist order or *saṅgha* as *theris*. The Buddha himself accepted women after persuasion by his disciple Ānanda. However, women could join the *saṅgha* only after obeying the eight norms that were prescribed — some of which were difficult — which put them in an inferior position in relation to the monks (*theras*).[66] Fulfilling these difficult principles was a way of discouraging women from joining the order. Further, women had to undergo the struggle of leaving the space of domestic confinement to join the *saṅgha*. The *theris* composed lyrics about the transformation that their life underwent after embracing Buddhism. As Verma (2000: 82-84) observes, these compositions reflect Buddhism's positive image of women. They express the desire to be free from domestic drudgery or mental grief or anxiety. They also contain criticism of class and caste in the course of revealing the urge for liberation (*nirvāṇa*). The songs were orally sung for about

---

65 The following discussion is derived from Chakravarti and Roy (1991) and Verma (2000).

66 See Verma (2000: 73-74) for a detailed enumeration of these eight rules called *gurudhammas*. Also see Horner (2001: 91-98). Verma contests the view that the Buddha himself prescribed such rigid norms against women's entry into the order. She argues that the monks who came after Buddha wove in the patriarchal social norms of their times while codifying the teachings of the Buddha.

five centuries, where itinerant *theris* would modify them according to context. Thus, one of the *theris*, Mutta proclaims:

> So free am I, so gloriously free,
> Free from three petty things
> From mortar, from pestle and from my twisted lord
> — Chakravarti and Roy 1991: 68

Mutta, the daughter of a poor brāhmaṇa, was married off to a "hunchbacked brāhmaṇa (ibid.), but she persuaded him to allow her to leave domestic life. She, thus, questioned the social norm of being confined to the domestic space to be feminine. Yet, in so far as Mutta adhered to the *saṅgha* by following the gender specific *gurudhamas*, she remained within the fold of the feminine. Feminist scholars such as Chhatre argue that gendered hierarchy arises because women attach themselves to a specific self-image such as "wife" that are provided by society (ibid.: 126-27).[67] Since all such definitions are passing rather than permanent, Buddhism urges that there be both "mental and spiritual changes" in women and society through detachment to specific self-image.[68] Chhatre remarks

---

67 The attitude of the individual to his or her self is called *kleśavaraṇa* (Chhatre 2003: 126-29), while that of society to the individual is called *jñeyavaraṇa* (ibid.: 130-31).

68 Chhatre has argued that the Buddhist account of the self as a bundle is a safeguard against essentialist notions of the self that naturalize the feminine. The human being is an aggregate of five psycho-physical elements (*pañcaskandhas*) that determine all events including human embodiment. These are also called *nāma-rūpa* (changing names and forms) that prevent the human being from assuming any as permanent. They are *rūpa, sañjnā, vedanā, saṁsāra and vijñāna* (Chhatre 2003: 127). This *nāma-rūpa* constitution of the human self implies that the human being transcends gendered distinction. Thus, rather than just change society, Buddhist philosophy suggests that one goes to the roots to tackle the base underlying social structures (ibid.: 136-38).

that the Buddha urged detachment from such attachment to specific forms of the self.

The Vedic tradition too has women like Gārgī and Maitreyī as ardent participants in the quest for philosophical knowledge. Gārgī is mentioned in *Bṛhadāraṇyka Upaniṣad* as a woman who ceaselessly questioned the philosopher Yājñavalkya till he asked her to remain silent (Sarma 1961: 7; Nikhilananda 1957: 221-22; Delhi University Forum for Democracy, 2001: 20). The kind of questions that Gārgī had raised can be seen as an instance of scepticism which was also present in Lokāyata and Buddhism. Gārgī had anticipated the method of infinite regress that became a part of the Buddhist twelve-fold cycle of causation.[69] However, one must not read too much of contemporary feminism into the figure of Gārgī. For one, *Bṛhadārayaṇka Upaniṣad* was not written by Gārgī. Further, as Chakravarti and Gill observe, the silenced Gārgī reappears as a learner who obediently learns about the imperishable Brahman from Yājñavalkya in the latter part of the Upaniṣad (2003: 20; Nikhilananda 1957: 228-34). In the same Upaniṣad, Yājñavalkya's second wife Maitreyī enters as his disciple who learns about the ephemerality of the material wealth on the occasion of his distribution of property between his two wives (Nikhalananda 1957: 174-84, 308-13). Chakravarti encapsulates the Upaniṣad's complex attitude to women,

> Yājñavalkya had two wives: Maitreyī and Kātyāyanī. Of these Maitreyī was conversant with the knowledge of *Brahman*, while Kātyāyanī had an essentially feminine outlook (ibid.: 308).

Moreover, out of the over one thousand hymns from *Ṛgveda* only about twelve have been attributed to women (Delhi University Forum for Democracy, 2001: 20).

---

69 I am grateful to Kanchana Natarajan for bringing this point to my attention in the course of a discussion.

In a contrary vein, Vanita (2003) argues that Hindu philosophical principles do have space for women. She cites instances of debates (*śāstrārtha*) between men and women in scriptural texts (ibid.: 80). To prove her point, Vanita narrates the case of two debates in *Mahābhārata* between a woman and man. Sulabhā, a single woman from the kṣatriya (defence personnel) community had a debate with a man, namely King Janaka to correct his anti-woman bias.[70] The woman ascetic is not typical of the Hindu tradition which treats women as active embodied nature (*prakṛti*), while men in contrast are spiritually oriented to wisdom as in *puruṣa*. The metaphysical principles of the *puruṣa* and the *prakṛti* structure the universe and influence gender roles. But, according to Vanita, Sulabhā, a wandering mendicant, is a counter-example to this. She meets Janaka who is acclaimed for having spiritual powers by taking the form of a beautiful woman. Doubting his emancipatory powers, she subjects him to interrogation. In response, Janaka wonders about her background and proclaims to her that he has immense spiritual powers because of his lack of attachment to the throne. Further, he also tries to prove to Sulabhā that being a woman she is incapable of achieving spiritual renunciation because she is inevitably attached to the world. Janaka turns to the gender divide between men and women to prove his point regarding his own ascetic superiority. He makes a case for Sulabhā's inability to renounce the world, given her delicate and youthful physique. Janaka also imputes a sexual dimension to her debate with him through her yogic powers, and calls her sinful. His sexual analogy refers to the mixing of castes, ways of life, ignorance of clan and his lack of desire for her.[71]

[70] This debate takes place in the Śānti-Parva section of *Mahābhārata* (Vanita 2003: 80).

[71] Janaka who is a kṣatriya thinks that Sulabhā is a *brāhmaṇa*, her unmarried status and his own married one make their union inappropriate according to him. Besides neither of them know the clan (*gotra*) of the other — Hinduism prohibits marriage within the same clan.

Sulabhā responds to Janaka by pointing out that the primordial elements that constitute the body are the same in all persons. Further, given that bodily identity is in a state of constant change, differences between the sexes are not essential. Sulabhā also points out to Janaka that emancipated persons are not hostile to others, that is women. On the matter of detachment, Sulabhā opines that kings can never be detached like householders given that they have to preserve their kingdom. Her union with Janaka is not sinful, according to Sulabhā, because she has only interacted with him intellectually. On the grounds of these arguments, she proves to him that as per Hindu principles, there is no difference between men and women. Despite their differences in bodies, they have the same *ātman* (self). Vanita remarks that unlike Gārgī, who is silenced by Yājñavalkya, Sulabhā silences her male interlocutor with her convincing arguments. Her point is that, differences in body are not central to human beings who are all the same because of a shared *ātman*. The fact that she won the argument with words and logic, rather than through manipulation and violence, is significant according to Vanita. For it shifts the register for women from goddesses like Kālī who won against their opponents through violence. ". . . Sulabhā's logical victory in debate has the potential to make the oppressor see the folly of his own thinking" (Vanita 2003: 91).

However, whether one should interpret Sulabhā's arguments as providing a legitimate position for women within the ambit of Hindu metaphysics is debatable. For she does not question the dichotomy between the body and the intellect, she only tries to show that women too have intellectual prowess. Besides, she does not question the prohibitions of Hindu scriptures on marriage across caste and clan, but only demonstrates that she did not have sexual relations with Janaka. Sulabhā does not question the principle of detachment from the material world, but remarks that she herself is detached unlike the king who is bound to his kingdom. Her whole point is that the sexual difference between her and the king is immaterial from the point of view of spiritual seeking. This is in principle commendable. However, for it to become materialized the differences in sex that are obstacles to spiritual growth will have to be problematized. This is precisely what Sulabhā does not do — hence spirituality remains outside the reach for most women.

Vanita narrates another instance of the voice of a wife's devotion that asserts the agency of women in the Hindu tradition (ibid.: 89-90). She quotes the instance of a married woman in *Mahābhārata* wh despite a life of domesticity wins an argument against sage Kauśika. Kauśika gets annoyed with her for not paying attention to his needs because she is busy serving her husband. In response to his rage, she replies that she has a responsibility to her husband which is her virtue. Besides, those who have wisdom will not fly into rage like Kauśika. However, in this instance the married woman's virtue of serving her husband overrides her duties to the sage. One cannot really view it as an assertion of the woman's voice; rather she prioritizes her patriarchal duties. Further, with devotional agency too, one needs to be cautious and not exaggerate its efficacy. There is a thin line segregating devotion from subservience to the existing social order. One needs to at least choose devotion, which is not done when one merely fulfils it in a self-conscious way.

An alternate example of the saint-poet Mīrābāī (*c.* 1498–1565) opened the space of wifely agency in a more feminist-oriented sense. She did so not through an aware service to her husband but through her service to Kr̥ṣṇa, a divine being who she considered as her husband. Ramabai described this act as:

A woman rejecting the worship of the husband and the

> enslavement it implies, choosing instead a higher symbol of the divine in which her passionate heart can find something more satisfying and enlarging.[72]

Mīrābāī's life and poetry reveal a struggle with the domestic sphere in order to enter public spaces. She attempted to convert her inner *bhakti* (devotion) to a tangible world of multiple social relations. Mīrābāī emerged against the background of conflict-ridden social relations in a war-torn world. She herself was married to a Rājpūt ruler. In the late fifteenth and sixteenth centuries, the leaders of the Mārwāṛ region of Rajasthan (to which Mīrābāī belonged) were enmeshed in wars with rulers from other parts of Rajasthan and the Mughals. In this context, the clan (*kula*) became important along with its supplement, the family. The clan maintained acceptable social relations by regulating marriage, in which women were exchanged. The men were loyal to their clan and women to their families. Service became a central virtue for women, underprivileged castes, as well as those who worked as house-hold help.

There are several versions of Mīrābāī's life. According to one, she rejected her husband, while another claims that she was a widow. However, in all stories she repudiated domesticity to pursue the path of spirituality in public, destabilizing the view that the woman's natural place is in the domestic sphere. Mīrābāī's protest is individualistic at one level; it is based on speculative metaphysics with a commitment to the law of *karma* (where one's current situation reflects reward or punishment for actions or *karma* from one's past life) and deliverance.[73] Yet as her line *strī puruṣa ke sambandh*

---

[72] As quoted in Tharu and Lalita (1991: 244).

[73] This was one of the reasons why the medieval Bhakti movement and its spiritual egalitarianism did not translate itself into a material one.

[74] The socially sanctioned relation between men and women is false.

jhūṭhe . . . " (Sangari 1990a: 1467)[74] shows she has a feminist aspect as well. With her dedication to Lord Kṛṣṇa as a personal God, Mīrābāī brought together masses of people from different sections of the society for which she suffered social ostracism. As Sangari observes:

> She breaks with "outer", "ephemeral" social systems of kinship and political power only to rejoin the community in another capacity — as critic and commentator.
>
> — ibid.: 1467[75]

The history of spirituality and philosophy reveals anticipations of feminist consciousness and collectivities of resistance to the feminine. The devotional writings of the *theri*s, Gārgī, Maitreyī, Sulabhā, the wife who argued with the sage Kauśika, Mīrābāī and several others have all gradually contributed to the space for feminist consciousness.

Extending Sangari's point, women's philosophical history represents "a struggle, not a victory".[76] One cannot over estimate these instances as the rule. Indeed, Vanita herself is well aware of the extraordinary and individualized dimension of these contributions. She observes that unlike other parts of the world ". . . when exceptional women have made such choices in India, they have usually found some acceptance, not just on the fringes but on the mainstream of such society" (Vanita 2003: 90). Alas this is not quite the case in India, for even Mīrābāī has been mainstreamed as a devotee, rather than as a woman with agency, who struggled to embark on her spiritual journey. As Sangari notes, she does not have a school of followers unlike Kabīr, the weaver saint who commands a following in India even today. Gārgī, Maitreyī, Sulabhā and

75 Indeed, women saint poets of medieval India, such as Bahinabai and Lal Dêd among others also forged new solidarities from diverse social strata by entering the public sphere.

76 Sangari's remark about Mīrābāī is extended in this statement (1990b: 1551).

the wife who argued with Kauśika are hardly central to canonical Hindu literature that is available to philosophy students. Vanita is well aware of this point as she claims:

> Who is Sulabhā? Not many people, not even many Sanskrit scholars, recognize the name at once. — ibid.: 76

She observes that women's studies have also not heeded the figure of Sulabhā.

Vanita believes that Ramabai herself is a proof of the liberalism of the Hindu tradition. For she was given the title "Pandita" because of her erudition in Hindu scriptures which was acknowledged openly (ibid.: 90-91). Yet Ramabai's own life was a struggle against the Hindu and Christian patriarchal order so that the freedom of Indian women can be affirmed as a mass group. The liberating moments for women in religion are few and far between. One cannot overgeneralize a few instances of dialogue between men and women in the scriptures as a sign of women's emancipation. More research would have to be done to arrive at conclusive judgements on the subject.[77]

The unique efforts of a few individuals for voice, space and visibility cannot be read as a collective feminist act. For they have not spoken on behalf of women as a whole. Yet these individual efforts over the centuries made it possible for activists such as Ramabai to protest against the social inequality of gender, class, caste, as well as, imperialism. But then as the following chapter on Wollstonecraft argues, exemplary women both during the modern and premodern period are not unique to India as Vanita assumes. The West too has its share, and so does the rest of the world.

---

[77] Natarajan's work on the contribution of Avudai Akkal, an eighteenth-century spiritual seeker from Tamil Nadu, to Vedānta throws light on this subject (2013).

2

Feminine/Feminist Gestures in Colonial England

– Mary Wollstonecraft –

> Unfortunately, Mary Wollstonecraft's arguments, dated though they should be, have more than historical importance, for her particular battle has not altogether been won. — Korsmeyer 1988: 297

RAMABAI'S affirmation of women's education is to some degree inspired by Wollstonecraft, when she remarks:

> Its almost a hundred years since the English woman, Mary Wollstonecraft, stated publicly that women of England should receive an education. — Kosambi 2000: 201[1]

Wollstonecraft resisted the logic of empire-building by drawing an analogy between family loyalty and patriotism as extensions of self-love. Thus, there is an intersection between Ramabai's early feminist critique of British imperialism, the latter's imposition of dogmatic Hindu-Indian tradition and Wollstonecraft's critique of the empire. Moreover, feminists both in Britain and India, interrogated the notion of domestic care, which gained ascendency in India and Britain during the colonial period.

---

1 Wollstonecraft made her plea for education in 1799. Ramabai also quotes Hannah More with appreciation.

Ushering in several new themes in feminist philosophy, Wollstonecraft critiques philosophies such as those of Rousseau which confined women to domestic spaces and denied their rights. She connected the materiality of women's rights with their participation in the public institutional sphere and upheld education as a key tool in the transformation of their psyches. Contrary to de Beauvoir's apprehensiveness (2010: 142), Wollstonecraft's defence of the rights of women — perhaps one of the first statements on women as a collective group — had an impact on the feminist movement, both in Britain and India. Wollstonecraft enunciates her philosophy through her involvement with British intellectual life in the eighteenth and nineteenth century. In the course of exploring Wollstonecraft's delineation of the feminist argument through her struggle with femininity, this chapter discusses the intersections between her position and that of Ramabai's. It concludes by locating Wollstonecraft within the premodern women's intellectual history in the West.

British Radicalism, Critique of Empire and Female Manners

Wollstonecraft grew up in a farming family with an alcoholic father who often traumatized her mother.[2] She struggled to acquire an education and become economically independent. In this endeavour, Wollstonecraft taught at a school and worked as a governess in aristocratic households. She opened a school for girls in a suburb of London, which she could not sustain for a very long period. Wollstonecraft wrote, published and even earned an income with her writing. She married philosopher William Godwin, had two daughters, one of

---

[2] The following brief sketch of Wollstonecraft's life is culled from Taylor (2003: 1-22, 145-75).

whom, Mary Shelly, wrote the scientific fiction novel *Frankenstein*.

Wollstonecraft was exposed to the ideals of modernity through her contact with English radicals who were influenced by the French Revolution. These included Thomas Paine, William Goldwin, William Blake, Mary Hayes and William Wordsworth among several others. This eighteenth-century (1789-95) radical group adulated the French Revolution, upheld universal love, critiqued the narrow aspects of British constitution and stood against Burke's conservative outlook (Taylor 2003: 145-53). Wollstonecraft's own entry into the radical fold was through her approving review of Richard Price's "enlightened patriotism" and "criticisms of the British constitution" (ibid.: 145).[3] She promoted "revolutionary democracy"[4] which entailed spreading the message of the French Revolution as the spirit of freedom and progress.

Radicalism spread throughout the working class and artisan population of Britain during the 1790s. It was ". . . a rich brew of disparate political traditions and aspirations" (ibid.: 149). The working class from the London Corresponding Society interacted with intellectuals and Unitarians who upheld economic liberalism and religious reform. Parliamentary reformers interacted with poets and communitarians. The various groups formed militant associations, which engaged in grassroots struggle for freedom. Richard Price, for instance, even upheld the possibility of annihilating private property so that human beings become naturally equal. Though Wollstonecraft did not engage in such grassroots activism, she and her intellectual

---

3 Price wrote his piece *A Discourse on the Love of Our Country* about four months after the fall of the Bastille (Taylor 2003: 145).

4 Expression from Taylor (2003: 149).

circle (Godwin, Paine, Priestly, Blake) joined the political struggle through their writings. She wrote a defence of the French Revolution titled *A Historical and Moral View of the Origin and Progress of the French Revolution*. She circulated her defence despite its censure by British authorities. Her *Rights of Men* was written as a rebuttal to Burke, however, she was subject to severe attacks for this work, through which she changed from a literary writer to a philosopher.[5] A wave of counter-radicalism that banned public assembly and free speech spread throughout Britain. Though Wollstonecraft and Goldwin were never attacked physically, their friends were;[6] she settled down in France in 1795 after witnessing some degree of government terror. Her Utopianism was both critical and forward looking.

Capitalism and superficial civility amongst the privileged sections of society were branded as "civilization" in Britain during the late eighteenth century. Under the influence of the French Revolution and Rousseau, Wollstonecraft took this account of "civilization" to task.[7] She argued that it led to inequality, slavery, misery, ignorance and "refined" villainy.[8] Wollstonecraft turned her critical attention to the modern woman who was at the centre of this process of civilization. Modernity redeemed women from feudal mores to offer them better conditions of life. However, it also contributed to the process of civilization through their genteel ways and an

---

[5] The opponents of radicalism hated philosophy because of Wollstonecraft.

[6] Joseph Priestly's house and library were demolished.

[7] For Wollstonecraft the French Revolution was a normative force that unleashed the spirit of reason "beaming with benevolence" (Taylor 2003: 3).

[8] Wollstonecraft as quoted by Taylor (2003: 155). The discussion that follows is derived from Taylor (ibid.: 154-75).

indolent lifestyle of luxury. As it has been argued in the above discussion of Ramabai, the British empire was expanded and sustained by control over women's capacity to be the moral authority at home. Thus, feminine nurture was central to such expansion.[9] Wollstonecraft discerned the patriarchal dimension of female manners which masqueraded as civilization. Thus:

> The passions of men have thus placed women on thrones, and, till mankind become more reasonable, it is to be feared that women will avail themselves of the power which they attain with the least exertion . . ..
>
> — Wollstonecraft 1988: 56

Consequently, Wollstonecraft called for a reform of female manners so that society is democratized.

Though her critique of "civilization" was influenced by Rousseau, Wollstonecraft distanced herself from his male bias in directing her critique to women's manners. Further, in her attempt to make reason available to both the sexes instead of being the foundation of their hierarchy she critiqued Rousseau's account of education (ibid.). Rousseau's blueprint for education focused on perfecting the male citizen Emilus.[10] He distinguished Emilus's rational education for citizenship from Sophia's affective education in the arts so that she perfects herself as a woman. Rousseau took their difference in temperament as the hierarchical premise for his own educational theory (ibid.: 79). Emilus's mission was to pursue citizenship in the public sphere of culture. Sophia was meant

---

9 See Wollstonecraft (1988: 52-77) for her detailed critique of the degradation of women. Yet some defenders of the empire lamented the effeminization of men in the company of genteel women (see Taylor 2003: 158). But then territorial expansion and commercial strength formed the background to men enjoying luxury in the company of women whose primary interest was decorum.

10 See Gatens (1991: 11-26) for a detailed discussion of this point.

to complement Emilus through charm and manners in the natural domestic sphere. Wollstonecraft argued:

> Yet whilst wealth enervates men; and women live, as it were, by their personal charms, how can we expect them to discharge their ennobling duties which equally require exertion and self-denial.
> — ibid.: 141

She believed that all those who have written on female education from Rousseau to Gregory have only contributed to making women socially irrelevant (ibid.: 22).

In her foundational feminist text, *A Vindication of the Rights of Woman*, published in 1792, Wollstonecraft connects the emancipation of women with the eradication of "artificial distinctions" such as sex, age, race and wealth (Wollstonecraft 1988; Taylor 2003: 3). She was a part of a period where the aspirations of the individual could fit in with that of humanity (Taylor 2003: 3). By challenging the thesis that women have a "fondness for dress" (Wollstonecraft 1988: 28), she advocated a common public co-education for men and women. She extended Rousseau's insight to women as well, wherein the best education develops the heart and body through the exercise of reason (ibid.: 21). Thus, Wollstonecraft questioned the very premise that segregated feminine virtue of intuition and obedience from masculine virtue of reason and self-discipline (Korsmeyer 1988: 286), since it stratified the sexes.

Wollstonecraft resisted the view that women should be governed by men and their rational faculty because of their weak character (ibid.: 25). She deplored the degenerate condition of women where they were dependent on their husbands and were hypersensitive and narcissistic in their effort to please them. Wollstonecraft argued for the priority of reason, which in her opinion was common to women and men as moral agents. She followed Locke in holding that there is only one kind of virtue based on reason that should govern the public and private spheres. This alone led to "independence, self-regulation, self-reliance" (Taylor 2003: 9). Wollstonecraft upheld that the so-called virtue based on sensitivity was a façade (ibid.). According to Gatens, she, like Descartes and Locke, desexualized human reason to make it available to women as well. There is *prima facie* proof of this in Wollstonecraft's denial of female subjectivity in the writing style she adopted, emulating patriarchal philosophers such as Rousseau, whom she contested. However, Wollstonecraft's written form in her *Vindication of Women* also reveals that she affirmed male philosophical reason only through a complex process of problematizing women's difference. Thus, despite being critical of rhetorical flourish and style as "noise", she makes her point about the universality of reason between men and women through repetitions, anecdotes, passion, lack of precision and citational dialogue with male writers; in using such a style she also drew parallels between the domestic world of women and the public world of men (Finke 1992: 108-46). Thus, Gatens overlooks Wollstonecraft's struggle with male patriarchy through her own internal conflict between femininity and feminism.

Wollstonecraft maintained that the notion of feminine as frivolous was conditioned through women's exclusion from public institutions, lack of experience and education, rather than any pre-determined nature (Korsmeyer 1988: 289). On the ground of the association of ideas, she argued that it is because of their upbringing that women did not use reason (Wollstonecraft 1988: 115-21; Korsmeyer 1988: 291).[11] By being considered physically weak, women were restricted to the

---

[11] "So ductile is the understanding, and yet so stubborn, that the associations which depend on adventitious circumstances, during the period that the body takes to arrive at maturity, can seldom be disentangled by reason" (Wollstonecraft 1988: 115-16). Also see Gatens (1991: 22).

home where they nurtured their children under the supervision of their husbands. They acquired virtues of ". . . sensitive, yielding nature: kindness, humility, gentleness, protectiveness and so forth" (Korsmeyer 1988: 287). Consequently, women could not exercise full citizenship (ibid.: 288), for which reason was a prerequisite. "Lacking full use of reason, they could be unstable, capricious, wily, cunning, sensitive, and sentimental, and, it was thought, they had to be kept at home for their own protection as well as for the good of society at large" (ibid). Like Locke, Wollstonecraft maintained that human beings are *tabula rasa* where their minds reproduce what is fed (Gatens 1991: 22). Thus, women were deficient from men in reason only because of nurture and not nature.[12] Thus, ". . . the most salutary effects tending to improve mankind might be expected from a Revolution in female manners . . ." (Wollstonecraft 1988: 192).[13] Wollstonecraft suggests that both women and men cultivate their minds, since they have equal rational capacities. She argues that women's mental capacities should not be curtailed artificially nor conditioned by domestic "manners". Yet to condition them differently she points out that women should have the same education as men on a mass scale.

---

[12] Thus, "virtue is an affair of convention" (Wollstonecraft 1988: 85).

[13] There were paradoxical expectations from women at that time as Korsmeyer notes. As guardians of the domestic sphere, women had the task of rearing their children in the laws of God and decency. They were to have a superior intelligence and intuition for this. Yet they were also regarded as inferior in terms of having the same intuition whereby they were not considered morally able (1988: 294). As Korsmeyer observes, women who lived under this misguided credo had to live paradoxical lives. This paradox was even present in the Seneca Falls agreement. It was also responsible for stereotypical notions of women's hysteria (ibid.).

Wollstonecraft did not store too much in exceptional women who had a heroic capacity to achieve; thus, with reference to those such as Sappho, Eloisa and Catherine Macaulay she says,

> I shall not lay any great stress on the example of a few women who, from having received a masculine education, have acquired courage and resolution; . . .. — ibid.: 77[14]

Instead, committed to women's reason, rights and education as a class, she upheld that women should support themselves by their own industry in the public sphere by professional practice as physicians, managing farms or shops (ibid.: 149). Wollstonecraft supplemented an instrumentalist version of the need for education with argument that women are entitled to education. In her prefeminist work, she argues that only women whose "minds take a wider range"[15] can undertake frugal family finances, make good mothers and wives. Her argument was that in order to allow society to benefit from maternal management, women would have to be educated in the life of the mind, right from early childhood. In her feminist work, *Vindication of the Rights of Women*, Wollstonecraft proposes a network of state-sponsored schools in which boys and girls would get co-education. She suggests that they acquire the same free and open education till the age of nine (ibid.: 167). Subsequently, those who were inclined towards either domestic or mechanical work would be trained appropriately. Further, those with "superior" intellect would be allowed to partake of academics. Wollstonecraft also maintains that children be taught kindness to animals so that they can extend the same to human beings as well (ibid.: 172). She also believed that women should be taught anatomy and

---

14 "I wish to see women neither heroines nor brutes; but reasonable creatures" (Wollstonecraft 1988: chap. IV, n. 4).

15 Wollstonecraft quoted by Taylor (2003: 47).

medicine so that they could take care of their health, as well as become "rational nurses of their infants, parents and husbands" (ibid.: 177). Thus, ". . . make women rational creatures, and free citizens, and they will quickly become good wives, and mothers; that is — if men do not neglect the duties of husbands and fathers" (ibid.: 178).

Wollstonecraft was a critic of the British empire, which she perceived to be the other side of family loyalty. She perceived patriotism and excess love of the family as extensions of the ego (Taylor 2003: 224).[16] Wollstonecraft located the need for family attachment in the inheritance of wealth; further, being sequestered within the house women either fell into frivolousness or drudgery. She critiqued Burke's notion of the family as a "little platoon" (ibid.: 223),[17] which like nationalism owes more to "selfish passions than reasonable humanity". In her review of Richard Price's *Discourse on the Love of Our Country*, she compares soldiers of a patriotic army to parents who spoil their children. Thus, "like the parents who forgot all the dictates of justice and humanity; to aggrandize the very children whom they keep in a state of dependence, these heroes loved their country, because it was their country, ever showing by their conduct, that it was only a part of a narrow love of themselves."[18]

Indeed, Wollstonecraft argues against sexual difference through an analogy between dependent women and soldiers (Wollstonecraft 1988: 23-24). According to her, feminine charm and male gallantry have much in common. Both pursue acts of "blind obedience" in servility. Both are indoctrinated in social manners before education or morality. Both acquire their

---

16 Wollstonecraft articulates her critique in the *Vindication of the Rights of Men* (1790).

17 This critique is spelled out in the context of the French Revolution.

18 Wollstonecraft quoted in Taylor (2003: 224).

beliefs through "casual conversation". Both try hard to please. Both practise minor virtues with meticulousness. Standing armies comprise unthinking "disciplined machines" like domestic housewives. Both ". . . have a knowledge of life before they have, from reflection, any acquaintance with the grand ideal outline of human nature" (ibid.: 24). Both enjoy the superficialities of social intercourse without pursuing a point of view beyond the surface in deep argument and analysis. Wollstonecraft pointed out that the esteem given to soldiers in comparison to women in society is derived from their enjoying a greater mobility, which women do not possess. In this respect, she presents an alternative to the support of colonization in the "manners" of both middle class and aristocratic women.

Wollstonecraft's analysis of the relation between upbringing and virtue contributed to the rise of the early feminist movement to make women's participation in institutions a reality (Korsmeyer 1988: 295). In the nineteenth century, women became legal citizens. As a result of Married Women's Property Act, they entered bodies of higher learning and even struggled for suffrage. Wollstonecraft's 1792 text opened these possibilities through its rejection of male authority and critique of social hierarchy (Taylor 2003: 3).

Intersecting Spaces: "Entangled"and "Embattled"[19]

There are similarities between Ramabai's "entangled space" and Wollstonecraft's "embattled" one.[20] Wollstonecraft

---

[19] The phrase "embattled space" is derived from Chakravarti (2006: 238). It will, henceforth, be used with quotation marks to indicate the same.

[20] Wollstonecraft herself was not a part of the nineteenth-century women's rights movement, since she died in 1797, however, her treatise *Vindication of the Rights of Women* influenced it.

published her major treatise on women in 1792 and "a century-plus further on and she has become Western feminism's leading heroine" (ibid.: 9) Ramabai published her feminist text, *The High Caste Hindu Woman,* in 1888. Thus, Ramabai and Wollstonecraft were both pioneers of feminist consciousness.[21] They wrote treatises on women's etiquette and restricted their analysis of women's problems to upper-class women who were privileged by race and caste. They earned a living as women writers when women did not have access to the public sphere of dialogue and opinion formation. They critiqued feminine stereotypes and worked towards feminist spaces. Maintaining that women have to articulate their interests outside the domain of their home, they initiated women's entry into the public space of debate. They confronted severe criticism from the public domain for their radical views and critiqued colonialism.[22] Given all of this, Ramabai and Wollstonecraft had to contend with the predicament that "From Plato's Diotima onward, the figure of the woman intellectual — the learned lady, the female pedant, *femme savante, precieuse, femme philosophe* (English writers often retained the French labels to underlie the exoticism of the phenomenon) had hovered on the margins of Western intellectual life" (ibid.: 28).[23]

Precisely because of this predicament, they led exceptional lives. Wollstonecraft, like Ramabai, was convinced that the "mind had no sex"; yet she had to confront the specificity of her own sex to struggle to become a professional woman (ibid.: 4). She ". . . transformed a young woman's bitter sense

---

21 For an account of Wollstonecraft in this respect see Taylor (2003: 1-22).

22 See Taylor (ibid: 27-28).

23 Taylor's remarks about Wollstonecraft have been extended to Ramabai. Further, "Western" has been expanded to include Indian.

of feminine grievance, and fierce, unfeminine aspirations, into a critical philosophy and a visionary political programme" (ibid.: 5). Ramabai effected a similar transformation.

Ramabai and Wollstonecraft also have affinities in championing the cause of women by locating it within the canvas of other social oppressions. They both draw analogies between women and other forms of social disempowerment, reflecting the larger social reform concerns of their times. Thus, Ramabai points to the similarities between women and oppressed castes in not having access to education. Wollstonecraft's *Vindication of the Rights of Women* is filled with analogies between women's oppression and colonial slavery.[24] Indeed, both indict women for being complicit in the enslavement of their mind and suggest that women are to an extent complicit in their own oppression. Ramabai saw it as a symptom of bigoted minds, while Wollstonecraft of superficial manners. Both suggest individual resistance through gender-neutral education as a foil to such a predicament. The strength of connecting women's inequality with those of caste or slavery is that it connects several forms of inegalitarianism. Ramabai and Wollstonecraft were, thus, critics of prevailing social oppressions like caste hierarchy, colonialism and racism.

Despite the larger perspective of caste and slavery informing their writings, both Ramabai and Wollstonecraft adopt a reductionist approach to these diverse forms of inequality. According to them, gender, caste and slavery are all ultimately forms of servitude, mental and physical, which are externally imposed. Yet neither Ramabai nor Wollstonecraft paused to analyse the differences between the oppression faced on account of caste and race on one hand, and that of domesticated gender on the other. Midgley observes:

---

24 See Ferguson (2001) for the political possibilities that this opens.

> Wollstonecraft's support for abolition of slavery emerges from her use of the metaphor of sugar, over whose production slaves were tyrannized in the West Indian fields by imperialist policies; sugar that was used to sweeten up life in the domestic domain by subjugated women was thus, associated with captivity.[25]

Consequently, feminists correlated the British male's public world with his domestic realm, through the literal presence of the slave that subsequently, became a metaphor. Such a correlation was a way of politicizing the domestic space occupied by women. This can be traced since the 1760s to the rise of the sentiment of sympathy towards African slaves in literature that was directed to female readership. British women were moved to sympathize and care for the slave through an expansion of their domestic virtue by discussing the perils of slavery and abstaining from sugar in tea parties. Wollstonecraft, in spite of expressing solidarity for the slave resistance in San Dominigo, makes claims about slaves having the tendency to overdress like women and showing no interest in non-Western cultures which she terms as "savage" (Midgley 2007: 17-19). Similarly, as it has been observed,[26] Ramabai's problem with colonial education policies for Indian women was that they mixed castes. Besides, her feminist text is founded only on the experiences of upper-caste women. Consequently, she overlooks caste and gender as overlapping forms of exploitation of women in the public sphere.

Ramabai and Wollstonecraft were also caught in the bind between the domestic femininity and the public dimension of feminism. Wollstonecraft initiated some of the key themes of modern feminism: education, entry into professions, economic autonomy and legal equality. ". . . yet, despite her often

---

[25] This discussion is derived from Midgley (2007: 41-64).

[26] See Chapter 1.

inflammatory rhetoric, the core of her manifesto remains middle-class motherhood, a feminist, republicanized adaptation of the female role normative in late eighteenth-century bourgeois notions of the family" (Myers 1988: 336). Okin and Gatens argue against Wollstonecraft in a similar tone (Gatens 1991; Okin 1997). Okin observes that Wollstonecraft's thought has a certain "ambivalence" about families (Okin 1997: 14). On the one hand, she is critical of Rousseau reducing women to pleasing figures in the lives of men and the unjust relations this breeds in the family. On the other, she advocated women's development through education, equality in marriage and paid work so that they could be strong mothers on whom families could rely. Though this criticism is sweeping in its claim about the "core" of Wollstonecraft's philosophy, it has a point. Wollstonecraft is critical of strait-jacketing all women as emotional, yet she upholds that women have a primary duty in childcare, which becomes the "lynchpin of a new society" (Myers 1988: 337). According to Wollstonecraft, education makes women realize their natural maternal vocation. Women who manage their families, educate their children, maintain civil relations with neighbours and even work for their families help in the common welfare as active citizens (ibid.). Thus, she sees "motherhood as public service in the national interest" (ibid.).[27] Public freedom and universal happiness depend upon the domestic value of the family. She does not confront the basic opposition between women's duties to themselves and to their duties to others as mothers (ibid.: 338). Wollstonecraft also urges men to take a lead to

[27] The belief system of "republican motherhood" upholds that the mother is a political educator who inculcates notions of patriotism in her babies (Taylor 2003: 223). As Taylor observes though Wollstonecraft gesticulates in this direction, it does not form the cornerstone of her philosophy. Her purpose was to remind elite mothers of their responsibility towards childcare, rather than appearance!

"generously snap our chains, and be content with rational fellowship instead of slavish obedience. . ." whereby women become "better citizens" (Wollstonecraft 1988: 150). Thus, rather than have intrinsic value, women's education becomes the basis for a more intelligent domestic life. In this respect, her kinship with Ramabai's own defence of motherhood and its role in the formation of the nation are explicit.

Wollstonecraft also made overt overtures to feminine ideology. Like Ramabai, she wrote a prefeminist work conduct *Thoughts on the Education of Daughters* (1787). This work was devoted to the development of reason and the control of instinct (Taylor 2003: 32). Wollstonecraft prescribed feminine conduct in her ladies anthology *A Female Reader*[28] and a children's book called *Original Stories*[29] (1788). But during this period she also forayed into women's use of reason (ibid.). In *Vindication* Wollstonecraft critiques the very femininity and manners that she propagated in her earlier work (ibid.: 33). She wrote these works to guide parents so that they attend to children. Taylor observes:

> The genres to which Wollstonecraft first contributed-conduct — books, children's stories, ladies' anthologies — were all ones that late eighteenth-century cultural arbiters approved as properly feminine. — ibid.: 33

Though there is a proclivity towards ushering the possibility of reason of women in these works, Wollstonecraft articulates a world of ". . . women fulfilling traditional female educational obligations: mothers, governesses, teachers. It is only as pedagogues instructing their inferiors — children, servants

[28] This was published under a male pseudonym (Taylor 2003: 33).

[29] *Original Stories from Real Life, with Conversations Calculated to Regulate the Affections, and Form the Mind to Truth and Goodness* (Taylor 2003: 34).

or less rational women — that the young Wollstonecraft permitted women intellectuals to speak" (ibid.: 34). Yet she offered a "model of adult authority" that was "feminine" (ibid.: 35). She argues that mothers will be able to take better care of babies instead of handing them over to wet nurses (Wollstonecraft 1988: 150). A woman who only thinks of her beauty and its admiration has "sinned against herself" by neglecting the "useful and happy" affection that comes from her being a mother (ibid.: 142).[30]

It is from the perspective of the feminine that privileged women occupy a hegemonic position in both Ramabai and Wollstonecraft. Wollstonecraft's universal benevolence as the basis for citizenship reproduces altruism as a catalyst of British imperialism. Ramabai's Indian women who produced sons for the nation, controlled *dāsīs* during the Vedic era and translated themselves into middle-class women in the context of the

---

30 As the above discussion shows, Wollstonecraft has an "explicit critique" of the relation between the sexes according to Rousseau (Gatens 1991: 21). Yet her "ontological commitments" differed from Rousseau in that the rational mind is not dependent on biology and is universal (ibid.: 23). On this basis Wollstonecraft also has an "implicit critique" (ibid.: 21) of Rousseau's version of human subjectivity as founded on biology whereby men are rational and women are affective. As Gatens observes, she follows Descartes and Locke in taking a biologically neutral stance to the mind. In which case Wollstonecraft cannot merely extend Rousseau's education for boys to include girls as well. For as Gatens observes the purpose of education for Rousseau was the negotiation of nature and culture. While Wollstonecraft believed that education was directed towards human perfection which was the same in boys and girls. Thus, she does follow through the ramifications of her critique of Rousseau. Indeed, Wollstonecraft's tension between the feminine and feminist dimensions assumes Rousseau's premise of rational men and affective women.

altruistic civilizing mission of the British empire. The same women could also be displayed as trump cards of India's past glory by Indian nationalists. Wollstonecraft in Britain and Ramabai in India subscribe to the problematic view of the home that is aptly characterized by Sangari as a "benign pedagogue" (1994: 102). In such a home, the middle-class woman herself became a reformer ". . . of prostitutes, servants, lower classes of colonial subjects" (ibid.). Middle-class women taught men not to be barbarians at home, the men in turn did the same in their colonies (ibid.). Neither Ramabai's nor Wollstonecraft's notion of motherhood could be marshalled to critique patriarchy. The nurturing functions of their "mother" coincided with patriarchal expectations. They simultaneously prescribed the concept of self-reliance through public institutions as a feminist alternative to feminine domesticity. They did not challenge the assumptions of self-sufficiency that governed public institutions during their periods. Thus, in straddling the poles of femininity and feminism, both Wollstonecraft and Ramabai unintentionally endorsed conservative patriarchy and colonization.

A moot question to be addressed with reference to Wollstonecraft (and Ramabai) is that given their affiliation to privileged women their critique of domesticity has limited relevance. Ramabai's treatise categorically bears the name of the upper-caste woman, while Wollstonecraft's worry about weak and delicate ladies pertains to bourgeois women. As Korsmeyer observes "the narrow and sometimes maddeningly unproductive sphere" was the basis "of the popular notion of a 'lady', and not of a farmer's, a fisherman's, a miller's wife, nor of a female slave in the south" (Korsmeyer 1988: 296). Thus, the whole notion of domestic space, the censure of widows and the investment in female manners have a class, race and caste bias. Women from diverse strata of Indian and British society had antithetical relationships with the domestic feminine.[31] As Davis notes, the nineteenth-century "housewife" was restricted to the upper and middle income sections of society in Europe (Davis 2011: 229). She argues that women from the economically and racially disadvantaged sections of society could not afford to fulfil their duties as home makers. They did work in the homes of the well-to-do, as well as in their own homes. But despite moving out of their perceived "'natural' sphere . . ." (ibid.: 229), socially vulnerable women were not treated as complete workers as they did housework. Consequently as Davis concludes, they were exploited from their gender and class, and in many cases, racial, points of view. But despite this disparity in women's lived experience of the domestic domain, ". . . nineteenth-century ideology established the housewife and the mother as universal models of *womanhood*" (ibid.).

However, despite their paradoxical position of critiquing and participating in this ideology, Rambai, and Wollstonecraft have both personally worked for the underprivileged women (though this too could be interpreted as patronizing charity work). In addition, following through Davis's argument, even though the woman from the working class or underprivileged caste functions within the productive sphere, she is still restricted by the sexual division of labour. She performs domestic tasks outside her home and gets paid to do so. Hence, despite their bourgeois location, Ramabai's and Wollstonecraft's critique of domesticity can address some of the problems faced by working-class women who are forced to adhere to the notions of domesticity — albeit outside their home. Following Korsmeyer progressive ideals have often emerged in hegemonic contexts,[32] they can be extended to non-hegemonic ones.

---

[31] See Chapter 1.

[32] She cites Juliet Mitchell at this point.

Wollstonecraft shares yet another similarity with Ramabai, namely, that of opening spaces for women in the public sphere. She could engage in a feminist critique of domesticity to carve a "counter public"[33] space for women, precisely because she was enabled by Irigaray's "female ancestry" (1994: 91) of women thinkers — who were not necessarily feminist — to which the following section turns.

Female Ancestry

Like Ramabai, Wollstonecraft too crystallized her ideas in relation to the history of philosophy. The tension between the feminine and feminist dimensions in her life and works is not radically new, but consonant with women mystics such as St. Teresa. Thus, Wollstonecraft too had access to a legacy of women's assertion and visibility. One of the early woman philosophers, mathematicians, scientists and teachers in the Western tradition was Hypatia of Alexandria (*c.* CE 370–415).[34] The Roman empire was on its ascendancy during the fourth century, when Christian dogmatism was also gaining force. The period following Hypatia's death by a mob of fanatical Christian monks was regarded as the dark ages in the West. Hypatia's father Theon was the librarian of the Library of Alexandria that was destroyed by intolerant Christians. Theon, a mathematician of repute, nurtured Hypatia to become a

---

33 Terry Eagleton's term quoted in Finke (1992: 118).

34 The exact date of Hypatia's birth and death cannot be ascertained as different versions are given by different scholars. The following discussion has been derived from Deakin (1994, 1995), Hermit (2003), Hubbard (1928). They have all observed that much of Hypatia's writings have not survived; her life has been pieced together from the fifth-century Christian church historian Socrates Scholasticus or the tenth-century *Suda Lexicon* which have contradictions and grammatical errors (Deakin 1995). Thus, much fact and fiction are mixed in the various accounts of Hypatia's life.

"perfect human" both physically and mentally. She trained in rhetoric, mathematics, literature, astrology, politics and philosophy among an array of other disciplines. Hypatia edited Theon's *Commentary on Ptolemy's Almagest* at a young age. She travelled extensively and studied in Plutarch's School of Mathematics at Athens and returned to Alexandria to teach mathematics and philosophy, and excelled as a scholar. Hypatia wrote research works on mathematics (though most of her works were destroyed) and contributed to science as well. She propagated neo-Platonism without heeding the empire's call for compulsory Christianity. Hypatia is said to have proclaimed:

> Neo-platonism is a progressive philosophy, and does not expect to state final conditions to men whose minds are finite. Life is an unfoldment, and the further we travel the more truth we can comprehend. To understand the things that are at our door is the best preparation for understanding those that lie beyond. — Hubbard: 1928

Hypatia was also actively engaged in administration and politics during her period (Justice 2002). Her fame was the source of consternation for Cyril who was the "unnamed bishop of Alexandria" (Hubbard 1928: 292).[35] Besides following "pagan" religion, a major reason cited for Hypatia's assassination was her violation of the domestic creed. Her enemies were offended by her repudiation of the "Pauline doctrine" that women had to obey men and remain silent in public spaces.[36] An instance of individual resilience in

---

35 He was later canonized. Some versions of Hypatia's story also attribute her death to him.

36 This is derived from Judy Chicago's exhibition *The Dinner Party* which pays homage to Hypatia for her "contribution to womankind" (see Justice 2002). This response has been characteristic of feminist appropriations of Hypatia. Raphael has Hypatia in his mural *School of Athens*, where

→

philosophy, Hypatia pre-empted many feminist concerns through her rejection of domesticity and participation in the public sphere.

In the sixteenth century, the Spanish mystic St. Teresa of Avila (1515-82) was another instance of a nascent feminist heritage that opened the way for those such as Wollstonecraft. Having to make a choice between marriage and convent, St. Teresa opted for the latter.[37] She rejected domesticity for the convent and applied herself to the pursuit of spirituality. At first her choice was governed by a mixture of pragmatism and fear; she feared for her life since she was diagnosed with a major illness. St. Teresa was also compelled to enter the convent because of her commitment.[38] However, she accepted the religious way of life for its own sake and underwent an intense struggle with her feminine tendency to please others, do what is expected of her and protect her "honour". Further, she often struggled with her own failure to pray despite giving such advice to the followers who came to her.

St. Teresa, finally, realized her spiritual experience when she turned forty, after which she took charge of her life and did not dwell on expectations that others had of her. She took the risk of travelling extensively all over Spain and interacting with many persons. Subsequently, St. Teresa wrote many literary spiritual treatises such as *The Interior Castle* and *The Way of Perfection* among many others and became established in the Golden Age of Spanish literature. She advised other

→ she occupies the space with pre-Socratean philosophers, Plato and Aristotle. But when he submitted a draft of his plan to the Church, he was told not to include her image. Yet Raphael included her in a surreptitious way.

37 St. Teresa's life sketch is derived from Giles (1982).

38 It is precisely to honour her commitment that St. Teresa joined the convent even though her father did not permit (ibid.: 20).

sisters that they follow their heart over their mind, even though the heart could be that of a woman's and the mind that of a man (Giles 1982: 24).

de Beauvoir argues that there is a unity of the mind and the body in St. Teresa's mysticism which is captured through the metaphor of eroticism by sculptors like Bernini (2010: 729).[39] The metaphor of earthly love is borrowed to depict spiritual ecstasy that is nevertheless in tune with the body in a unity of subjective experience. Thus, the body becomes an inherent part of the subject. Yet she points out that one cannot reduce this to erotomania or sublimation of sexuality as one would do so with other mystics. St. Teresa, in de Beauvoir's view, does not experience her sensuality first to subsequently pour it on an object. Rather, her writings disclose her experience of intense embodied faith and emotion in her quest for union with God. Hence, her body does not get subjugated in this process. Thus, "St. Teresa situates the dramatic problem of the relationship between the individual and the transcendent Being in a highly intellectual way; she lived an experience as a woman whose meaning extends beyond any sexual specification" . . . (ibid.: 730). de Beauvoir contrasts St. Teresa's experience of mysticism with her other sisters who did not seek transcendence from their situation of femininity but rather its redemption in salvation. Unlike them, for St. Teresa a mystical experience is not a subjective subjugation of the body. She did not turn to mysticism because an earthly love failed her — for St. Teresa mysticism was not just a relation with the unreal (ibid.: 734).[40] Rather its validity lies in its objective scope.

Despite de Beauvoir's interpretation, one cannot

---

[39] This discussion is derived from de Beauvoir's account of the mystic (2010: 726-34).

[40] Nor was it an unreal relationship with a real being who is deified as God by patients who undergo "erotomania" (de Beauvoir 2010: 726-27).

characterize St. Teresa as a feminist in the modern sense of the term. For one, she did not undertake her spiritual path in order to transcend her condition as a woman. Rather passages from her autobiography indicate that she pursued spirituality in spite of being a woman. Consider her appeal to God's love "For the rest, the mere thought that I am a woman is enough to make my wings droop. How much more then the thought that I am not only a woman but wicked!" (1957: 75). Further, she believed that her fellow sisters needed to take advice since they were weak women. Her own conflict between her lack of an impeccable education, her reliance on experience and her consequent reticence in turning to the counsel of those who were established, underlies this belief. Moreover, despite her periodically expressing her mystical experiences in erotic vocabulary, she treats embodiment as a hindrance that needs to be overcome since all persons have the same soul. This is problematic given the association of women with bodies in both philosophy and theology.

Yet following de Beauvoir, the communion with God remains at the level of interiority for some women, while for St. Catherine, St. Teresa and St. Joan of Arc they propel them to pursue the path that they have set for themselves (2010: 733-34). They integrated their mystical feeling into "active and independent lives" whereby they freely acted upon the world in which they lived (ibid.: 734). They transcended the "supreme vocation of love" that is given to the woman to transform their situation — but they do so with love. As predecessors they made Wollstonecraft's own exceptional struggle for all women possible. Her protest against the social inequality of gender, class, caste, as well as, imperialism was backed by the legacy of both Hypatia and St. Teresa.

Like the previous chapter, this too has attempted to reveal the tension between feminism and femininity in the texts and lives of women spiritualists, academicians and activists, but with reference to the Western context.[41] The *therīs*, Hypatia, Mīrābāī, St. Teresa, Ramabai and Wollstonecraft prove de Beauvoir's point that women, unlike men, are explicit about their subjectivity in the work they do (ibid.: 15). Their philosophical reflection emerges from their lived experience as women. Therefore, since the term "woman" does not signify the universal human being, women have stressed their gender difference to rewrite the very notion of the universal human being. Their experiences find expression in the matrices of the feminine and the feminist within the background of history, politics, economics and culture. It is because of this relation that women such as Wollstonecraft and Ramabai, who have philosophized during the eighteenth and nineteenth centuries, have contemporary relevance. Wollstonecraft's narration of the difficulties of becoming political, like Ramabai's, can be traced to the obstacles that confront women at their very birth. Despite the passing of centuries these lived experiences persist even today.[42]

> Then, as now, the politics of the women's rights movement proceeded less from a systematic political theory as from a recognitionof personal oppression and injustice. Naturally as women became conscious of and actively dissatisfied with their place in the social order, their oppression as they perceived it was explained in the context of the prevailing ideas of the time, and, accordingly, prescription for change mirrored much contemporary political philosophy as well.
>
> — Korsmeyer 1988: 285

---

41 Besides the tradition is by no means exhausted with the women philosophers who have been discussed so far. Constraints of space disallow a discussion of Ann Conway (1631-79) for instance, who has contributed to Platonism and Cartesianism, while offering a concept of monads. Warren (2009) offers an overview of the history of women philosophers.

42 Abortion of female foetuses is rampant in India, as well as, in its diaspora.

At first sight personal experience seems to have a foundational status in women putting forth their experiences in an activist (Ramabai), theoretical (Wollstonecraft), academic (Hypatia) or devotional (St. Teresa/Mīrābāī) forms to philosophize. Most of the women who entered the life of the mind or spirit did so because they were motivated by personal experience. Further, the above discussion reveals that women who initiated feminism led extraordinary lives. In this context, it is tempting to maintain following some of the feminists, that first-hand experience of oppression is central to women affirming a feminist stance.[43] Bell hooks claims that attributing expertise to experience was initially empowering by allowing her to bring in her experiences of oppression into the academy (hooks 1994: 89-90). Yet she observes that years later she also realized its capacity to exclude and silence those who are not experienced. Hooks argues that despite this she believes that she does not want to "relinquish the power of experience as a standpoint on which to base analysis or formulate theory" (ibid.: 90). She maintains that this is especially the case with suffering that is marked on the human body. One cannot know or name it from a distance, one needs to experience suffering so that one can theorize it.

However, the notion of an authentic experience, especially suffering, as the validating ground of feminist theory is problematic. It reproduces some of the problems of empiricism that have been critiqued since Kant.[44] To quote Kant:

> But though all our knowledge begins with experience, it does not follow that it arises out of experience.
>
> — 1965: A1: 41

[43] Feminists from diametrically diverse positions such as Susan Gubar and Gilbert, as well as, hooks have defended the notion of first-hand experience as primary to feminist theorizing.

[44] Other philosophers who have critiqued the primacy of immediate experience include Hegel, Marx, Husserl, Harding and Quine.

Thus, raw data of experience received through the five senses is incoherent, it has to be processed or mediated through concepts that connect and interpret it so that it is comprehended. Kant also guards against an exclusive reliance on concepts to avoid the opposite extreme of speculative thought that does not refer to experience. Thus, he upholds that percepts and concepts are both needed to arrive at knowledge. Experience is laden with language, convention and theory itself. To return to the experience of gender oppression, it has to be processed through a conceptual framework and history. If first-hand experience is taken as the fulcrum of feminist theorization, all women would be feminists. Yet, there are instances of women who are not convinced by feminism despite being excluded or oppressed. Thus, one cannot even out the distinction between the biological factor of being female with the cultural behaviour of feminine (Moi 1997: 114). Nor can such "amalgamated femaleness/femininity" be equated with feminism (ibid.).

Female experience does not necessarily translate itself into feminism, since as Moi points out there are innumerable instances of women "who become solid defenders of the patriarchal *status quo*" (ibid.). An exclusive focus on female and feminine can thus be problematic. Moreover, as diverse examples of Mill and Engels reveal, men who have not been victims of first-hand oppression have taken sides with feminism.[45] Again, the appeal to first person experience would restrict feminist philosophy to women and would privilege the victim's perspective. The experience of oppression and exclusion is connected with male privilege. Hence, it cannot be remedied without addressing the hierarchy between men and women; women's experience of the loss of privilege affects

---

45 Also see Morgan (1994) for perspectives on men's relation to the feminine and feminism.

both men and women. It is a reminder of the interrelated character of experience and subjectivity. Neither experience nor the self, exist in separate compartments; instead, both are linked with the selves of others — their experiences, lives and conceptual schemes. The relation of dependency between the self and the others mandates that feminism concerns both women and men. After all, men have to unlearn their privilege, since it depends on women's exclusion and oppression.

If the first person experience of oppression is accorded primacy then its subject becomes a sovereign entity. The subject of experience would be completely transparent — an entity who knew herself thoroughly. This in turn would rule out all contradictions within the self. More importantly, feminist philosophy has emerged through a critique of such a transparent subject which was taken for granted in the history of philosophy and which excluded women by not articulating the possibility of embodiment. Wollstonecraft transforms Locke's notion of association of ideas into a social activity of learning and conditioning. Ramabai does not take recourse to notions of subject in the classical Indian philosophical tradition, which takes either the substantive or non-substantive versions of consciousness as central.[46] In order to assert the gender neutrality of reason, both Ramabai and Wollstonecraft begin by making an issue out of difference in subject perspectives. Such an embodied subject is divided between the perspectives of femininity and feminism. Thus, rather than a unitary subject of experience,[47] feminist theory has grown out of a subject

[46] Both Buddhist *anātmā* (no-soul approach) and Lokāyata's materialism are counter examples.

[47] For a critique of notions of unitariness, wholeness and loss in this appeal to female tradition see Tharu and Lalita (1991: 21-33). Unlike hooks, Tharu and Lalita see the stress on first person experience of female as an obstacle to women without privilege as it reinstates male authority with that of female.

that has a fragmented and fluid, rather than a ready/made solid entity.

As Miller (1995) has argued, feminists do not have to choose between the traditional philosophy's essentialized self and the post-structuralist selflessness. Both options are patriarchal. The authorless or selfless attitude is detrimental to women's interest, since its inchoateness and anonymity do not permit one to attribute specificity to women's injustice. Hence, one cannot know oneself but can only be oneself (Kant 1965: B155-59). Women who write as subjects divided between femininity and feminism, have to admit their ". . . ongoing contradiction, the gap and (and perhaps permanent) internal split that makes a collective identity always a horizon, but a necessary one" (Miller 1995: 207). Both experience and subjective identity are fluid, vulnerable, responsible and unpredictable. Since women as females or feminine beings do not necessarily write as feminists, their experience does not automatically dictate any specific political position (Moi 1997: 115). Hence, besides evoking women's lived experience, feminist theory has also evolved by reconstructing male thinkers (ibid.: 105). Ramabai reconstructed the male social reform from a gender-sensitive point of view. Wollstonecraft was inspired to make a case for feminism by reworking some of the patriarchal ideas of the French Revolution. Ramabai and Wollstonecraft linked the domestic sphere with that of the public, through their critiques of femininity. They also opened the space for women reflecting on gendered identity by speaking and writing. As a result, they provided impetus to both activism and theory from a gendered point of view.

Moi's thesis is instructive at this juncture: "the point is not the origins of an idea but the use to which it is put and the effects it can produce. What matters therefore is not so much whether a theory was formulated by a man or a woman, but whether its effects can be characterized as sexist or feminist in a given position" (ibid.). In writing as women, they need not be confined to an expressive confessional mode that is at the other end of anti-reflective theorizing (Moi 2005: 249).[48] Rather by writing through both the personal and the philosophical, they brought in everyday practice, historical background, lived experience to question the view that the feminine is a limitation that prevents women from speaking or writing. In doing this they affirmed their righ to be activists, mathematicians, mystics, philosophers and enter the domain of knowledge, politics and religion. It is precisely because of this that the women discussed above who came from different domains such as activism, science, philosophy and spirituality were divided between feminism and femininity.

The following chapters will examine the theoretical treatment that has been given to the tension between the feminine and feminist perspectives with respect to the care debate in postcolonial contexts.

---

[48] This discussion is influenced by Moi's account of women's writing (2005: 236-50).

Part 2
Postcolonial Contexts, Perspectives

3

The Ethics of Care

– Carol Gilligan –

> Yet in the different voice of women lies the truth of an ethic of care, the tie between relationship and responsibility, and the origins of aggression in the failure of connection.
>
> — Gilligan 1982: 173

BOTH Ramabai and Wollstonecraft exemplify the tension between the feminine virtue of nurture and its feminist critique. They renounce domestic femininity and its concomitant virtue of care, so that women can enter the public sphere as equals to men. Yet, despite this, they end up accommodating the prefeminist feminine dimension in affirming nurturing motherhood as a remedy to the ills that beset nation and civilization. The contemporary postcolonial debate regarding the ethics of care among feminists reflects this paradox at the intersection of pioneering Indian and Western feminism, during the colonial period.

The ethics of care has both a continuity and rupture with the preceding discussion's conflict of the feminine and feminist perspectives in colonial India and colonizing Britain. It upholds the difference in position, where it emphasizes women's difference from men. Similarly, though Ramabai and Wollstonecraft believed women to have the same virtues as men during their feminist phase, they did defend motherhood as the differentiating virtue of women. They, thus, struggled in their commitment to women's equality and yet pointed towards the aspect of women's difference. However, they did not explicitly spell out the theoretical aspect of women's difference, in terms of motherhood, as care or nurture. Nor did they consider the possibility of the virtue of care as an antidote to the patriarchal notions of equality and freedom. The ethics of care differs from Ramabai's and Wollstonecraft's approaches to motherhood in precisely these respects. It brings the culturally prevalent feminine aspect of nurture to the forefront as a central theoretical virtue that has the resources to critique patriarchy.

The theorization of care from a feminist point of view can be traced to the Western context of the United States with Gilligan's care ethics in the early 1970s. This chapter will explore the continuities and ruptures between Gilligan's context and that of her predecessors in the colonial context, namely, Ramabai and Wollstonecraft. It will also examine the extent to which Gilligan's theorization of care remains relevant to women's location in countries such as India, which had by the 1970s become postcolonial.[1]

Gilligan responds to the exclusion of women's experiences by investing feminine cultural traits such as interdependence and nurture with normative worth. Arguing that they emerge from women's situation of involvement in the household and family, she labels the virtue attached to such tasks as care. Gilligan believes that cooperation and benevolence constitute the moral perspective of women, in contrast to what she sees as a masculine emphasis on entitlement and impartiality. She grounds the ethics of care in the different psychological development of women, who she believes are inclined towards responsibility, context and connection. Gilligan differentiates such feminine development from masculine orientation

[1] India attained Independence from British colonization in 1947.

towards abstraction, rights, autonomy and separation. The discussion that follows starts with Gilligan's critique of mainstream ethics grounded in rights as represented by Kohlberg's developmental psychology. It proceeds to examine her own normative position of care that is informed by her feminist standpoint to conclude with a discussion of its relevance to women's struggles in postcolonial India.

Critique of Mainstream Ethics

Gilligan defends a moral perspective of care based on feminine psychology on grounds of the inadequacy of mainstream ethics. She admonishes Kohlberg for advocating a patriarchal account of moral development under the guise of a psychology that is gender-neutral.[2] Indeed, since he himself traces his antecedents to Kant and liberal theory, Gilligan's critique is simultaneously pertinent to Western ethics whose overt gender-neutrality reflects a bias towards the male perspective. As she argues, Kohlberg roots his generalization about adults in the developmental processes of privileged male adolescents and adults (Auerbach et al. 1985: 152). He offers a six-stage process of psychological development that is also a cross-cultural sequential classification of moral judgement, wherein the final stage is the culminating point of moral adequacy.[3] He believes that his account of development is universal.[4] Kohlberg also professes to avert the is–ought problem through an isomorphism between psychological and normative theory,

---

[2] See Gilligan (1982: 5-23) for a discussion of male bias in the psychological theories of Freud, Piaget and Kohlberg.

[3] See Kohlberg (1971, 1973) for a detailed account of these six stages from which the following is derived.

[4] Universality is not proscribed by ethical tolerance which believes in equal worth of all cultures for ethical tolerance itself is a universal value (ibid.: 158). In upholding universality, Kohlberg takes middle-class children to be the yardstick of moral development. According to him, it is a matter of fact →

where philosophical criteria of the adequacy of moral judgement define psychological adequacy and vice versa (Kohlberg 1973: 633).[5]

> This implies that the *philosopher's justification* of a higher stage of moral reasoning maps into the psychologist's *explanation* of movement to that stage, and vice versa" (ibid.).[6]

According to Kohlberg, the psychologist cannot study cognition or morality in an epistemologically neutral way and vice versa (1971: 154). Further, he believes that such an isomorphism is credible, if one adheres to the view that the

---

→ that middle-class children are morally more advanced than their counterparts from underprivileged classes (ibid.: 160). Yet both share the same values such as honesty; but underprivileged children have to confront circumstantial limits which makes it difficult for them to achieve this value all the time. Yet he points out that one cannot consequently ascribe a collective guilt to the entire group since moral judgement and action take the individual as the primary unit. Further, Kohlberg cites empirical evidence to show that "There is very little correlation between situational cheating tests" (ibid.: 277). Variations in individual behaviour in situations show the limits of assuming virtues to be the character traits. Hence, in Kohlberg's view one cannot endorse Aristotle's dictum that virtue is habit.

5 Thus, he observes that the context of discovery of moral points of view and the latter's context of justification are reciprocally related to each other (Kohlberg 1973: 633). The former is studied by the psychology of moral development, while the latter by moral philosophy.

6 See Kohlberg for a discussion of the vacuity of the is–ought problem since Moore's ushering in of the naturalistic fallacy. The is–ought gulf is premised upon the assumption that facts are value neutral. Hence, Kohlberg's first step is to link the two, whereby facts reflect values and vice versa, which thereby avoids the dichotomy between them. For instance, Kohlberg points out that the thesis that moral values are assessments of an action upheld by the members of a given society is not →

developing human being and the moral philosopher are engaged in the same task. He delineates stages of moral judgement that parallel psychological development, wherein each new stage incorporates aspects of the previous ones and transforms them to arrive at a more stable equilibrium.

According to Kohlberg, at the preconventional level the child begins by absorbing cultural categories of good and bad that are interpreted in consequentialist terms of seeking pleasure or avoiding punishment or subservience to those who are more physically powerful. At stage one of this level, there is a tilt towards punishment and obedience. Thus, bypassing punishment and submission to power are viewed as intrinsically valuable, rather than the moral framework that underlies them.[7] The second preconventional stage involves an instrumental–relativist approach, where right action instrumentally satisfies one's own needs and at times that of others. According to Kohlberg:

> Human relations are viewed in terms like those of a marketplace. Elements of fairness, of reciprocity, and of equal sharing are present, but they are always interpreted in a physical pragmatic way. — 1973: 631

Thus, there is a limited attitude to reciprocity whereby children meet the needs of others, only if others meet their needs. The conventional level, Kohlberg upholds, comprises the individual's duties to the social order of the family, community and nation, which are regarded as inherently valuable. The individual not only conforms to the social order but also internalizes it. At stage three of this level, there is "The interpersonal concordance or 'good boy–nice girl' orientation" (ibid.). Here adolescents follow prevailing norms to secure

→ metaethically or epistemologically neutral but wrong (1971: 154).

7 It is at stage four that this order is taken into account.

the approval of others with sincere intentions. Stage four involves a "'law and order' orientation" (ibid.). For Kohlberg, this entails that adolescents respect authority, follow fixed rules and preserve social order for its own sake. According to him, the postconventional level recognizes the universal applicability of impartial moral principles independent of the groups holding them and the individuals who identify with the groups. At the fifth stage of this level, there is an orientation towards a legalism based on social contract (ibid.: 632). Adults, thus, adopt a utilitarian approach whereby individuals can do as they please, provided they refrain from harming others. The personal dimension of values is separated from legal procedural norms for arriving at consensus. The sixth stage is an orientation towards the universal ethical principles, according to which, "Right is defined by the decision of conscience in accord with self-chosen ethical *principles* appealing to logical comprehensiveness, universality, and consistency" (ibid.). Kohlberg points out that abstract ethical principles, rather than concrete ones are applicable to this level. Thus, this stage can be illustrated with the Golden Rule and the categorical imperative, rather than a specific code like the ten commandments or those in the *Laws of Manu* (Doniger and Smith: 1991). At this level, conventional morality is transcended through universal principles of justice, reciprocal and equal human rights, as well as respect for the dignity of each human being as an individual person. Thus, adults are no longer ruled by self-interest, the opinion of others, or fear of legal punishment, but follow their own autonomous perspective.

According to Kohlberg, each new stage includes parts of the previous stage to gradually develop into a more stable and extensive equilibrium. The graduation to each stage entails a moral perspective of ideal role-taking, of adopting the point of view of the other. He remarks that the rational moral agent (who is not just an average agent or an impartial spectator) ". . . is fair, not saintly . . . " (ibid.: 640).[8] He maintains that there is a correlation between rights and duties whereby the rights of every individual are safeguarded by the duties of others. According to Kohlberg, this is captured by stage six for which the outcome of moral judgements is reversible, consistent and universalizable. Further, moral judgements are reversible in the sense that those who can put themselves in the shoes of the other, have to ponder over the consequences of the principles of choice. Kolhberg regards all those who do not fit into his scale as morally deficient.

However, Gilligan argues that this is problematic since his six stages are neither universal nor invariable.[9] According to her, there is a deep bias in Kohlberg's methodology in favour of men, whose experiences he reads as universal. His original data was masculine, since it was comprised fifty-two subjects from a private Chicago boy's school who were periodically interviewed every three to four years for a period of thirty-five years (Puka 2010).[10] He subsequently added some more samples, whereby the development of eighty-four boys was followed through for a period of twenty years (Gilligan 1982: 18). Thus, according to Gilligan, the female sex has no place in Kohlberg's foundational data. Yet Kohlberg's response is that the data of children and adolescents do not show significant differences in moral reasoning (Benhabib 1992: 150;

---

8 The Kantian echo is clear, as Kant points out that his moral theory appeals to the human will and not the holy will. "Therefore no imperatives hold for the divine will, and in general for a holy will; the *ought* is here out of place, because the *would* is already of itself necessarily in agreement with the law" (Kant 1983: §414).

9 See Gilligan (1982: 18-23).

10 Gilligan points out that those who have not even been included in Kohlberg's samples hardly reach the higher stages (ibid.: 18).

Kohlberg and Levine: 1984). He concedes that the data of adults do reveal such differences in favour of males, and remarks that the ideal role-taking mandated by stages four and five becomes possible for those who have been able to participate in public institutions. These often turn out to be men's privilege, given women's traditional exclusion. But this does not lead Kohlberg to either question the validity of his own findings or investigate the causes that underlie women's obliteration. In fact, he believes that factors pertaining to education and employment should be controlled while exploring differences in moral reasoning (Benhabib 1992: 150).

Indeed, if one were to follow through the thesis of isomorphism between empirical data and moral theorizing, the bias against women in the Western tradition in ethics gets reproduced by Kohlberg.[11] As Gilligan argues, Kohlberg sees interpersonal relationships as falling under the purview of abstract rules (stage four), which in turn are subsumed under universal principles of justice (in stages five and six). He integrates diverse accounts of moral reasoning at each of these stages. Kohlberg (1973: 635) cites stage six as representing "a family of theories" in mainstream ethics, ranging from Kant to Rawls.[12] Benhabib observes:

---

[11] See Held (1998) for a detailed account. Also see Gilligan (1984).

[12] He also cites Gandhi as exemplifying this stage (Gilligan 1982: 104). Invoking Gandhi reproduces similar problems as those with Western ethics. Gilligan herself endorses Erikson's critique of Gandhi as a paradox of violent absolutism in the domestic sphere of relationships and a non-violent relativism in the public sphere. But she fails to locate the source of this paradox which is a symptom of Gandhi's adoption of traditional feminine metaphors such as the suffering chaste Sītā, which cut both ways. There are aspects of Gandhian thought that are gender sensitive; for instance, he introduced the spinning wheel as a symbol from the domestic sphere into the public domain of politics. However, his defence of the traditional Hindu law of *dharma* tends to reproduce the →

> Kohlberg proceeds from a definition of morality that begins with Hobbes, in the wake of the dissolution of the Aristotelian–Christian world-view. — 1992: 154

Rather than derive morality from the human position in the cosmos, morality became a matter of what human beings agreed upon in contract. The latter stressed justice, as opposed to the good life. Feminists have diagnosed the history of Western ethics as treating women in a functionalist way, where they have only instrumental value in relation to men (Okin 1979; Benhabib 1986; Jaggar 2000: 349). Such instrumentalism was justified by upholding that the feminine sphere of care was less than human and confining it to the private sphere.

Kohlberg's response to Gilligan reveals such prejudice against women. He distinguishes between ego and moral development observing that the former is necessary for the latter (Benhabib 1992: 151).[13] According to Kohlberg, the perspective of care does not open up a new mode of moral reasoning. Rather, it only reveals a different kind of ego development which can be examined independently of moral development. Further, Kohlberg can also claim to assimilate Gilligan's care approach within his theory of justice by agreeing that it "enlarges" the sphere of morality to uphold that care and justice do not represent two diverse orientations (ibid.: 153-54). Like the tradition of moral reasoning from Hobbes onwards, Kohlberg views care or sympathy for family and friends as the domain of decision-making in personal relationships, which presupposes justice (ibid.: 150, 153).[14]

→ oppressive dimension of traditional femininity. Feminists have pointed to these patriarchal limits in Gandhi (Patel 1988; Leonard 2010).

13 See Kohlberg and Levine (1984) for his response.

14 See Benhabib for a perspective on social contract theories in this respect (1992: 154-55).

Indeed, the mainstream philosophical justification of moral reasoning in the public domain has reiterated the psychological explanation of findings such as those of Kohlberg's. Typically moral reasoning is said to involve reason, form and knowledge that have been associated with maleness. It is expected to control emotion, matter and reproduction, which are associated with feminine traits in the private sphere of the household. The household is the site of reproductive work and natural needs to which women are central. This perspective persisted through diverse conceptions of reason, such as the Platonic in ancient thought, and the Kantian one in modern philosophy and continued into the twentieth century with analytic ethics and Rawls.[15] Consequently, mothering and family care were neglected by Western ethics. Virginia Held, therefore, observes that the dichotomy between reason and emotion, the private and the public divide[16] and the concept of the autonomous self are all constitutive of a patriarchal moral theory (ibid.: 98); each of Held's dichotomies are reproduced by Kohlberg. Women's moral development appears deficient since their "judgements seem to exemplify the third stage in his six stage sequence" (1982: 18), on which none of Western philosophical theories has a foundational bearing. Most women tend to cultivate interpersonal relationships of pleasing and helping others, which Kohlberg considers as applicable in the domestic space. Consequently, his theory implies that women can become able moral subjects only if they perform activities traditionally enacted by men. But then this in turn implies that women have to renounce their own developmental paths and moral concerns. Gilligan points out that conventionally, the virtue of good has been

[15] See Held (1998: 95-96) for a detailed account; also see Mahadevan (2013).

[16] This distinction coincides with the one between nature and culture.

ascribed to women because of their ability to be sensitive and caring to others; this distinguishes them from men whose experiences are individualistic. Yet from Kohlberg's point of view, since these traits impede women's moral development they should be renounced.[17]

Kohlberg's psychology of disconnection and separateness leads to a notion of individuation in which autonomy is seen as entitlement and non-interference is a virtue.[18] Moral reasoning by such autonomous agents has to abstract from interpersonal involvement to resolve conflicts in an impartialway. Kohlberg gives the instance of a moral predicament faced by Heinz who has to choose between stealing an expensive drug or losing his wife to cancer. Since the chemist is not prepared to lower the price, Kohlberg explores whether Heinz should steal the drug. Yet Kohlberg's is not the only solution to the problem. Gilligan observes that this dilemma was tackled in different ways by two eleven-year olds: a boy and a girl. When an eleven-year-old boy was asked to resolve Heinz's quandary, he concentrated on solving the problem through abstract reasoning once and for all (Gilligan 1982: 25-63). He treated moral reasoning as a "sort of math problem with humans" which depends on a backdrop of social consensus and agreement. The world in this case comprises people who stand alone and function through a system of rules which differs from morality. The boy according to Gilligan demonstrated a reasoning that is a mixture of stages three and four. The dilemma for the boy is one of a conflict between property and human life, in which the latter is important. Hence, he is confident that Heinz should steal the drug.

The girl, on the other hand, was not too sure whether stealing is the only way of procuring the drug, although she is

---

17 See Held (1998: 97) for a discussion.

18 This is in keeping with liberal tradition from Hobbes to Rawls.

sure that the wife's life should be saved. She suggests that Heinz could borrow the money or then persuade the chemist to lower the cost. The world for her comprised human relationships that bond through feeling rather than rules. Her responses, thus, contain a mixture of stages two and three. Rather than a dispute between life and property, the eleven-year-old girl sees it as schism in human relationships that can be cemented. The problem in question is that of an uncalled-for exclusion, namely that of the chemist's failure to take Heinz's wife into consideration. The girl's perspective is not an individualistic one comprising autonomous agents and their entitlements like the boy's. Thus, "the voice that set the dominant key in psychology, in political theory, in law and in ethics, was keyed to separation: the separate self, the individual acting alone, the possessor of natural rights, the autonomous moral agent" (Gilligan 1995: 122).

Gilligan observes that when confronted with a moral dilemma, Kohlberg's male subjects prized their own freedom and its non-interference with those of others. In contrast, her female subjects took the perspective of collective responsibility towards themselves and their family members (or the ones who were affected by their decision) in a moral conflict.[19] Further, they reasoned in a context with sensitivity to feeling without assuming singular rational solutions on behalf of others. They tried to fulfil their obligations to others without injuring them, to reconcile their concern for others with their own freedom. In her empirical research Gilligan interviewed twenty-nine pregnant women from a metropolitan area between the ages of fifteen to thirty-three, who were from diverse ethnic and class groups, some of whom were married and some single, but all of whom were in the process

---

[19] Gilligan also points out that interviews with male and female subjects revealed that men had a narrower sphere of responsibility than women (1984: 79). Also see Gilligan (1986).

of making a decision about abortion (Gilligan 1982: 3, 71).[20] She found that though women often don't get past stage three, men routinely ascend to stages four and five (ibid.: 3).[21] Gilligan interviewed women who were at various levels of deciding whether or not to abort. Her conclusions were that no matter what their age group or racial or class background each of these women exhibited a remarkably non-Kohlbergian way of thinking. Instead of approaching abortion as individual entitlement, they perceived it as an issue that concerned all those it impacted. They took into account the relation between the fate of their foetus, their spouses, parents and themselves. Hence for Gilligan:

> The elusive mystery of women's development lies in its recognition of the continuing importance of attachment in the human life cycle. — ibid.: 23

These differences between men and women are not the outcome of biology; rather it is the result of women, for the most part, being responsible for the primary care-giving, given their association with reproductive processes (ibid.: 7). In the course of her research, Gilligan discovered a feminine

---

20 Gilligan has called this as her "abortion decision study". Participants were all women in their first trimester of pregnancy. They participated in the research for different reasons. Some sought to resolve a conflict while making their decision, while some responded to the counsellor's concerns about repeated abortions. Others simply wanted to make a contribution to on-going research (1982: 91). In this work, Gilligan includes a study of twenty college students who did not continue with a course on moral and political choice. Her findings revealed that sixteen out of them were women. Finally, she also examines gender orientation towards rights and responsibilities in a study of men and women between six to sixty (ibid.: 2-3).

21 They were doing this in the aftermath of Roe *vs* Wade (Gilligan 1995: 122).

psychology of interpersonal relationships and emotion which valued care as a virtue. Consequently, the possibility of theorizing connection in psychology, which plays a role in the different moral reasoning of women had become concrete (Gilligan 1988, 1995).

The Perspective of Care

According to Gilligan, there are two modes of judging, one that is traditionally linked to the masculine public world of authority and the other to private domestic interaction.[22] She points out that developmental psychology has prioritized the former as the culmination of the latter. This, she believes, is the outcome of biased fieldwork that focused on boys and men. But she also attributes it to women not articulating their perspective, given their internalization of disempowered domestic femininity of selflessness (Gilligan 1993: ix-x). Consequently, women often did not know what they wanted or feared expressing it because of the dangers of disapproval, hurt or confusion. Moreover, besides women's silence, Gilligan locates several obstacles in the reception of their speech (Gilligan 1982, 1973). She points out that although women passively accepted this hierarchy through several epochs by sacrificing their autonomy, recent history of women's resistance reveals the contrary. It is replete with instances of the conflict between autonomy and concern for others that manifests itself through a tension between adulthood and femininity. She observes that cultural glorifications of the "good" woman stress the latter, while the former is emphasized by the "bad" woman. Yet, according to Gilligan, the two modes of judging have to be resolved without sacrificing one for the other. Further, she says,

> Women's moral weakness, manifest in an apparent

---

[22] This point is derived from Gilligan (1982: 69-71; 1986).

> diffusion and confusion of judgement, is thus inseparable from women's moral strength, an overriding concern with relationships and responsibilities. — ibid.: 16-17

In her early work (1982), Gilligan argues for a moral perspective grounded in the psychological differences between men and women. She does so, on the basis of listening to the voices of women who were not yet heard (1993). She believes that women are inclined towards responsibility, context and connection, while men lean towards abstraction, rights, autonomy and separation. This is so because women situate themselves in the context of human relationships. They describe their own identity in the context of a relationship such as mother, wife, child and so forth (Gilligan 1982: 159); thus, women tended to think of themselves as selfless and without desires in their quest for being in relationships (Gilligan 1993: xiii). Women, therefore, traditionally have a place in the life cycle of men as care providers and as a ". . . weaver of those networks of relationships upon which she in turn relies" (ibid.: 17). Yet men severed themselves from these relationships to think of their identities as autonomous (ibid.: xiii). Consequently,

> the moral imperative . . . with women is an injunction to care, a responsibility to discern and alleviate the 'real and recognizable trouble' of this world. For men, the moral imperative appears rather as an injunction to respect the rights of others and thus to protect from interference, the rights to life and self-fulfilment. — Gilligan 1982: 100

For Gilligan, women's moral judgements are, therefore, based on the criteria of relationships, responsibility and nurture. She maintains that women's morality emerges from their fundamental awareness of the experience of connection, which they make explicit. Hence, for women, morality is not based on the logic of fairness, as much as that of inclusion or relationships. Human beings are inextricably connected to each other psychologically, socially, politically; hence for Gilligan, the basic questions of human life ae questions of how one lives with others and how one deals with conflict (Gilligan 1993: xiv). She found that these questions are answered differently by men and women. Despite her recognizing the "different voice of women", Gilligan believes that there is no absolute relation between gender and the moral perspective of care. In her early work she points out that the association of the different voice with women is not absolute (ibid.: 2). In fact, she argues for a "dialectical mixture" of autonomy and care where women and men both change their position (Gilligan 1982: 100; 1991; 2000 and Auerbach et al. 1985: 158). Gilligan has specifically claimed that she termed her work as "different" rather than "woman's" voice (1986). However, in her later work (1988), she ascribes superiority to the ethics of care and the reasoning associated with it.[23]

Gilligan offers a multi-layered conception of moral argument that takes women's relational experiences into account.[24] An approach that takes the self-sufficient subject as its foundation is committed to the individual's rights and abstract impartiality. Such an approach tends to be absolutist and negligent of women's experiences. The alternate approach takes the point of view of the other to which the self is responsible. But such an approach could become an apology for the sacrificing woman that is idolized in patriarchal contexts. A middle ground between these two extremes of ego-centricity and self-sacrifice would take the reciprocal

---

23 See Gilligan (1988) and (1991). Yet as critics have observed, Gilligan ascribes superiority to the ethics of care in a tacit way even in her earlier work *In a Different Voice*. This is evident from her claim that a "progressively more adequate understanding of the psychology of human relationships . . . informs the ethic of care" (Gilligan 1982: 74). See Auerbach et al. (1985: 157-58) for a discussion.

24 Mahadevan (2013) discusses this in the context ethical theory.

relationship between the self and its other as the basis of moral thinking (Gilligan 1982: 171, 173).

On the basis of her empirical studies, Gilligan upholds that morality for women entails minimizing suffering in interpersonal relationships (ibid.: 65). This is precisely why, according to her, they have the tendency to constantly seek approval. Interviews with women reveal an obligation towards interpersonal relationships and sacrifice of the self, over the values of entitlement and equality. Gilligan's subjects upheld peaceful coexistence without hurt as the basis of justice (ibid.). Further, women who were interviewed by Gilligan tended to display hesitance and apprehension, rather than an eagerness to make absolutist judgements, when it came to the morality of controversial issues such as abortion, draft or monogamy (ibid.: 102).[25] Her observation of boys and girls showed that boys tended to be more competitive with games, they upheld rules rigidly and enjoyed solving the disputes that cropped up. Girls, on the other hand, did not like to enter into disputes and preferred to end the game. They were also more flexible when it came to the matter of upholding rules. Hence, Gilligan's women subjects believed in examining moral conflict in a situation-sensitive way, by heeding exceptions, rather than taking an abstract absolute position regardless of context. They believed that laws were pragmatic instruments. On the other hand, interviews with men reveal a contrary perspective of their moral task as one of protecting their own rights and balancing these with others.

Gilligan introduces the notion of a self as relational and corporeal, which is articulated and sustained through language and society (ibid.: 64-105; Benhabib 1986: 405; 1992: 148-96).[26]

---

25 One of Gilligan's subjects maintains, "If there is any absolute for moral decisions, it is human life" (1982: 66).

26 " . . . women repeatedly are observed in the literature on psychoanalysis and personality psychology to blur the →

She is in tune with many feminists for who in the self is to be found between the familial and social spaces of egotistical individual self-interest and that of abstract humanity (Held 1998: 104). To quote Gilligan:

> . . . the central metaphor for identity formation becomes dialogue rather than mirroring; the self is defined by gaining voice and perspective and known in the experience of engagement with others. —1988: 17

She questions the conventional model of development as separation, by citing instances of adolescent girl subjects. They resisted separateness and saw engagement as the key to their identity formation (ibid.: 13).

Gilligan's interviewees often responded to not being heard by dealing with its ensuing conflict through silence, so that they are not invalidated further. For them listening and disagreeing was crucial, according to Gilligan, to distinguish between what is true and false, and to engage in relationships through processes of involvement and re-involvement. Thus, dependency, Gilligan observes, implies that there is an acquisition of autonomy through the processes of speaking and listening (ibid.: 15). Benhabib remarks that this in turn entails locating the self in a larger social world differentiated by sex-gender (1986: 405; 1992: 148-96).[27] Further, the latter distinction is not just a description, but rather represents unequal relations between the sexes based on exploitation by patriarchal symbols. Besides critiquing traditional ethics for assuming women and simultaneously denying them, feminist

→ distinction between self and others . . .(Gilligan 1984: 80). Mahadevan (2013) also has an analogous discussion on the care-based approach to personal identity and its ethical relevance.

27 Other patterns of differentiation include class, ethnicity, caste and so forth.

ethics also offers its own account of moral reasoning as Gilligan's case demonstrates. For Gilligan, moral maturity involves striking a balance between the self and the other, where neither is given up for the other (Auerbach et al. 1985: 153).[28] It is in this spirit that she urges men and women to dialogue and complement each other.

Care in Patriarchal and Colonial Contexts

A standard criticism against Gilligan's position is that in privileging care as a feminine virtue she ignores the extent to which it victimizes its provider. The previous discussions of premodern, colonial and postcolonial India, as well as the West, show that patriarchal relations treat care as a family value.[29] Care for infants, elderly and the infirm within the family was not regarded as work, in terms of either social status or income generation, till the twentieth century. Yet income determines access to resources, which is a precondition for social and political participation and contribution (Kittay 2001: 528). But no income is available to women doing dependency work in their homes. Nor is such work adequately compensated through women's participation in the economy. The latter often involves doing double-duty, both at the workplace and at home. Hence, according to Kittay,

> . . . it is when women move out of the "private" sphere of the family that the dependency hidden from public view becomes visible and is revealed as having the social dimension it has in fact always had. — ibid.

Nurses, day-care centre workers or secretaries perform dependency work that is not compensated in a fair way in the

---

28 Also see Gilligan (1982: 62).

29 As Kittay observes, "Historically the family has been the site of every form of dependency work" (2001: 528). See Chapters 1 and 2 above for a detailed discussion of nurture and family during these periods.

public sphere. In India, much of the dependency work belongs to the unorganized sector. Thus, those who do such work are for most part women from underprivileged class and castes who tend to occupy a fragile position in relation to others. Care-giving has often led to the sacrifice of the giver. Hence, most of the women in this context confront what Carol Pateman has termed as "Wollstonecraft's dilemma".[30] According to the latter, there is incommensurability between women's participation as equals in the public sphere and their losing out on equal opportunities because they provide care in the private sphere. It is in effect the tension between femininity and feminism that both Ramabai and Wollstonecraft faced. As Kittay points out, this dilemma arises because the self-sufficiency and formal equality of the adult male earner is taken as the yardstick (ibid.: 530). It ". . . is the failure to include within political theory the concerns of fundamental human dependency and the gender-specific way in which concerns of dependency have been allocated" (ibid.). The problem is to balance one's own pursuit of freedom with responsibility for the welfare of others, without compromising on the former.

Sandra Lee Bartky observes that an emphasis on care as a normative value based on women's psychology ignores how women often choose care through an identification with cultural expectations of the feminine that are patriarchal. She points out that one cannot assume all women to inhabit in the victim mode through the activity of care whih is necessarily imposed on them from the outside (Bartky 1990: 33). For very often women choose to preserve rather than challenge existing relations and have a desire to please, as Gilligan's stage three demonstrates. Consequently, the caregiver often ends up sacrificing her autonomy for the sake of the larger whole.

[30] This phrase is derived from Kittay (2001: 530, n. 22).

Indeed, women tend to be narcissistic about identifying with their feminine roles that estrange them from their own sexuality, body and freedom (ibid.: 33-44). Bartky points out that women can be distinguished from stereotypical male workers in their tendency to seek out modes of femininity and even follow instructions in popular culture on how to be better at feminine tasks (ibid.: 36).

As discussed above, Ramabai and Wollstonecraft, who were pioneering feminists, both wrote popular guides on the feminine in their prefeminist phase. Bartky's point about not equating the feminine with universal victimization is relevant. Indeed, Gilligan's whole point against the standard criticism is that the approach of care is enabling and empowering. However, Bartky, for her part overlooks that women's tendency to narcissistically identify with the feminine is a way of gaining recognition in a society which devalues care. Hence, rather than treat the caregivers as victims, following Gilligan's critics, one needs to comprehend their function within the larger whole. Functionally, caregivers retain civil and social bonds. Moreover, given the expectations of a patriarchal society, they are, for the most part, women. Gilligan does not defend this function as a virtue in the normative sense in the manner of the Aristotelian tradition represented by MacIntyre, for instance.[31] Instead of advocating the function of care as a chosen virtue for the cohesiveness of the community, she interrogates its secondary status in a patriarchal world from a feminist point of view. The type of care that one encounters in a patriarchal world reduces women to self-sacrifice. Indeed, in such a world, Gilligan explicitly notes that women are obstructed from actively speaking their minds and taking decisions. This is because an

---

31 MacIntyre concedes to a plurality of virtues which are unified through the "virtue of integrity or constancy" (2007: 203).

> internal or internalized voice told a woman that it would be 'selfish' to bring her voice into relationships, that perhaps she did not know what she really wanted, or that her experience was not a reliable guide in thinking about what to do
> — Gilligan 1993: ix

Hence, relationships of care are not about selfless sacrifice, which renounce voice, and responsibility (ibid.: x). Gilligan, thus, differs in this respect from the colonial context of Ramabai and Wollstonecraft in their pre-feminist phases. Rather, her whole point in according a place to care in moral reasoning is to question its subordinate function in a patriarchal society as a unifying force. Thus, care has a critical function in Gilligan's scheme, since it is about women choosing to speak, being heard and listening, so that their subservient status is transformed.

Gilligan is well aware of the patriarchal aspects of women's lives, through their exclusion from social participation and forced adherence to masculine judgements on which they are dependent (Gilligan 1982: 67; 1986). Indeed, against her standard reading, she does not propose a substantive virtue ethics of a good life or self-realization in place of the self-determinism of a formal procedural one of justice (Habermas 1989-90: 181).[32] Nor does she, as Habermas observes, conflate the justification of a moral point of view with its application (1990: 177-78, 181-82; 1989-90: 42, 50-51). Rather, Gilligan's whole point is to articulate a different moral point of view or reasoning that is based on hitherto neglected women's experiences and subjectivity. She does not enlist care as an exclusively feminine virtue or as an antithesis to freedom. In fact, for Gilligan "The questioning of separation has nothing to do with questioning freedom but rather with seeing and speaking about relationships" (1993: xiv-xv). Hence, she uses the term "care" to convey a form of moral reasoning based on

---

[32] Also see Habermas (1990: 176-78).

women's experiences, to accommodate a plurality of perspectives sensitive to the other person's point of view. It is a way of thinking about relationships. Such a mode of reasoning takes the particular context into account rather than abstract universality. Further, it is oriented towards sensitivity to others, rather than individual entitlement. Gilligan opposes this reasoning to what she sees as Kohlberg's absolutist, separatist and individualistic approach, which she argues, implies that women are not as developed as men. Kohlberg's contribution emerges from a masculine set of experiences, which are comprised rules and universality that eclipse the feminine way of reasoning, based on relationships and particularity. Further, Gilligan justifies her account of different moral reasoning through an appeal to women's experiences within the domestic sphere and their subjectivity as relational. This differs from the application of principles to arrive at specific virtues.

Gilligan would well agree with Habermas in several respects[33] that in a pluralistic world, self-realization depends on individual preference, which is not random, since it is regulated by the moral point of view which is impartial to competing versions of good life. She makes Habermas's point:

> Since valid norms cannot but embody generalizable interests, it follows that the . . . principle of care and responsibility . . . are already contained in the meaning of the term normative validity. — 1990: 181

Those of Gilligan's commentators, who believe that she articulates the perspective of good life, overlook her non-

---

[33] Benhabib analogously observes that Habermas's notion of recognizing the other in the moral point of view is similar to Gilligan's acknowledging the other in care. She also notices an overlap between Habermas's generalized other and Gilligan's concrete other (1992: 190).

teleological approach.[34] She does not give an account of the outcome of moral reasoning as her examples regarding the abortion decision; each of her subjects has a different answer depending upon her position in society. Rather than specify a concrete list of virtues, Gilligan recommends a mode of moral judgement and reasoning based on women's perspective. Indeed in this respect she does share with Kohlberg and Habermas, and through them with Kant, the commitment to a larger moral perspective than a specific account of virtues.

These similarities notwithstanding, Habermas indicts Gilligan for dichotomizing between postconventional formalism geared towards justice and a care-oriented postconventional contextualism to maintain that they are unequally distributed between the two sexes (Habermas 1990: 180). He points out that she opposes the former perspective of justice to the latter approach of care. But Gilligan's point in articulating a postconventional moral perspective is to provide "an integration of rights and responsibilities through the discovery of complementarity of these disparate views" (Gilligan 1982: 100). She believes that such integration cannot

34 This includes Habermas. Indeed, it is MacIntyre (2007) who enumerates a list of moral virtues that is derived from the various tasks of participation in the community. Against the alleged individualism of existentialism and vacuity of emotivism, he suggests a turn to virtues in a functionalist sense. Virtues allow the individual to pursue good life through membership in the community. But MacIntyre's position and that of communitarians in general (though MacIntyre rejects the communitarian tag does share some commonalities with it) has some similarities with that of Gilligan. These include the rejection of individualism, a non-atomistic notion of the self and a rootedness in relationships. However, there is a major difference in that Gilligan would not affirm virtues as a unity in the functionalist sense of the terms like MacIntyre. Nor would she turn to existing tradition and community as alternatives to individualism. Kittay also acknowledges the distinction between feminism and communitarianism.

be achieved by leaving responsibility to the private domain of interests following Kohlberg.[35] Habermas on a similar note upholds the relation between an impartial justice and solidarity, where the latter entails taking the welfare of dialogue partners into consideration (1989-90).[36] This is a transition from Kohlberg's postconventional formalism which looks at moral reasoning as an abstract social contract type of process to postconventional contextualism (Benhabib 1992: 149). The latter involves taking the situation and its specificities into account while reasoning. It also entails taking the standpoint of the "particular other" since "women appear more adept at revealing feelings of empathy and sympathy . . . " (ibid.). For Gilligan, women's development and cognition are not deficiencies or confusions but strengths, in the process of mature adult moral reasoning, of which entitlements are also a part. Hence, the virtue ethics interpretation of the ethics of care too has this danger. Instead, feminist consciousness proceeds through both an interrogation and an expansion of the domestic. But then, this requires going beyond Gilligan's

---

35 Benhabib observes that Habermas veers in the same direction as Kohlberg in treating matters pertaining to the good life as personal rather than moral and relegating women's experiences and care to the periphery of the moral (1992: 183-85). However, although Habermas does treat questions of self-realization as preferences, one need not read it as an anti-feminist move, as Benhabib does. For feminist ethics is not restricted to the virtue of care or the good life alone. Indeed, Gilligan herself utilizes the concept of care as an umbrella for interconnectedness, responsibility, emotions and an openness to the point of view of the other. Habermas is well aware of her inclusive use of this term, which he tries to weave into the moral point of view. He attempts to combine the good life.

36 However, although Benhabib recognizes this similarity between Gilligan and Habermas only in his later paper on justice and solidarity, their similarity can be traced to Habermas's discussion of Gilligan in his earlier work (Benhabib 1992: 190).

developmental perspective which assumes women's psychology to be naturally given. Instead of investigating the conditions under which co-operative and preserving qualities are acquired by women, Gilligan simply considers these to be their distinguishing traits. In this sense, she tends to naturalize care as a feminine virtue without historicizing it.

Thus, the problem with Gilligan is rather that she tends to universalize the notion of care and treat it as an abstraction by assuming that its pursuit leads to peaceful coexistence. In her recent work with Richards, Gilligan reiterates her abstract account of non-violence in claiming that "this tension lies at the heart of the struggle between democracy and patriarchy, one relying on voice, the other on violence. In plumbing the wellsprings of voice, we have been led repeatedly to our desire for love and to the foundations of deliberative democracy" (Gilligan and Richards 2009: 265). Gilligan argues that shame in not living up to the ideal of manliness — that comprises of pride, autonomy and so forth — has motivated violence and militaristic aggression. She remarks that the roots of intolerance based on race, gender or class, emerge from the breakdown of "intimate relationships that marks the initiation into patriarchy, so the splits between mind and body, thought and emotion, self and relationships signal a dissociation that keeps us from knowing what we otherwise would know" (ibid.: 266). Consequently for Gilligan, the voice of experience that takes embodiment, feeling and relationships grounded in the body, fosters a democratic humanity, in which men integrate women's experiences and vice versa. Many feminist moral philosophers have followed by endorsing this thesis (Benhabib 1992).[37]

However, such an equation of care with peace tends to be both ahistorical and simplistic. A historicization of the abstract

[37] Held (1998), Ruddick (1989) and Benhabib (1992) are instances of this view.

discourse of care/sympathy, following Rai (2002) and Narayan (1995), reveals that it is not always as benign as Gilligan maintains in her abstract context. Caregivers can dominate their recipients — albeit tacitly. Rai (2002) and Narayan (1995) have documented the manner in which the concepts of sympathy and care were used to further colonial ends. They point out that the economic motivations of colonization did not merely conform to what Narayan terms as "crude self-interest"; rather they were justified through spiritual, material and cultural benefits for the colonized (Narayan 1995: 134). The colonizers believed that sympathy allowed the superior white race to have control over those they perceived as inferior: Indians, women and animals.[38] Indeed, from the gendered point of view, ". . . colonial attempts to get 'native women' to conform to Victorian/Christian norms of respectable dress, sexuality and family life were regarded as in the moral interests of the women" (ibid.). As it has been argued above, the ideology of the sacrificing woman within the family emerged through the interface between colonization

---

38 The eighteenth-century philosopher David Hume, as Rai observes, makes this point in contrast to the contract tradition of Hobbes and Locke (1983: 35-43). Indeed Hume's view that reason is the slave of the passions echoes the feminist perspective of care. Further, he upheld sympathy to be a universal natural feeling — an internal sense — whose combination with justice would lead to social well-being (ibid.: 16-20). Hume maintains that this virtue has a central significance in the domestic sphere. However it is only when it is extended beyond that humanity as a whole can get its benefits (ibid.: 18). This duty to society also takes an explicitly patriarchal turn when Hume identifies chastity as women's primary social duty (ibid.: 54). Further maintaining that the British have the onus on initiating sympathy against barbarians, he subscribes to its civilizing empire building ability.

and nationalism.[39] The family in turn plays a role in regulating the population through the caregiver. Thus, from the colonial world-view "white women" had the onus of protecting their husbands from being absorbed in the colonies, in addition to fulfilling paternalistic roles towards people in the colonies who were treated as children (ibid.: 136). As Wollstonecraft observes, women were indoctrinated into a lifestyle of manners so that the civilization process could continue smoothly. In the context of both Western feminism and colonization, the paternalistic construction of femininity was challenged by the movement through exposing its hidden exploitative component (ibid. 137).

Colonization or other hierarchies shift the relationship of care from particular individuals to those between groups (ibid.: 134; Fraser 1986: 427). Thus, groups or collectivities are defined in terms of hierarchical relations to each other or in terms of their position within the larger social hierarchy. Hence the nature and justification of interdependency would depend on where one is located. As Narayan observes:

> The paternalistic moral vision of colonialism was sustained by the discourses of religion, philosophy, science, and art-cultural practices that collaborated to make a sense of Western superiority part of the collective world-view of people in the colonizing countries. — 1995: 134

Yet, Western feminism did not always critique the logic of empire building during the period of British colonialism. Indeed, as Narayan observes many working-class and feminist movements in England favoured colonization. The women from the colonized world were depicted as helpless and in need of protection from the guidance of Western men. In fact, the care-giving work done by women in the colonies were

---

[39] See Chapter 1.

often effaced by transferring them to Western colonial men. Wollstonecraft's ambivalent attitude to slavery discussed above is testimony to this.

Such a problem of hierarchy reveals that one cannot simply replace Kohlberg's abstract other with someone concrete, whom one encounters in face-to-face relations (Bartky 1990; Fraser 1986).[40] The choice is not between an insulated egoistic self and one that is related to others in abstraction.[41] For such an alternative only focuses on the domain of the intimate within which the feminine plays a significant role. Gilligan's relational self cannot be based on close-knit relationships, as Held believes. For women are conventionally socialized to feel more responsible to their immediate circle of family and friends. Consequently, the sphere of concern would not be able to acquire a political status, which is necessary for taking women's lives into consideration. However, a critique of the feminine requires both an interrogation and expansion of the domain of domestic relationships. Thus, the conditions under which women acquire the attitude of co-operation need to be investigated. This in turn demands that the family be located within the non-intimate sphere of the social and political. Else one would be replacing the Kohlbergian separateness of the individual with that of the family. In fact, as de Beauvoir observes, women tend to be more loyal to the men of their own community rather than to women from others (de Beauvoir 2010: 8). This hinders them from forming collective associations that cut across their sphere of proximate relationships. In order to explore the possibility of what Fraser has termed as a concrete collective other, the family would

---

40 As Fraser observes, this is the problem with Benhabib's attempt to combine rights with care (1986: 427).

41 Thus, the choice is not between Hobbes's egoism and Kant's altruism.

have to be located within larger social networks. The resultant interface between the domestic dimension of responsibility to others, and the public value of freedom leads to bonds of solidarity between women. Such bonds inevitably require diverse communities so that feminist collectivities are constituted. Thus, overcoming the intimate domain — without losing its insights which have to be brought into the non-intimate spheres — is necessary for feminist consciousness.

Solidarity becomes possible only because individuality is attained through socialization processes, following Habermas. He argues that individuals acquire their sense of specificity through language acquisition and being socialized in speech communities (Habermas 1989-90: 46). Hence, sharp boundaries of individuality imply a deeper entanglement in reciprocal social ties. It also reveals that vulnerable individual identities can be protected and developed through the welfare of others with whom they are bound. Gilligan's self is similar to Habermas's, in that the individual aspect of the self presumes the larger domain of social relations and vice versa.[42] The inevitability of dependency work in every community is because there always are people — infants, old, infirm — who are not capable of self-support, both at the private and public level. But care-giving is also necessitated by the interrelation between the self and society, which makes the self vulnerable, rather than self-sufficient. Habermas's notion of "double-aspect" identity allows for integrating the insights of both Kohlberg's rights-based approach and Gilligan's responsibility orientation. ". . . There emerges instead a close connection between concern for the welfare of one's fellowman and the interest in general welfare: the identity of the group is reproduced through intact relationships of mutual

---

[42] Kohlberg too concedes to such a relational self through empathy, as a response to Gilligan.

recognition" (ibid.: 47). As Habermas observes, sympathy, benevolence or care are restricted to the dimension of personal relationships and this can lead to its own kind of asymmetries (ibid.: 45). Hence, with reference to Kohlberg's endeavour to accommodate Gilligan, Habermas points out that he ". . . formulates the correct intuition with the wrong concepts when he ascribes to the principle of equal respect for every person an expanded meaning that includes both equal treatment and benevolence" (ibid.: 46). Rather concern should be directed to both justice, as equal freedom of individuals, and solidarity as the welfare of an inter-subjectively shared form of life (ibid.: 47). In this way, what Habermas terms ". . . the boundaries of a concrete lifeworld of family, tribe, city or nation . . . " (ibid.: 48) should be broken (ibid.).

As Ramabai's instance reveals, pioneering feminism itself evolved by transcending such boundaries through the solidarity between women in the West and its colonies. Such a solidarity became possible only by overcoming the restricted circle and its implied hierarchy in the ethics of care, to adopt the perspective of what Fraser has termed the "collectivized concrete other" (1986: 428). According to Fraser, the latter avoids the extreme positions of the generalized abstract and the individualized concrete other. Women encounter each other ". . . as members of groups or collectivities, with culturally specific identities, solidarities and forms of life" (ibid.), rather than as unique individuals. Further, rather than presume a given concrete life story for arriving at the good, it broadly commits itself to the good of all members of dialogue who are in solidarity with each other. Indeed, to privilege the good life over the procedure, as interpretations of Gilligan suggest, would be problematic because traditional accounts of the good life confine women to the position of the feminine.

Yet one might argue that these criticisms overlook Gilligan's distinction between a feminist and feminine ethics. The perspective of care emerges as a feminist ethics by taking hitherto neglected women's experiences into account (Jaggar 2000: 349-53).[43] The ethics of care emphasizes interconnections, rather than patriarchal relationships. Going beyond Kohlberg's differentiation between good life and justice, Gilligan believes that men, as well as, women, have to avoid the extremes of total self-sacrifice or rigid individualism. For Gilligan, the ethics of justice is based on equality, which believes that all persons should be treated in the same way (Gilligan 1982: 174). In contrast, care is based on non-violence, which is committed to not hurting anyone. Yet since both inequality and violence are wrong, the two perspectives have to be integrated. Both men and women have limits that have to complement each other, so that they can communicate with greater understanding. Further, Gilligan questions what she terms "two long-standing equations, the equation of human with male and the equation of care with self sacrifice" (Gilligan 1988: 18). For "this dialogue between fairness and care not only provides a better understanding of relations between the sexes but also gives rise to a more comprehensive portrayal of adult work and family relationships" (Gilligan 1982: 174).

As Bartky points out, there are several empirical studies to show that women and men lead different lives, but rather than just being differently situated from men, ". . . women are actually subordinated to them within it" (Bartky 1990: 84). Thus, although Gilligan makes a distinction between feminine and feminist approaches to care, she does not discuss the specific way in which care contributes to a "phenomenology of oppression".[44] Further, she also does not articulate how

---

43 As Jaggar (2000) and Held (1998) note, the domain of feminist ethics is heterogeneous.

44 This expression is derived from Bartky (1990: 84).

care can be integrated with autonomy or justice; nor does she investigate the extent to which the notion of care would get transformed in the course of interacting with those such as justice. It is perhaps this ambivalence that has allowed both the conservative and feminist minded to imbibe Gilligan's work.[45] Feminists see it as a source of tolerance in a militaristic world, while managers view it as offering a humane division of labour in institutions (Auerbach et al. 1985: 159).

Indeed as critics observe, by basing her research on the premises of developmental psychology, Gilligan tends to reproduce the notion of linear progress to higher stages. It is just that the number of stages in her scheme is fewer than Kohlberg's. With the notion of linearity Gilligan does not focus on the factors that drive women to other stages. In fact, she does not consider why nine out of twenty-nine women she had interviewed for their abortion decision had not changed their perspective and stage (ibid.: 153).[46] Nor does she examine why some women had reverted back to their previous stage. By assuming that the conflict between self and other is automatically resolved at the third stage of moral development by integrating the individual self of entitlement with responsibility for the other, Gilligan adopts a "naturalistic concept of development" (ibid.: 153).[47] Given that the

---

[45] Gilligan's book has had a very good reception in the United States both in the academic world and in non-academic circles such as politics, corporate and the popular media. Thus, *Ms Magazine* conferred Gilligan with the title of the "Woman of the Year 1984" for "a new appreciation for a previously uncatalogued female sensibility, as well as possibilities for new understanding between genders" (quoted in Auerbach et al. 1985: 149).

[46] See Gilligan 1982: 108.

[47] Habermas analogously observes with respect to Kohlberg, ". . . I do not see why the highest moral stage would have to be conceived as a *natural* stage — that is, conceived in the same sense as stages 1 through 4" (1989-90: 32).

arguments used by philosophers do not have a "hard status" like psychologists, one cannot resolve the controversy between moral philosophers over the validity of Hobbes and Kant with a "psychological assertion" over the latter's superiority (Habermas 1989-90: 33-34). Yet, in this respect, Gilligan treads Kohlberg's path. In doing so, she overlooks the fact that moral debate, following Habermas, addresses the explanation of a universally shared moral intuition through a specific procedure and set of concepts (ibid.: 34). Thus, the philosophical perspective reflects on the intuition so that "this contest can be settled only on the field of philosophical argumentation, not on that of developmental psychology" (ibid.). Habermas rightly observes that developmental psychology itself should drop the assumption of "natural", especially at the postconventional level. This is because the psychologist as an interviewee becomes a dialogue partner with the subjects who reflect on their moral conflict. Hence, rather than provide a disinterested report on an object domain, research becomes a "joint venture" (ibid.).[48] In fact, from the point of view of women scientists such an engagement is central to their task of questioning value-neutral methods in science. But then Gilligan does not pause to address this issue. Although she does discuss social factors as playing a role in the formation of gender identities, Gilligan tends to overlook this in turning to the concept of a linear development through stages.[49]

Moreover, critics have maintained that Gilligan ignores differences among women. For in her small sample of data, she does not provide the details of the race or community of her subjects. Hence, all the differences that she can discern

48 Although Kohlberg has expressed his apprehension about foraying into philosophy as a psychologist, Habermas is keen on taking "the insights of Kohlberg the philosopher just as seriously as those of the psychological author" (Ibid.: 35).

49 See her "Introduction" to her *In a Different Voice* (1982).

are attributed to gender. Critics have observed that this homogenization of the different voice is also "to hypostatize illegitimately the 'voice' of professional, heterosexual, white women to be the voice of all women" (Benhbaib 1992: 191). Hence, "it is also not clear whether Gilligan attributes gender difference to culture or biology" (Auerbach et al. 1985: 155).[50] However, in her subsequent essay "Letter to Readers 1993", published in the 1993 edition of her *In a Different Voice*, she explicitly takes racial difference among women into account (Gilligan 1993: xiii-xiv). In an example that resonates with Davis, she refers to the African-American mother in Toni Morrison's *Beloved* who kills her own daughter so that she does not have to face slavery. In this context, Gilligan points out that the meaning of care for a loving mother who lives in a racist and violent society has to be examined. For such a society is injurious to both women and men. Hence, for her rather than a separate ethic, the non-violent approach of care is a counterfoil to such racist violence. However, Gilligan does not examine the specific contours of a care that manifests itself through the violence of its society as a choice for Morrison's protagonist.

Gilligan's demand for an integration of autonomy and care is important. However, considering that she has the tendency to attribute the former position to men and the latter to women, their dialogue is a key to such integration. Yet, there are structural barriers to such dialogue. Moreover, if men are viewed as autonomous and women as relational, there is a tendency to preserve the *status quo*. After all, the care-giving industry is filled with women who labour.[51] Perhaps the

---

50 She relies upon both the reproductive roles of women and Chodorow's psychoanalytic–sociological frames in arguing for a different voice. Gilligan's ambivalence between biology and culture has been similarly critiqued by Linda Kerber from a historical perspective (Benhabib 1992: 92).

51 It has been argued that Gilligan's perspective can be used to →

problem with Gilligan's work is not that it advocates conservative or bad politics, but that it rather lacks politics (Auerbach et al. 1985: 161). For contributing to progressive politics the concept of care should be situated in concrete social and political contexts. In her 1993 edition of *In a Different Voice,* Gilligan remarks that this book was written in the 1970s, a time of political turmoil (1993: ix). She enumerates the anti-Vietnam movement, student demonstrations and the subsequent crisis at the Harvard University, the US Supreme Court making abortion legal with Roe *vs* Wade in 1973, the revival of the women's movement as forming the backdrop to her book. Yet, given her analysis of care in terms of relationships, Gilligan does not address how her care ethics can impact institutions to question militarization or be exclusively committed to a politics of the disenfranchized. Further, the sustained focus on children as recipients of care and the family as a centre of care-giving should be re-thought (Kittay). Care cannot only lead to moral development in the domain of intimate relationships; it should rather transcend the "privatization"[52] of the personal sphere so that it acquires a political voice. This in turn mandates that care is integrated with justice and freedom or autonomy. This is especially so with respect to non-Western contexts such as India, which despite undergoing the decolonization process have to contend with the problem of social justice. The latter is felt most acutely

---

→ defend a gender hierarchy between men and women in institutions. "Given their better relational capacities, women are likely candidates for middle management and personnel positions that require extensive supervisory work, but men would continue to be slotted into positions offering more autonomy. Women may be in there 'relating' to people, while men will continue to run the organization" (Auerbach et al. 1985: 160).

52 This term "privatization" is borrowed from Benhabib (1992: 152).

by women from underprivileged castes and tribes, which are often also economically deprived.

Critics have argued that there is an overlap between feminist and conservative understanding of motherhood (and care) as perfection (Thorne 1982: 12; Chodorow and Contratto 1982). A glance at Ramabai and Wollstonecraft reveals as much. However, Gilligan's theorization of care is an advance over Ramabai's and Wollstonecraft's advocacy of motherhood; the former is a critical notion that questions patriarchal individualism. She arrives at her account of care only through a nuanced critique of Western ethical theory and its psychological assumptions. Gilligan also distinguishes between care and motherhood; her abortion studies show that women who care may not necessarily choose motherhood. Thus, Gilligan does not idealize care. Neither Ramabai nor Wollstonecraft, who literalize and glorify motherhood, understand its implications for becoming a critical concept that can replace patriarchal individualism. For them mothers have the moral responsibility for the nation and civilization. They do not pause to reflect on the conflict between such a motherhood and their struggle for women's self-reliance. However, despite her advance over them, the tension between the feminine and feminist perspectives which is played out in Wollstonecraft's (and Ramabai's) dilemma remains unresolved within Gilligan's framework. For Gilligan does not convincingly integrate care with justice. The following chapter, therefore, turns to Okin's attempt in this direction by taking the family as an institution of justice.

4

Integrating Justice and Care
– Susan Okin –

> . . . many of the respondents whom Gilligan identifies as speaking in a "different voice" use it to express as fully universalizable a morality of social concern as respondents who express themselves in the language of justice and rights.
> — Okin 1989a: 247

GENDER equality requires women's participation in public political life. However, their involvement with the responsibilities of care work hinders women from exercising their entitlement to equal freedom and justice. This is true of both the colonial and postcolonial periods. Though Gilligan's care-based approach discusses the possibility of employing care within non-patriarchal relationships, its reconciliation with freedom and justice has not been explored in detail. Okin attempts to embark on such an exploration by integrating care with freedom and locating the family as a central political institution. To examine her contribution to the perspective of care, this chapter will begin with her critique of Rawls who has been held in high esteem by Kohlberg.[1] It will proceed to delineate her account of justice in the family that is connected to liberal economic and state institutions. In conclusion, it will argue that Okin's emphasis on the state regulation of the family reproduces some of the pitfalls of liberal theory, in particular

1 See Chapter 3.

the capitalist economy and the bureaucratic state. In the resultant tension between femininity and feminism, Okin tends to undermine the former.

Justice and Family: Critique of Rawls

Okin discerns an ambivalence towards families in feminism itself. During its late eighteenth- and nineteenth- century phase, Wollstonecraft, John Stuart Mill and Harriet Taylor have all acknowledged the fact of injustice in the family. However, none of them envisaged its abolishment (Okin 1997: 14-15); on the contrary, they offered solutions to reform its existing form. Okin discerns a similar attitude in second wave feminism. Liberal, socialist and psychoanalytical feminists did not eschew the family despite critiquing it. Hence, for Okin, the feminist view is that ". . . families, being neither all bad nor all good, need to be critiqued and reformed, rather than discarded" (ibid.: 17). Thus, feminist aspirations need not be detrimental to the family. She also points out that the 1970s divide between liberal, Marxist, socialist and psychoanalytic feminism is not very sharp anymore. In fact, feminist debates centre around the issue of differences between sexes or between women, traceable to their families and communities. Additionally, feminists of all hues are united in their critique of the dichotomy between the private sphere and the public (ibid.: 17-18). Feminists have made visible the power relations that operate within the private domestic sphere. Again, the very notion of the private sphere and its limits has been decided in the public one of state and society. Following psychoanalytic feminism, Okin claims that the earliest form of social life is experienced in the family. Hence, its impact on gendered subjectivities cannot be neglected. This critique itself is an outcome of treating family as a necessary dimension of human life.

Okin observes that political theory right from ancient times to liberalism has excluded women from the domain of justice by banishing the family as an ethical domain.[2] This neglect, she upholds, can be traced back to an assumption articulated by Aristotle who relegated women and slaves to the sphere of the home (*oikos*) without access to political justice. The household is understood in a patriarchal way, with a male head. Moreover, traditionally thinkers have assumed that women are determined by their biology and are too disorderly to develop in the direction of justice. This view, as has been argued in Chapter 3, is upheld by Kohlberg as well, who approvingly cites Rawls in his account of moral development. Okin believes that to address this exclusion, the household has to be taken into account as a sphere of justice. She notes that Rawls addresses this neglect by giving the household a status in his theory of justice. He identifies the monogamous family as an instance of what he views as a major social institution which has a deep impact on people's lives depending upon how they are placed with reference to it (Okin 1989b: 7).

A primary social institution ensures evenly distributed fundamental rights and duties, which form the basis of advantageous social co-operation. Thus, all those who are a part of such institutions have their liberties guaranteed and the least advantaged amongst them are given priority when it comes to the distribution of resources. Such institutions differ from "private associations", "less comprehensive social groups" and "various informal conventions and customs of everyday life" (Rawls 1971: 18). Besides the family, Rawls considers the political constitution, legal protection of essential freedoms, competitive markets and private property, as instances of primary social institutions.

Okin observes that Rawls is well aware that the sex of the individual has no normative implications and he also treats

[2] See Okin (1987 and 1989b) from which most of the arguments in the following paragraphs are derived.

the institution of the family as a basic social institution. But in her opinion he fails to develop the gender equal implications of either of these premises. Thus, "the problem for a feminist reader of Rawls's theory as stated by Rawls himself, however, is encapsulated in that ambiguous 'he'" (Okin 1987: 65). His use of language in keeping with the tradition of philosophy is masculine, as he uses the terms "man" and "individual" interchangeably. According to Okin, though Rawls explicitly denounces discrimination against women in a formal and legal manner, his use of a gender-biased language casts a doubt over the applicability of his theory to women. Further, Okin argues that Rawls does not interrogate the gender divide within the family, where women perform care-giving activities, often without access to income. The latter is often the privilege of men who enter the public sphere with a sense of entitlement. The male bias in Rawls's use of the generic masculine becomes clear, Okin argues, in his concept of the original position. The latter is an impartial starting point to arrive at the principles of justice. Its impartiality entails maintaining a veil of ignorance over social standing, class, fortune, intelligence and so forth. Yet, as Okin points out, Rawls does not explicitly mention sex difference as irrelevant. Further, he claims that the participants in justice are not just individuals, but heads of households. As she observes, Rawls urges the members of the original position to imagine themselves as heads of families and allocate goods as per their entitlement and what they need to set aside for their successive generation (ibid.: 128-29).[3]

Okin points out that Rawls refers to the family as a domain of justice. He links the family with justice when he assumes that the family is the first school of moral development (Rawls 1971: 490). According to him, such just families play a role in

---

[3] However, Rawls also makes it clear that though this is not a necessary interpretation, he follows it (1971: 128).

the moral development of the child (ibid.: 462-67). A reciprocal relation between a child and parent gives a sense of self-esteem to the parent and a role model to the child (ibid.: 466). Love, trust, affection, guidance and being good role models are basic to a balanced moral development. Yet, as Okin argues, Rawls's assumption is "unwarranted" on his own terms. For, if the members of the original position are heads of families, they are not in a position to determine justice in the families, since this requires their ignorance of their own position (Okin 1987: 490). She acknowledges that though Rawls does accept the possibility of a woman heading a family, he does so rather casually. Besides he also claims that favouring men over women is justified, only if it works to the advantage of women.[4] Further, Rawls concedes that racist doctrines are also characteristic of sexist ones.

Thus, from Okin's point of view, there is a vital tension in Rawls's oversight on justice in the family and his own theory of moral development which requires that families be just (Okin 1989a: 238).[5] She traces Rawls's neglect of the family to his Kantian heritage (ibid.: 231-35).[6] Kant's moral philosophy upholds that a morally valid action is motivated by duty and not by feeling. Okin points out that Kant distinguishes between two different types of love, benevolence and affective love or attraction. He holds the former in higher esteem because it is "practical love", a consequence of doing one's duty to help others. Thus, in his doctrine of virtue, Kant proclaims that to

---

[4] This is an extension of his difference principle.

[5] Rawls assumes that families are just.

[6] Although by giving the family a role in moral development Rawls's theory according to Okin is not as sterile as that of Kant (1989a: 236). Kant has in contrast delineated a model of moral development between a tutor and a pupil that is based on memorizing rules and following them through habit (ibid.: 232).

love one's neighbour as one loves oneself, "does not mean: you should immediately (first) love him and (afterwards) through the medium of this love do good to him. It means rather: do good to your fellow-man, and this will give rise to love of man in you."[7]

Okin upholds that Kant did not take into consideration the possibility of a love that is between duty and affect, such as that of the love of a parent for his or her child, which is neither duty-centric nor passion-centric. Such a love develops gradually as the parent nurtures the child, "It is fed by attachment, continued intimacy, and interdependence" (Okin 1989a: 233). Given that women have been mostly nurturers, this type of love is a significant part of women's lives. By failing to take this love into account, Kant neglects both women and the family. Rawls's tendency towards rational choice that does not take feeling into account is founded on Kant. For Rawls, the impartial standpoint produced through an ignorance of one's specific social status and so forth "achieves the same purpose as benevolence".[8] Women for Kant are not capable of moral development because they are confined to the domain of the affective. Thus, according to Okin, Kant reproduces the sexual division of labour between the rational man and the affective woman at the conceptual stage. To the extent that Rawls relies on Kantian foundations, he too veers towards such "gender regimes".

A Feminist Reinterpretation of Rawls

Despite these flaws, Okin believes that Rawls can be appropriated in a feminist context. She draws upon some of the central aspects of his *A Theory of Justice* to challenge the gender-structured character of contemporary society. She

---

[7] Kant quoted in Okin (1989a: 232). Kant's malecentric terminology has been retained without qualification.

[8] Rawls quoted in Okin (ibid.: 235).

defends his account of the original position, as the impartial standpoint from which justice can be delivered with reference to women. Further, Rawls's difference principle too can be interpreted in a feminist light.

Rawls's original position represents the moral point of view from which norms can be determined. It allows individuals to arrive at norms on the basis of a certain type of knowledge and the deprivation of a different type of knowledge (Rawls 1971: 17-21, 142-50). Within the original position, agents have knowledge of various general facts. These include the sociological, psychological and economic conditions surrounding primary goods. The latter are universally applicable resources that are instrumental in the pursuit of any private, individual goal. Rawls specifies primary goods concretely as the right to basic liberties of thought, expression, access to opportunities and powers, self-worth and the right to accumulate property. They allow each individual to acquire his or her particular goods. The fair distribution of limited resources is guaranteed by the primary goods. Thus, the Rawlsian capacity for rationality aims at prudentially maintaining the self-interest of all agents. The norms which result from the original position are meant to give all agents their share of primary goods and the resultant freedom.

Rawls further maintains that agents should also arrive at impartial norms without capriciously privileging the standpoint of a particular person or a group of people. To enable this, there is a veil of ignorance thrown over the legislating agent's particular interests, socio-economic position and psychological dimension (ibid.: 136-41). Such a deprivation of the particular facts pertaining to the moral agent would, according to him, enable a non-discriminatory choice of norms. For Rawls, individuals who engage in the reflective exercise of the original position arrive at the two principles of justice (ibid.: 150-61).

These include the liberty principle wherein the right of all individuals to maximum freedom is compatible with the like freedom of others. It also includes the difference principle in which any inequality in society should promote the interests of the worst off people in society. The original position and the two principles of justice constitute the framework of justice as fairness, which Rawls maintains is the basis of social institutions. Okin suggests that Rawls's original position is not just mutual disinterest, but a perspective of equal concern for others (Okin 1989a: 246). She places his theory within his account of moral development in the family and points out that for Rawls it is a matter of relating oneself to others. For this the disembodied persons in Rawls's original position have to be replaced with concrete human beings, who are not under a veil of ignorance, but have full knowledge of their specific situations (ibid.). Okin also argues that although Rawls presumes that the sex of the participants in the original position is male, under the rubric of "general facts" one can include the disadvantages that women face in a patriarchal society (Okin 1987: 66). The original position is a framework that allows for securing self-esteem, which is a primary good. Hence, if the parties in the original position were oblivious to their gender they would be able to bring about social relations that would not undermine the dignity of either men or women. The original position demands that the moral point of view entails considering every other human being who is different in terms of identity, achievements and goals to be an equal. In fact the knowledge of each one's specific situation requires ". . . capacities for empathy and powers of communicating with others about what different human lives are like. Since we know who we are, and what our particular interests and conceptions of the good are, we need as well a great commitment to benevolence; to *caring* about each and every other as much as about ourselves" (Okin 1989a: 246).

Such an interpretation of the original position in turn would highlight the family as a central institution for propagating gender inequality (Okin 1987). Okin also traces the original position to the family as a site for benevolence which is very central to the making of an impartial just order (Okin 1989a). She observes that the original position can be interpreted in a gender-sensitive way. She begins by replacing the disembodied persons in the original position with women. Those placed under the veil of ignorance do not know their goals, hence, the original position is not merely an instrument for securing goals. Rather, it can be seen as a moral point of view — particularly benevolence — which is sensitive to concrete situations and differences. Okin remarks that Rawls himself understands the original position in this way as his following quotation reveals:

> . . . the combination of mutual disinterest and the veil of ignorance achieves the same purpose as benevolence. For this combination of conditions forces each person in the original position to take the good of others into account.
>
> — Rawls 1971: 148

Okin's reading has yielded a feminist reinterpretation of Rawls's original position. She argues that it is not a weak stipulation (as Rawls holds), but a strong one for the veil of ignorance that demands that instead of self-interest one has to be concerned for others. It is clear (as Rawls believes) that since one is not sure of the person that one is going to be (when the veil is removed) one's rational self-interest directs one to be concerned equally for all persons. Therefore, one must have the knowledge of different types of people and all the different types of social positions. As Rawls himself admits, this is not so simple. For without knowledge of one's particular situation, one thinks from the position of everybody in turns, rather than the position of nobody. For example, in order to arrive at the liberty principle those who are non-believers should think from the perspective of believers. Similarly, with the difference principle, one looks at the system of inequalities from the point of view of the least advantaged. Okin concludes that the original position is not an abstraction from life, but an appreciation of human differences. Nor is the self in the original position devoid of relations and attachments, since benevolence requires attachments.

Rawls's account of justice is relevant from the feminist point of view in three ways, according to Okin (1987: 66-68). According to Rawls, the principle of liberty for all has intrinsic value. The only condition under which inequalities can be endorsed in public office is when they benefit those who are least advantaged. Okin argues that the difference principle can help redeem the right to occupation, which is often compromised when women have to bear the responsibilities of household duties. They either become confined to the margins of paid work or depend on their husbands economically. Further, men's subsequent responsibility of supporting their wives prevents both men and women from exercising their right to occupation freely. According to Okin, both men and women end up doing jobs that they find mechanical because of the basic sexual division of labour in a patriarchal society. She points out that for Rawls, formal political liberties, such as participation in the public sphere for all classes, can occur when the difference principle is followed (ibid.: 67). Similarly, she points out that the difference principle should be adhered to from the point of view of encouraging participation by women who belong to the least advantaged section of society.

Okin also points out that Rawls has introduced the family in discussions of justice. She observes that Rawls's recognition of the family as one of the just social institutions is also very significant from the feminist point of view, since just families are sites of moral development. A family, according to Rawls, is a small association of rights and duties where our moral understanding increases because we are constantly exposed to what others have to say. We take up their point of view by adopting different roles and positions. Indeed, the attitude of benevolence is cultivated in the family. Thus, according to Okin, Rawls can be understood in a feminist way by paying heed to the notions of concrete situation, differences, benevolence and family.

In this context, Okin argues that from the point of view of such a reading of Rawls, the dichotomy between an ethics of care and that of justice is unfounded:

1. One can have a theory of justice which makes room for concrete situations and differences.
2. One need not replace justice with care. It is not rules and rights *per se* that constitute the problem, but the way in which they have been arrived at.
3. Okin sees herself as freeing Rawls from Kant's "arid" (1989a: 232) intellectualization.[9]

Okin also appreciates Rawls for his efforts to incorporate the gendered dimension into his theory subsequent to his *A Theory of Justice* (1994). She notes that in the light of her criticisms, in his subsequent work Rawls does not refer to "men" and "mankind". Nor does he label the parties to the original position, the hypothetical situation in which fair principles of justice are chosen, as heads of households. He also adds a person's sex to the list of morally irrelevant contingencies not to be known within the original position. Moreover, he includes the family in the basic structure of society, to which the principles of justice are to apply.[10] Yet Okin's attempt to

---

9 See Okin (1989a).

10 But Okin's assessment of Rawls changes with respect to his later work *Political Liberalism* (1994). She argues that Rawls has undermined his feminist gains given his focus on social →

connect care with justice ends up increasing the power of the state, which could often work in an adverse way with respect to women.

Gender Justice: Liberalism and the Family

According to Okin, discarding gender is necessary for a non-sexist humanistic theory of justice that reaches out to both men and women (Okin 1989b). She contends that for unanimously adopting the principles of justice, human beings should develop universal psychological and moral characteristics that are at the same time indifferent to social status. Okin maintains that Rawls's strength is his potential to contribute to such a humanistic vision, for he assumes sex to be morally irrelevant to human beings who are free and rational (Okin 1987: 68). However, as Okin rightly notes, the problem with Rawls is that he assumes that male psychology represents human psychology. Hence, his humanism is flawed. Rawls's humanistic potential in her view can be actualized only when sex differences are problematized so that they can subsequently be abolished.

Okin's critique of Rawls is also a critique of institutions that propagate gender inequality.[11] For her, Rawls's position is compatible with feminism in so far as he considers the family to be the location of moral development (Okin 1989a: 236-37).

→ stability and neglect of the family. Though he regards the family as part of the basic structure, he is ambivalent regarding its adjudication by the principles of justice. For instance, Rawls does not enter into a discussion of women's rights in the household. Consequently, Okin argues that he overlooks women's asymmetrical and vulnerable position within the family that inhibits their entry into the domain of public reason as free and equal citizens. Okin maintains that Rawlsian liberalism becomes suspect in its attempt to achieve social stability.

[11] The first section of this chapter discusses this critique.

Yet as Okin also notes, Rawls assumes the family structure to be just and does not take into account the relation between the family and other institutions such as the economy or the state (ibid.: 237-38). However, for this he would have to consider the sexual division of labour's relation to the state or the economy to surpass the oppressiveness of the private–public dichotomy. To the extent that he does not do so, Rawls confines himself to the typically liberal way of viewing the home as a blissful hearth.

In her search for what differentiates women from men, so that the dichotomy between the private and public is addressed, Okin turns to Gilligan and Chodorow amongst others (Okin 1989a: 246-47). She remarks that their studies indicate that in a society stratified by gender women have a standpoint that differs from men. The perspective of care articulates women's moral development on the basis of their role as nurturers (Okin 1987: 69-71). According to Okin, the care perspective does have a close relation with universality and a concern for others (Okin 1989a: 247). A constructive approach to such difference would entail taking the formative influence of female parenting on the psychology of children into account. The nurturer does not think of herself as outside the bond of relationships that she sustains. Rather a mother or a wife who provides care for others within the household comprehends her own self through the web of relationships. Hence, Okin points out that those aspects of Rawls that encourage relationships should be developed, while those that do not should be renounced (ibid.). As argued above, she herself has interpreted Rawls's original position and the difference principle in this light. Integrating difference and equality, she observes:

> The notion of a standpoint of women, while not without its own problems, suggests that a fully human moral theory can be developed only when there is full participation by

> both sexes in the dialogue that is moral and political philosophy.
> —1987: 70

Thus, difference is a crucial and necessary step towards equality.

Okin is also aware that an equal participation of women and men in political processes that respects differences mandates institutional changes. The latter would initiate dialogue between the perspectives of care and justice or women and men. Hence, differences that are a result of existing institutions which propagate gendered parenting and sex differences would have to be critiqued. Subsequently, institutional changes would have to be effected so that they are ". . . replaced by genderless institutions and customs" (ibid.: 71).

As a remedy, Okin suggests several public policies for ushering in humanistic institutions by diminishing sex differences.[12] These policies must assume that both women and men are equally responsible for maintaining their children. They do not assume that men have a nurturing structure responsible for their well-being at home. As a policy matter, Okin suggests that day-care centres be funded. Second, she also recommends flexible hours at the workplace, so that those who pursue pregnancy, parenting or care for the aged (mostly done by women), do not sacrifice their career growth. Third, schools must try to include greater equality between sexes and not leave their children's education and development to women alone.[13] Besides appointing men on an equal part with women, schools should also concentrate on removing gender stereotypes in their curriculum. Hence, "No assumptions would be made about 'male' and 'female' roles; childbearing

---

[12] See Okin (1989b: 175-80).

[13] Most of the primary level courses are taught exclusively by women.

would be so conceptually separated from childrearing and other family responsibilities that it would be a cause for surprise, and no little concern, if men and women were not equally responsible for domestic life . . ." (Okin 1989b: 171). The division of labour between men's work and women's work has adversely affected women and children by weakening them through a deprivation of their participation in public life. Okin's policy recommendations require that men participate in what were erstwhile women's bastions and vice versa. An equitable distribution of men and women participating in all spheres of life would prevent men who are cut off from domestic duties to be making decisions regarding marriage, divorce and rape — as is the case with the present legal system.[14]

In her proposal for a "humanistic justice" that shapes institutions, Okin assumes that the family is the "lynchpin of gender" (ibid.: 170).[15] It is central, she believes, to the reproduction of gendered identities and the site of moral development. Okin concentrates on the absence of justice in the family, as a problem to remedy it with proposals for equal sharing of work between the sexes outlined above. However, there are several difficulties with imputing such a foundational

14 Most of Okin's suggestions have attained legal cognizance in many societies.

15 Despite acknowledging this significance of family, Okin holds Plato in high esteem because of gender justice in his *Republic* (Okin: 1979). She sees this as a strength in Plato despite the misogyny in his writings otherwise. Okin attributes the Aristotelian denigration of the household as the basis of women's inequality in subsequent political theory. However, in this distinction she overlooks that Plato gives women a role in the public sphere only on the basis of sacrificing their femininity and adopting masculine virtues of the political sphere. Indeed, it is through the dismissal of the family that Plato achieves this. But unlike Aristotle he does not delineate the characteristics of the *oikos* (household).

role to the family. From the point of view of moral development, taking the perspective of the other within the family does not necessarily guarantee its implementation in non-familial contexts. As has been argued in the previous chapter, the practice of morality within the intimate domain is based on personal affection and loyalty, which might not necessarily expand to non-familial contexts.

Okin resolves the question of women being sidelined within the family — itself by making men responsible to women in the home. However, this is rather problematic from the point of view of women-headed households, which often involve single parenting. Okin does admit that the case of single parents gets "more complicated" than the picture that she has presented (ibid.: 78). But, she believes that this aspect too can be assuaged if sex differences are not given primacy in society as per her proposals of state involvement. In the case of single mothers, who have never been married, she suggests the reduction of teenage pregnancy through development of self-esteem, self-assertion, contraception and sex education. All of this would convince girls that there is more to life than motherhood. As for the boys, they would not indulge in "careless sexual behavior until they were ready to take on the responsibilities of being parents"(ibid.). With respect to single mothers who are divorced, Okin recommends that the parent who is not in physical custody of the child is required to compulsorily contribute to the child's support so that despite divorce both parents are active in the child's life.

For Okin, incentives of shared, rather than gendered work at the institutional level can contribute to rearranging personal relations on the basis of political principles of justice. To quote:

> The way we divide the labour and responsibilities in our personal lives seems to be one of those things that people should be free to work out for themselves, but because of its

> vast repercussions it belongs clearly within the scope of things that must be governed by the principles of justice.
> — ibid.: 171

Okin argues that this is analogous to labour relations: In cases where there is inequality of sexes, one cannot leave matters to individual decision or free contract (ibid.: 173). For given their position of vulnerability in terms of depending on men, they would not have the freedom to bargain as they do not have bargaining power. For Okin, justice, which has hitherto been confined to men in the public sphere, should also address the issue of unrecognized labour in the private sphere. She believes that women matter to a society because the well-being and the moral education of children depends upon them (Okin 1995: 281). Thus, following Mill, Okin claims that justice in the family is of prime importance because the family is the most important aspect of moral development (ibid.: 282-83).

Yet Okin's counsel for the distribution of work in the private and public sphere between the sexes makes several assumptions. It assumes that the two spheres acquire their identities independently of each other. Thus, women are assumed to care for their families in a universal and almost natural way. Heterosexual family ties comprising spouses and children are taken as the norm and the moral growth of children is taken as primary. In this respect, Okin assumes that women's primary task is feminine nurture, as Ramabai, Wollstonecraft and Gilligan do. She also assumes that her policy recommendations for families would hold for relations that are not always bound by marriage, same sex families and women-headed households. She believes that having a law is tantamount to it being enacted. Yet, legality has to constantly confront the lack of will in material realization. She advocates the regulation of the private domain by the public; for her the issue is not one of regulation *per se*, but rather of "how" — the terms and conditions that govern it — it takes place (Okin

1997: 14). But such a one way regulation of the intimate sphere by the public dimension defined as the state and economy is problematic. For one, it does not imbibe the care-giving virtues of the private sphere, but assumes its own authority in regulating the private sphere.

Moreover, Okin neither interrogates the political dimension of the state nor the economic dimension of capital that influences personal care-giving relationships. The state is mostly administered by patriarchal forces all over the world so that the insensitivity of bureaucracy to gender issues stems from its larger masculine character. In addition, there is a widespread withdrawal of the state from welfare commitments, under pressure from an economy oriented towards profit.

Thus, the liberal premise that separates the family from the state and economy needs rethinking. Zack remarks:

> Perhaps "the family" as an institution within an inegalitarian society can never be completely separated from public political issues. — 1997: 48

The family as a mode of social reproduction is not autonomous, its very functions link it to other institutions, such as the economy and the state in a reciprocal way.[16] It lays down the boundaries of social interaction, nurtures workers, reinforces gendered roles, consumes products and provides support to the old, ailing and vulnerable. In poorer families such support is difficult to provide and in disenfranchised ones it is virtually absent. This is because of the absence of purchasing power in the economy and the lack of state support. Thus, the family is not experienced by all individuals in the same manner, nor is

---

16 Although Okin admits that the private sphere is not autonomous, its relation to the public sphere is one of being regulated by it. It is in this spirit that she proposes her policies as well.

it a universal natural phenomenon (Zack 1997).[17] Engels upholds that the advent of civilization with commodity production is characterized by metal money, capital, middlemen between producers, private property and slave labour (1970: 332). He discerns its corresponding family structure as monogamy in which men are superior over women and "... the individual family as the economic unit of society" (ibid.). Hence, according to Marx and Engels:

> In its completely developed form this family exists only among the bourgeoisie.
> — 1959: 24

Among the poor working sections of society, ties among family members are severed because they are absorbed in the economy as labour. Thus, women in these contexts hardly have the opportunity to focus on moral development as Okin assumes.

Okin points out that in poorer countries women are hindered from earning a livelihood to mitigate their problem because of cultural barriers such as religious laws (Okin 1995: 285). She suggests that the solution to these problems is similar to that of Western countries, where state policy blurs the divide between the public and the private, and women are given employment opportunities with men (ibid.: 289). For this women should be given support such as parental leave during childbirth, day-care centres and flexible working hours. Yet such policies, Okin believes, should have the individual, rather than household as its unit of analysis so that women's individual voices are not lost (ibid.: 290). But, poorer countries that follow liberalism are not welfare states, yet they do have welfare policies for the disenfranchised. Such policies have not eradicated the divide between the public and private spheres, given their assumption of liberal individualism.

---

17 This was Engels's insight in the nineteenth century. He connected the monogamous family with rigid marriage bonds, patriarchal control and property transfer to paternal heirs (1970: 237).

Mahasweta Devi's short story "Ma, from Dusk to Dawn" (2004a) reflects the problems of reposing faith in the liberal state from the perspective of disenfranchised women. Devi narrates the obstacles that confront a nurturing tribal mother hailing from a remote region in India both at home, as well as, in the state at the structural, rather than cultural level.[18] Its protagonist Jaṭeśvarī belongs to the Pakhmara tribe of bird hunters, which is a nomadic and homeless tribe that lives a subsistence life by working in salt-pans and cashew plantations. Jaṭeśvarī leaves the tribe for the city after her marriage by choice to Utsava who belongs to another tribe. She and her husband achieve a status that is better than their previous one through seasonal work in cashew orchards and fish markets. Jaṭeśvarī's comforts are short-lived, as Utsava dies suddenly due to over-consumption of alcohol. In order to nurture her mentally challenged son, she is forced to suppress her personal affection for him in the course of the day, to earn her livelihood as a spiritual mother. But she compensates for this through her affection for him from "dusk to dawn". Although the Government of India has instituted several welfare schemes for underprivileged tribes, she has no access to them. During his short life, Utsava tries to avail of some of these schemes for upward mobility, but had to confront the hurdle of bureaucracy. Devi's fictional account sums up the abject condition of tribal people in India. The state has undertaken charge of tribal welfare of almost 500 tribes which is about 140 million of the population.[19] Eighty million people from Scheduled Tribes have been recorded, while about 60 million of them who have not been counted by India's census are called "denotified and nomadic tribes". Thus, Jaṭeśvarī's

---

18 See Devi (2004b) for four short stories on the theme of the unavailability of bourgeois motherhood from the point of view of the destitute.

19 This point is derived from Jacob (2009).

Pakhmara tribe did not even fall into the government register given its nomadic status for welfare benefits.

Jaṭeśvarī is the antithesis of domestic femininity that emerged during the Indian nationalist movement, which largely neglected tribal culture in India following the footsteps of the British. She does not have access to the domestic space within the framework of institutional structures such as the state, the school and so forth, which get attention in Okin's reforms. Jaṭeśvarī dies of malnutrition because there is nobody to nurture her or provide emotional solace. Yet even after her death her son evokes her spirit in order to get his bare meal. This story reveals that the rubric of nurture plays itself out differently in various contexts and depends on what lies outside the context.[20] It also reflects the shifts in the trajectory of the women's movement in India and the West, with respect to the family and its relation to other broader institutional structures. Although Okin believes that the various phases of the feminist movement depict a certain homogeneity in the normativity of the family despite critiquing it, she overlooks the specificities of discontentment between them. During its early period in the nineteenth and twentieth centuries, the women's movement emerged in different parts of India as a critique of oppressive traditions.[21] Its focus was on social reform with respect to diverse matters such as satī, child marriage, seclusion of widow and so forth. "But precisely with all this diversity, it becomes all the more striking as to how frequently the sphere of the home, family and marriage

---

[20] A recent state finding on Indian mothers (published in the newspaper on mother's day!) reveals that India has the highest number of deaths during reproduction. Further, one out of every one forty women in India face the risk of dying during childbirth. See Sinha (2011).

[21] This discussion is derived from John (2005). Also see Chapter 1 above for a detailed account of the gendered intervention in colonial India.

relations were critical institutional sites for social reformers and for the first generation of feminists" (John 2005: 712). As John observes, neither the diversity of sexuality, nor the intersection of gender with caste, class and community, were interrogated by early feminists in detail. Against the oppressiveness of traditional families, new subjectivities that were embodied individuals in a social domain were projected.[22] The role of the state in perpetuating stifling notions of femininity was not the focus of the reform movement, except indirectly given its alliance with the anti-imperialist nationalist movement.[23] Thus, the specific way in which the colonial British government and the nationalists (in response) entrenched traditional notions of the feminine as domestic — albeit without the overt oppression — was not interrogated by the women's movement during this period. In India, during the first part of the twentieth century, the nationalist movement and women's organizations struggling for the rights of domestic women, overlooked that for some women — from the impoverished sections of society such as the tribes — nurturing motherhood was an impossible ideal.[24] Further they also failed to connect the state with welfare in the family.[25]

---

22 John remarks that the questioning of obsolete traditions is linked to the women's movement with the anti-caste movement — a matter that is often not acknowledged.

23 One can discern a similar perspective in the women's movement in the Western world which was restricted to reforming the state through greater inclusiveness through female suffrage and the like. See Chapter 2 above for a discussion of the emergence of the women's movement in the West.

24 See for example Chakravarti's (1989) discussion on the Vedic *dāsī*.

25 See Sinha (2007) for an overview of the debates that surrounded the Hindu Code Bill during the 1930s and 1940s in India.

But John discerns that "a distinct gap — temporally, conceptually and politically — is apparent when we consider the post-Independence rebirth of the women's movement in the 1970s" (ibid.: 713). It acquired a critical, rather than just a reformative tone, in questioning marriage and family for "violence against women". Rape and dowry were key issues addressed by the movement during its second phase. However, the second phase of the movement went beyond the family to pinpoint the state, class, caste and community as coercive factors in abetting violence. Thus, for instance, dowry besides being an oppressive traditional practice was also linked to the type of modernity that entered India through active state support, namely a consumerist one, which sustained itself through dowry.[26] Besides the state the community also entered the debate as a factor that influences patriarchal behaviour.[27] Since the 1990s, the women's movement in India has concentrated on activism in the law, for restructuring gender relations. In recent years, sexuality has been visible as an issue of contention in the women's movement. It can be contextualized against the transformation of identity and desire in an era of globalization.[28] The latter development of the women's movement in India bear Wendy Brown's point that a feminist perspective "rooted in female identity may be irreconcilable with the diverse and multiple vectors of power constructing and diversifying identity; however, feminist

---

[26] Feminists have been divided over the prioritization of the dowry issue. Poor women hardly experience dowry as an evil because of their lack of property.

[27] John (2005) cites the example of the Shah Banoo case in this instance.

[28] A similar trajectory of turning from state reform to state critique can be discerned in the feminist movement in both England and North America (Brown 1995: 168-69). Also see Chapter 2 above for the early Western feminist perspective of reform.

claims about masculine domination do not thereby disintegrate" (1995: 166).

Questioning masculine domination, since the later part of the twentieth century in particular, has often taken the form of being critical of the liberal state's role in maintaining oppressive gender relations. The state in the sense of government organizations — such as the legislature, its executive and judiciary — is not a fixed entity with set boundaries. It is a ". . . multifaceted ensemble of power relations and a vehicle for massive domination" (ibid.: 174). Hence, its impact can range from the economy to ecology and the family. Besides, the latter institutions in the so-called private sphere also impact the state. Rather than overt forms of violence — except on rare occasions — the state maintains itself through the law, economy and welfare. Its power is constituted through the hierarchies of caste, class and gender. Given that Jaṭeśvarī's fate is unfortunately not an exception, one cannot merely turn to the state as an institution for reforming relations of gender in the family as Okin does. Rather its role in social and cultural marginalization due to its relationship with other institutions, such as the economic, needs to be examined.

In defence of Okin, one could argue that she questions the autonomy of the two spheres, namely the public one of the state and the private one of family (1997: 17-18). However, she fails to see how state reform of the family might exacerbate existing gender hierarchies. Okin does not interrogate the paradox of the private within the framework of liberalism — although women are equated with the private, they are regulated as well.[29] As a result, her discussion of justice in the family is depoliticized. The turn to the state for introducing social policy as an agent of reform entails both protection and

[29] Brown (1995: 181) citing Mackinnon.

regulation (Brown 1995: 167-70). The state in its existing form — within the capitalist order — is increasingly abdicating its responsibilities to non-governmental organizations in civil society which are institutional forms of paternalism often supported by corporate funding. Further, considering that it legitimizes itself on the basis of a few interests — such as that of dominant class, caste, race and gender — the state disenfranchises women like Jaṭeśvarī. Hence, its protection and regulation come at the cost of increased control of the dependents through its paternalism. The latter is inherent to liberal theory right from its social contract models — individuals give up their rights in order to be protected by the state (ibid.: 169). Similarly, women who are assumed to be in a state of nature with respect to men in their personal relations turn to the state — controlled by men — for protection. "Protection codes"[30] have been used by the state to propagate specific forms of femininity and have often worked to the advantage of privileged women against the likes of Jaṭeśvarī.[31] Thus, women get divided as "good" or "bad". As Brown points out there is a "masculinism" in the state, both in its capitalistic and welfare-oriented *avatāras* (ibid.: 167). Male dominated power both administers the world and keeps a vigil on vulnerable sections, such as women, in the process. The propagation of the state — an abstract entity — that promotes welfare is particularly problematic from the point of view of the increasing numbers of impoverished women heading households — who depend on the state.[32] For it encourages state control over the lives of the vulnerable, through what Fraser has termed "expert discourses" (1989a: 303) applied to a population that is assumed to be passive.

30 From Brown (1995: 170).

31 See Mahadevan (2003) for a discussion.

32 See Brown (1995: 171-72) for broad statistical details in the US.

Okin's proposals for state intervention in the private domain do not lead to "oppositional discourses" which question the subordinate status of the vulnerable or speak about hitherto prohibited topics such as domestic violence in public to stimulate active agency.[33]

The basic problem with existing institutionalization of care-giving in the contemporary world, both Indian and Western is that these institutions are rigid and bureaucratic. State-driven welfare schemes treat their recipients as burdens and — as Devi's story reveals — the right to welfare often does not reach those who are in need. Bureaucratic logic in India operates in a way that differs from the picture sketched by Adorno and Horkheimer in their *Dialectic of the Enlightenment* (1979). Instead of administering the individual completely without care, it cares for communities in a selective way so that individuals are often dropped out of its ambit of care. Moreover, bureaucracy also professionalizes care to make it a form of control. Those who work in state-based welfare schemes offer "care" to recipients by treating them as dependents over whom they exercise control. Their self-understanding is one of wage earners and experts, who are individuals rather than as caregivers, for the underprivileged sections of society. As experts, or "specialized publics" they determine the needs of those who seek care from them (Fraser 1989a: 306).[34] "They are thus associated with professional class formation, institution-building, and social 'problem-solving'"

---

33 According to Fraser, when ". . . needs become politicized when, for example, women, workers, and/or peoples of colour come to contest the subordinate identities and roles, the traditional, reified, and disadvantageous need interpretations previously assigned to and/or embraced by them" one encounters an oppositional discourse (1989a: 303).

34 See Fraser (1989a) for a discussion of need interpretations by experts in welfare societies.

(ibid.).[35] Further, the logic of bureaucratic care is often one of control over the lives of others, reflecting the colonial roots of care. Again, the stigmatization of receivers of care as "dependents" persists in liberal and patriarchal societies. As Fraser and Gordon (1997) argue, the term "dependency" has a mystified ring in liberal welfare societies of the West.[36] It connotes a dichotomy between the "independent" competent wage earner and the incompetent person who depends on welfare schemes. Although this divide is not articulated clearly in the Indian context, it does not have the organized mass welfare of the West. Jaṭeśvarī's struggles do point to the valorization of independence, where those who receive care are perceived as burdens.

Further, the case of women-headed households in the Indian context is often one where there is no male figure to hold responsible. As Jaṭeśvarī's case reveals, many impoverished women in India raise families singly; often because they lose their husbands to alcohol, disease, natural calamity or because they are voluntarily or involuntarily abandoned. There are several structural barriers that inhibit men from choosing the ideal of the nurturing father. Pro-feminist male academicians are well aware of the possibility of an exclusive focus on gender deterring from socio-economic issues that prevent men from considering nurturing tasks (Greig et al. 2000: 13). "Collective action at community and societal level is needed in order to create not only the cultural but also the economic conditions that can make this re-negotiation possible" (ibid.). At the economic and political level, women are excluded from decision-making and planning

[35] Fraser has warned against the danger of these expert discourses percolating to social movements, which then cease to be critical and oppositional (1989a: 306).

[36] They distinguish several "registers of meaning" of the term, such as economic, social, psychological and political.

in key economic institutions.[37] Governments and transnational corporations in a globalized world operate through a flexible sexual division of labour, though they appear to be gender neutral.

A couple of examples can illustrate this. Women's participation in the market has led to underprivileged men working in mining and manufacturing sectors (Jacobson 2006: 18-19). As a result there is a reinforcement of aggressive attitudes.[38] This shift is the outome of there being no equivalent expansion of jobs in the profit-oriented market so that both men and women can be accommodated. Further, unemployment and migration affect men's marriage prospects, whereby they have often to do without or delay marriages. This in turn weakens their relation to their families and parenting (ibid.: 19-22). Thus, not all men can enter into families to perform the normative role as nurturing fathers. "Economic transformations, increased presence of women in labour markets, and increased demands for equity and the acknowledgement of women's rights, as well as cultural changes, have affected men" (Olavarría 2006: 38).

But the change caused by women's participation in the labour market is marginal compared to increased militarization and migration of men themselves. The National Commission for Women in India has discerned an increase in women-headed households in north-eastern states such as Manipur and Assam because many of the men have either abandoned their homes or been forced into insurgency or the military (PTI 2005).[39] Thus, men are not given opportunities for re-

37 This exclusion also applies to the sphere of reproduction and family which is largely occupied by women.

38 Also see International Centre for Research on Women ICWR 2002 for a relation between men's diminishing employment opportunities and their inability to connect to the family in non-violent ways.

39 That the military construes chores such as cooking as →

negotiating their masculinities in domestic contexts through fatherhood. Moreover, women in the family themselves are not empowered because of the lack of support from institutions of civil society and state. This is despite a strong woman's movement in these regions. Analogously, the increase in women-headed households in Anantapur, Andhra Pradesh is the result of mass male migration by landed and landless farmers to urban areas (Sainath 2004). Such migrations only left them with low-paid menial jobs, which prevent them from looking after their household.[40] As a result, men in these regions tended to take to drink and indulge in domestic violence.[41] Besides, studies have shown that members of female-headed households do not have the means to acquire state welfare help such as educational and health opportunities.[42]

Undeniably, men tend to choose to engage in activities traditionally associated with women (as Okin would prefer), only when they enjoy economic security. Celebrity fathers take paternity leave to be with their new-born babies. The ex-Prime Minister of Britain, Tony Blair, had taken such leave. Many corporate CEOs have expressed their desire to avail of paternity leave (Nashrulla 2008). Despite these privileged high-profile cases, men claim that there is often a stigma attached to paternity leave, where those who avail of it are not perceived as serious

→ effeminate and unfit for military service is well known (Singh 2008). In a culture where the army is valorized such domestic involvement cannot be sustained.

40 The feminization of poverty led to children getting impoverished as well.

41 Male violence is often linked to men undergoing similar experiences with other men, rather than a retaliation to women (see Jacobson 2006: 12-13 for a discussion of this subject and issues that confront male subjectivity in a developmental context).

42 See Panda (1997) for a discussion in the context of rural Orissa.

about careers; further, men cannot afford it especially when their wives have taken maternity leave (Ardnt 2003).

Another deterrent to men choosing the path of nurture is popular culture's image of the metrosexual. As Chaudhry (2006) points out, the term "metrosexual" was coined by the English writer Mark Simpson, to define a self-reflexive male identity that is obsessed by physical appearance and the pleasures of consumption. The "metrosexual" lifestyle of commodity gratification urges young men to be "lads" without responsibility.[43] It is the very antithesis of family involvement and responsibility which is demanded of caring fathers. This mass media ideal which is quite pervasive in urban upper-class circles, prevents men's participation in domestic tasks (ibid.). Like dominant masculinity's macho image, the metrosexual too is a product of corporate globalization that hems men into militarization, retrenchment and migration. There is an uneven exploitative relation between the metrosexual urban man and the migrant labourer. Yet this unevenness is played out on the even ground of both being alienated from the domestic sphere.

The structural barriers — social, economic and political — that inhibit men's participation in the domestic sphere are not addressed by Okin. She also overlooks women from poorer strata, such as Jaṭeśvarī, who do not have purchasing power nor do they enjoy the privilege of sharing work with men in their homes, due to colonial and postcolonial policies. "It is as gratuitous to dwell upon an impoverished single mother's freedom to pursue her own individual interests in society as it is to carry on about the property rights of the homeless" (Brown 1995: 183).[44]

---

43 Chaudhry (2006) defines this as the 1950s ideal of masculinity. Further, it is not limited to heterosexuality.

44 Yet in defence of Okin she does take up the issue of differences amongst women and the relevance of a feminist theory that →

This gratuity is reflected in Okin's rhetorical proclamation that a poor single mother who is dependent on welfare ". . . is working. She is doing some of the most important of society's work, albeit often under extremely difficult circumstances" (1997: 21-22).

But then perceptions of welfare recipients as lazy, dependent and non-industrious are linked to a capitalist economy and the liberal state, which is not questioned by Okin. Her stress on the institutionalization of care does not interrogate the basic premise of liberalism, namely that the family and economy form the private sphere, while the state maintains itself as public. Okin overlooks how the liberal state's intervention for poverty alleviation and the like since the nineteenth century in the United States aims at reinforcing the family (and the individual) as self-sufficient units.[45] Liberal institutions assume that the family is an isolated unit whose natural giving functions produce self-sufficient individuals for society and economy. Moreover, welfare institutions aim at reforming who they perceive as dependent individuals into independent ones. Thus, the institutionalization of care is based on the ideal of individualism, rather than interdependence, which explains their discriminatory ways.

Okin also does not dwell on the availability of welfare to women without social and economic privilege. Women such as Morrison's protagonist in *Beloved*[46] have no access to even a modicum of well-being that is provided by welfare institutions

---

→ emerged in upper class contexts to underprivileged ones (1997). She points out that empirical studies reveal that Chodorow's work on the reproduction of mothering, focusing on the differential experience of women as mothers like Gilligan, is reflected in the experiences of underprivileged families as well (1997: 20).

45 See Zaretsky (1982) for a detailed discussion.

46 Chapter 2 discusses this.

because of the state's implication in a profit-seeking economy. The liberal state is a key player in the construction of masculine freedom as individualistic, autonomous and separate (Brown 1995: 183). Hence, contrary to Okin, the liberal state is a part of the problem rather than a solution. This is especially the case during its present period of ubiquitous liberal triumphalism. For under the pressure of corporate finance all over the world, it is withdrawing from its welfare responsibilities that are constitutionally guaranteed.[47]

Yet, in the Indian context, there are many more obstacles to women such as Jaṭeśvarī seeking institutional welfare. Welfare has a weak constitutional guarantee because the Constitution of India views it as a directive principle, rather than as a fundamental right. Directive principles do not have binding power. With the advent of neo-liberal policies, welfare is gradually getting transferred to paternalistic non-governmental organizations, many of which have corporate backing. Indeed, one can discern two types of social welfare approaches in India, state schemes for formal organized labour and corporate social responsibility that mostly covers the needs of informal labour (Pendicini 2011). The 93 per cent or so of India's complex and vast unorganized labour force, to which Jaṭeśvarī belongs, are not evenly covered by corporate schemes.[48] In fact, their motive is mainly corporate advancement, rather than a commitment to social upliftment.[49] Both the state and corporates regard fulfilment of social responsibility as a burden and adopt a stigmatized attitude to needs. Consequently, Jaṭeśvarī does not have hope for

---

47 See Noronha and Sharma (1999) for a discussion of how neo-liberalism leads to a decline of welfare institutions.

48 See Pal and Dutta (2012) for the challenges facing the informal labour sector in India.

49 This point is derived from Pendicini (2011).

acquiring social stability under the corporate sector in her capacity as an unorganized worker.

Jaṭeśvarī's plight under the state, which has welfare schemes on paper for underprivileged tribes, is no different. Under Prime Minister Nehru, a five-point framework for guiding tribal welfare was proposed in India.[50] Constitutional safeguards for the protection of tribes were also made. However, there were several internal contradictions between these laws which alienated the tribals. Besides, it took several decades after Independence to identify the need for a comprehensive policy on Indian tribes as was spelled out in 2004 (Jacob 2009). Yet, this first version of the National Tribal Policy (NTP) advocated assimilation and development (as per the norms of modern science and technology) for tribes without taking their land, culture and circumstances into account. A new NTP was proposed in 2007, which did respect the tribal's right to the preservation of their culture and self-determination. Yet it too is worded rather ambiguously, especially with reference to their conflict with development. The new NTP too tilts in favour of development, in case of conflict. Further, it dichotomizes between the tribes and the mainstream Indian population in spirit. Above all, the new NTP did not encourage the tribal sections to participate in the making of this bill. Only twenty days or so were given to tribal leaders for feedback. As V.K. Srivastava puts it:

> The dynamic reality of tribal living is missing in the draft. It lacks the "tribal voice". Throughout the text runs the "we–they" distinction — what "we" think tribes should be given.[51]

All of this gets reflected in its discriminatory definition of Scheduled Tribes as "primitive traits, distinctive culture,

---

[50] This discussion regarding tribal policy in India draws from Jacob (2009).

[51] Quoted in Jacob (2009).

geographical isolation, shyness of contact and backwardness" (Jacob 2009).[52]

Fraser observes that genderless institutions that integrate care and justice become possible only when the opposition between domestic care-giving and public income earning is overcome (1994: 612-13). The perspective of public income tends to fare well in overcoming income equality and marginalization, but does badly in removing androcentrism.[53] While the care-giving model does well in removing androcentrism, it leads to marginalization and income inequality. But this dichotomy is inherent to liberalism in which the two sets of institutions are treated as separate self-regulating units. Their integration mandates an overcoming of liberalism, whose individualism and profit-oriented market regards the family as an isolated entity. Destigmatizing care entails commitment to an economy that is not profit oriented and is collectively owned. For, as Okin and Brown argue, the key lesson from the domestic sphere of women's work for feminism, which is the basis for Gilligan's difference, is relationality (Okin 1989a; Brown 1995: 183). Thus, individuals are not atomic beings, but have identities in the context of their relation to others. In their relational framework, individuals would have to be understood as both givers and recipients of care in diverse contexts. As Fraser and Gordon (1997: 629) note, the dichotomy between dependence and independence ignores the vulnerability of individual identity which is acquired in

---

52 Institutional care to the Cholanaickan hunter-gatherer people in Kerala is viewed as a "curse" rather than "care" because of such factors (see Kakkath 2009).

53 See Fraser (1994: 606, 611-12) for scale of evaluation of the feminine care-giving and the masculine bread-winning models in terms of poverty, exploitation, income equality, leisure-time equality, equality of respect, marginalization and androcentrism.

social contexts. This dichotomy has to be renounced as it is ". . . negated by the most essential characteristics of the modern world, which create ever higher relations of interdependence, based on an ever-increasing division of labour, from the global to the neighbourhood" (ibid.: 630). Moreover, the aspect of being related to the other should be extended to families as well — their resources for care depend upon their relation to the economy and the state. This is after all Engels's insight.

The feminist critique of Engels notwithstanding, he connects the state and the economy in his account of family relations.[54] In his analysis with Marx he is well aware that life that "involves before everything else eating, drinking, a habitation, clothing and many other things"[55] is the precondition for human beings being active historical agents. The "material base" of society involves both the production of commodities, and the reproduction of human beings in families. Humphries rightly evokes Engels at this point:

The social organization under which the people of a

---

[54] For the feminist critique see de Beauvoir (2010), Evans (1987), Hartmann (1997), Rubin (1997) and Nicholson (1997). Evans for instance argues that there are strong tendencies towards treating the relation between the sexes as natural in Engels's seminal work on gender. Besides, she upholds that several passages indicate that he saw women as instrumental in fulfilling men's needs in the domestic sphere. Yet the tenor of Engels's work is neither biologistic nor economistic. He argues that gendered identities are constructed within the intersection of the state, economy and the family. He does not argue for the priority of the economic, in fact his argument is precisely that there is a simultaneity between the family and other domains. Further that social reproduction and economic production go hand in hand and that they are distinct, but not autonomous. He also provides a powerful argument for how women's confinement to domesticity aids capitalism. For a sympathetic account of Engels, see Humphries (1987).

[55] Quoted by Humphries (1987: 13).

> particular historical epoch and a particular country live is determined by both kinds of production: by the stage of development of labour on one hand and of the family on the other.
> — 1970: 191[56]

Yet, besides human reproduction the family is also the site of social reproduction because it (along with religious institutions, schools, voluntary associations and so forth) also plays an ideological role in shaping social identity. Humphries notes:

> Engels was insistent that historical analysis must emphasize the interaction between these *two* aspects of material life. . . .
> — 1987: 14

Engels tends to view the changing forms of the family with those of property and treats monogamy as a basis for shielding private property within the family. This militates against his own insight that there are two aspects of material life, namely, reproduction and production. However, he maintains that women are confined to specialized tasks at home because of the rise of production outside the domestic sphere. In his essay with Marx, Engels (1959: 25-26) notes that women are simply "instruments of production" for the bourgeois, so that their common domestication already forms women into a community. Therefore, they argue that the critique of a profit-oriented economy is also a critique of the exploitation of women (ibid.: 26). Thus, the vulnerability of women has to be situated within the context of liberal capitalism.[57]

---

[56] Also quoted in Humphries (1987: 13).

[57] Feminists such as Hartmann (1997) or Firestone (1997) have tried to develop a dual systems theory of gender and class to correct what they perceive as Marx's economism. However, as Humphries (1987: 16) observes they tend towards the reverse error of treating sex/gender as primary. Further they do not engage with Marxist treatises on gender such as Luxemburg (1971) or Lenin (1965).

A historicization of the family within capitalism, following Engels, Marx and Brown, is needed for a change in perception towards recipients of care, so that there is a materialization of the right to welfare. This requires an attitude of treating welfare work in the public sphere as a mixture of both paid work and care. It demands a policy that takes into account the relationship between justice and solidarity because of the relational dimension of the self. This in turn mandates a reconstruction of the concept of autonomy by retaining the gains of the ethics of care. Such a reconstruction will also question an economy that is premised upon the profit motives of autonomous individuals. Although Okin hints at such a reconstruction, she does not spell it out.

In this context, those like Jaṭeśvarī, single poor women who experience the conflict between care and freedom, do so without having the security of either family or public institutions. They turn to institutions that offer care in order to support their families. However, in the process they neither get care nor freedom, as welfare institutions in liberal capitalist societies discriminate against them for their dependence. As seen above, during the colonial period, Ramabai and Wollstonecraft appeal to both self-reliance and motherhood as ideals for women. Their turn to public institutions for making women self-reliant, fails to comprehend the limits of these institutions. Like Okin, both Ramabai and Wollstonecraft assume that the virtue of self-reliance is an antidote to confinement in families. They fail to see how the family supports self-reliance and individualism in the public domain through women's unacknowledged domestic work. Nor do they interrogate the dichotomy between public institutions and the domestic sphere. Like Okin, Ramabai and Wollstonecraft do not address the conflict between self-reliance and nurture or care. Okin is critical of feminist liberals, such as Friedan,[58] who consider the family to be oppressive, as ignoring the predicament of poor single women for whom extended families might be liberating. Besides, she is also aware that the ideal of the housewife might be unattainable for those who suffer from poverty and race or caste discrimination (Okin 1997: 19). But she does not discuss these obstacles, which are outcomes of liberal individualism.

Liberalism cannot restructure private institutions, such as the family, and public institutions, such as the state, by integrating care and autonomy. For its understanding of freedom is individualistic. Freedom is seen as an individual's right to choose and pursue personal life plans without interference. As Brown argues, liberalism gravitates around the axes of the family, civil society and state (1995: 135-65). The association of the capitalist economy with liberalism forces institutions — both in civil society and the state — to be oriented towards profit, rather than care. Indeed, corporate social responsibility and philanthropy ensure that care is brought in only to serve the interest of profit. In a world driven by profit, care-giving institutions of welfare tend to be bureaucratized and hierarchized. Hence, a large chunk of the burden of care is shifted to the domain of the family. Yet, Devi's Jaṭeśvarī emblematizes the painful fact that not all families are in a position to perform nurturing functions. Families are differently located due to economic, social and political stratification and exploitation. Hence, Okin's commitment to a liberal conception of freedom has to be renounced to bring about an integration between justice and care. The following chapter will turn to the debate between community and freedom in order to rethink the idea of freedom and overcome liberalism, on the basis of some of the arguments offered by de Beauvoir.

---

58 See her *Feminine Mystique* (1984). Friedan later changed to an acceptance of the feminine and the family in her *The Second Stage* (1998).

5

Rethinking Freedom and Care
– Simone de Beauvoir –

> . . . the independent woman today is divided between her professional interests and the concerns of her sexual vocation . . . — de Beauvoir 2010: 752

OKIN's endeavour to assimilate care with justice raises questions about privilege from the postcolonial perspective. Disenfranchised women in countries such as India do not stand before the state as individual bearers of entitlements to bargain for what is justly due to them. Like Jaṭeśvarī, providers of embodied care-giving are susceptible to exploitation by the very society that depends on their labour. Their socio-economic vulnerability also makes them potential recipients of care from the state. However, considering the individualist notion of freedom underlying state institutions, they are perceived as burdensome dependents. Despite accepting Gilligan's care perspective, Okin does not adequately theorize the implications of the relational self for thinking beyond an individualist notion of freedom.

In this context, it is tempting to follow the ecofeminist Mies's proposal to abandon the concept of autonomy or freedom[1] as a Eurocentric Western feminist norm that is exploitative or at best irrelevant in the postcolonial world.

---

[1] The terms "autonomy" and "freedom" are used in overlapping ways.

Although Mies's target is de Beauvoir, one could well extend her critique of Western feminism to Okin who is explicitly committed to individual freedom. Mies proposes a "recreation of a living relation" (Mies 1993c: 228) with nature and community as appropriate for women who inhabit so-called indigenous cultures such as India; her position has affinities with Gilligan's ethics of care. With Mies, feminine care undergoes a major shift from its colonial period of disavowals and avowals, in the early feminism of Ramabai and Wollstonecraft, to a normative postcolonial concept in opposition to Western feminism. None the less, Mies's position is debatable, given the inequalities of the global intersection between women from Western and non-Western worlds. An interrogation of Mies's critique of de Beauvoir as an advocate of individualism, overlooks the latter's theorization of "interdependent"[2] embodiment and ambiguous situation that resonate with Jaṭeśvarī's predicament. Moreover, de Beauvoir's embodiment and situation have implications for rethinking freedom, which needs to be explored for reconciling an ethics of care with non-individualist freedom in a postcolonial context.

The shift from Okin to de Beauvoir is motivated by the need to enlarge the canvas of Western feminism, as well as discuss de Beauvoir in the context of a renewed interest in her writings since the late twentieth century. As a forerunner of feminist freedom and critic of the myth of femininity, de Beauvoir's position makes any discussion of femininity and feminism incomplete without an engagement with her. Yet, revisiting her concept of freedom as a relation between the self and the other, subsequent to the debate on care in a postcolonial context, is instructive. It reveals that she is not as

---

2 This term is taken from Fraser and Gordon (1997: 628) who have used it in another context.

much of a critic of the feminine as is assumed. Besides, it also opens the possibility of reading her as an ally of care as a critical concept. de Beauvoir's arguments on embodiment and ambiguity need to be scrutinized to examine the prospect of thinking about freedom in relation to care.

In this endeavour, this chapter interrogates whether the concept of autonomy or freedom needs to be renounced in postcolonial contexts such as that of India. It considers Mies's defence of the perspective of feminine care, to subsequently examine de Beauvoir's notion of freedom within embodiment and situation. The discussion explores whether the core insights of feminine care, through its trajectory from the colonial to the postcolonial points of view, can be reconciled with de Beauvoir's feminist concept of autonomy or freedom from a postcolonial point of view.

The Disquietudes of Individualist Freedom

Through the instance of reproductive rights, Mies diagnoses the individualist notion of self-determination as culturally unsuitable for non-Western women. It requires the position of privilege and the safety net of the welfare state for its preservation, neither of which are available to women in the so-called developing world. As argued above, Okin's suggestions for state-sponsored erosion of the private and the public spheres are out of reach for women such as Jaṭeśvarī. Their problems are not cultural as she imputes, but economic and political. In India, for instance, many poor couples see commercial surrogacy as a source of income, though not quite respectable because "marriage, pregnancy and giving birth are sacredly tied together" in Indian culture (Kaur 2009). Thus, against Okin, cultural barriers do not constitute hindrances to non-Western women choosing options such as surrogacy or testing for potentially marketable contraceptives because of their economic benefits. The obstacles to poor women's rights are built into the very structure of possessive individual freedom that is upheld by the liberal state. It is on the basis of such exploitation that Mies moves beyond Okin to argue that concepts like self-determination, freedom or autonomy have an equivalence within the framework of Western Enlightenment; they may have led to freedom and equality for the West, but have spelled colonization for the rest of the world (Mies 1993c: 223-24). Turning to the Western feminist movement's ideal of autonomy, Mies discerns its limitation:

> For only the owners of property could be subjects in the full societal sense. — ibid.: 223

Hence, their economic condition — rather than culture — hinders women from poorer income groups in India from exercising freedom over their bodies.

Under the influence of de Beauvoir's assertion that "Birth control . . . would allow women to control their pregnancies freely" (2010: 546), the Western feminist movement established reproductive rights. Citing the instance of de Beauvoir as a paradigmatic proponent of the concept of autonomy, Mies points out that as the right to self-determination, it consists in exercising control over the body (1993c: 221-26). In Mies's opinion, such a control is predicated upon a split between the body and consciousness or nature and culture. For Mies:

> She (de Beauvoir[3]) maintains alienation from the body, especially the female body which, according to her, hinders self-determination (transcendence). Our body is our enemy. — ibid.: 225

Accordingly, she concludes that de Beauvoir does not interrogate the split between mind and body, which is ". . .

[3] The parenthesis has been added.

the European man's project, particularly since the Enlightenment . . ." (ibid.: 226), that is presupposed by freedom. She argues that on this view women who have been traditionally perceived as the property of men press for the right to control their own bodies as property. This can be illustrated with de Beauvoir's argument that women's right to choose motherhood requires that they refuse it as well with the help of contraception (2010: 751-52).[4] Since such reproductive control is not available to underprivileged women, Mies argues that the ownership model of freedom is irrelevant to them.

In Mies's view, de Beauvoir's concept of freedom is also exploitative of women who are socially vulnerable. Institutionalizing Okin's or de Beauvoir's choice of motherhood has expanded the opportunity to have biological children across diverse sexual preferences. Single women, couples who cannot reproduce biologically or those with alternate sexuality, can all have children due to reproductive technologies. However, Mies upholds that these reproductive choices of the privileged Western world have to be situated in a more complex context. She argues that the international context of the global division of labour has led to a situation where Western women get well-paid corporate jobs, while women from the rest of the world provide cheap labour for the same corporate interests (Mies 1993c: 219-20). They are the outcome of a system where Western scientific and corporate research uses women from susceptible socio-economic backgrounds as laboratories for experiments on reproductive technologies before making it available in

4 "If the idea of artificial insemination interests women so much, . . .it is because they hope that voluntary motherhood will finally be accepted by society" (de Beauvoir 2010: 752).

5 As Spivak notes, "Bourgeois feminism, because of a blindness to the multinational theatre . . . can participate in the tyranny →

Western markets.[5] Women from poor countries voluntarily choose to participate in such experiments because of their economic impoverishment. The "globalization of motherhood"[6] is a phenomenon where non-Western countries provide children for adoption, nannies and surrogate mothers at inexpensive cost to privileged women who are mostly located in the West. Consequently, as Mies concludes, freedom or autonomy as self-determination results in inequalities among women, even though all women exercise choices.[7]

The exploitative relationships created by the elite feminism, of those such as Okin and de Beauvoir, can be illustrated with a detour into another short story by Devi, "The Breast Giver".[8] It is about Jasodā who lives in postcolonial (then) Calcutta. Devi calls it a tale of "motherhood by hire" to show how commercialization and capitalist exploitation have entered even the private domain of feminine care through surrogacy. Jasodā chooses motherhood as a career by serving as wet-nurse in a business household, thus blurring the divide between work and home like her counterpart Jaṭeśvarī.[9] She turns to earning a livelihood because of the loss of her husband's financial support due to an accident. Thus, Jasodā's household

---

→ of the proper . . ." (1987: 91-92). She cites the example of the Control Data telecommunications company which tyrannized women in South Korea despite granting affirmative action to American women workers (ibid.: 89-92).

6 This expression is derived from the title of a book edited by Chavkin and Maher (2010), it will be subsequently used with quotation marks to indicate the same.

7 See for example Tharu and Lalita (1991) and Spivak (1987, 1993).

8 The narration that follows is from Devi (1987).

9 See the discussion in Chapter 3 on Devi's short story about the social nature of motherhood. Also see Mahadevan (2010) for an interpretation of this story from the point of view of materialism in the history of philosophy.

too is female-headed, like that of Jaṭeśvarī's. The business family for whom she works, becomes a factory of nurture. Jasodā conceives seventeen children — out of whom only twelve survive — to continue with her professional motherhood. With advancing age she is forced to give up her occupation and become a cook in the same household. When Jasodā gets breast cancer, medical support is slow to come by. On finally being taken to the hospital after unsuccessful local medicine, both her professional and biological family members abandon her to die.[10]

Devi depicts Jasodā's work as analogous to Jaṭeśvarī's, for Jasodā is a blessing to the household where she works. The women in the business house were able to keep up with Western fashions, avail of contraception, live in nuclear families and even work in their husbands' offices. Above all, their exposure to what Devi terms as the "new winds" of change such as de Beauvoir's feminist ideas, became possible because of the free time they derive due to Jasodā's labour. Their refusal of motherhood mandated that Jasodā chose hers; her inability to determine the fate of her body is directly connected with the reproductive freedom of her wealthy employers. Jasodā, the postcolonial wet-nurse, has much in common with her precolonial and colonial counterparts.[11] Thus, "the colonial 'wet-

---

[10] Devi's story underscores a patriarchal culture's investment in the symbol of sacrificing motherhood. Jasodā is named after the mythical figure Jasodā, the foster mother of Lord Kṛṣṇa. Like the legendary figure Jasodā is venerated for nurturing sons, which profits the wealthy household. Yet her very existence is also a deformation of the myth. When the ailing Jasodā fails to fit into this image she is abandoned to her "fate".

[11] Chakravarti (1989) has discussed the neglect of the underprivileged woman by nationalists such as Dayanand Saraswati who urges women in colonial India to become mothers handing over child care to wet-nurses so that they →

nurse' only fed (and even emotionally mothered) the child; surrogacy outsources the entire process (and perhaps the joy) of bearing babies from rich to poor women" (Kaur: 2009).

Given such exploitative implications of individual freedom, Mies believes that there can be no singular solution to the gender problem and champions communitarian caring, as opposed to autonomy, as an apt route for "other women".[12] Women in so-called developing societies have strong communal and familial bonds, according to Mies; hence rather than look upon community and relationships of care as weaknesses, they should be seen as their empowerment (Mies 1993c: 220, 228-29). Consequently, she stipulates the community as the normative foundation for the feminist movement in countries such as Bangladesh and India.

Mies notably addresses the crucial relation between globalization and gender. Nevertheless, her repudiation of freedom, propagation of communitarian care and critique of de Beauvoir, all need further examination. The "globalization of motherhood" depends upon the labour of socio-economically vulnerable women from India and other so-called developing economies. However, denying freedom as a value and replacing it with care-giving will only subject such labouring women to further exploitation for one of the prime values for transnational corporations is domestic care. Mies merely transports such care to the community whose prospects for remedying social relations of domination are not encouraging. Any move for change would have to renounce domination, and take into account labour as a situation in congruence with

---

→ could serve the cause of nationalism. She traces the lineage of women freeing themselves by taking recourse to housework to the Vedic period.

12 The expression "other woman" is derived from Spivak (1987: 150).

the experiences of toiling women. Mies has drawn attention to the absence of homogeneity amongst women arising out of colonization, unequal economic relations and the like. However, since many of these differences generate domination, one cannot follow her path of forsaking autonomy for community, as it assumes that autonomy has only one absolute meaning as individual freedom that operates within liberal contract.

Indeed Mies has not freed herself from some of the Eurocentric assumptions plaguing de Beauvoir's position, while valorizing communal nurture in the non-Western context. If the freedom of privileged Western women is related to the victimization of those who are underprivileged, then the activities of care performed by the latter perpetuate their exploitation. Mies reifies the relationship between privileged Western women and their exploited others as natural.[13] By assuming the exclusionary features of the de Beauvoirian account of freedom to be decisive, Mies offers a problematic option of either adopting an exploitative autonomy premised upon ownership, or uncritically embracing the position of "otherness".[14] Communitarian "otherness", in accepting what atomic autonomy banishes, is hardly promising for women in the so-called developing world. Considering the difficulties posed by Eurocentrism in the gendered context, Mies's alternative leaves little space for critiquing gender roles or altering the situation of "other women".

---

13 Indeed, Mies sees the northern and southern continents as culturally irreconcilable. Like many Indian nativists, she has a monolithic conception of an acquisitive Western world, against which she juxtaposes Indian traditional practices. The latter obliterates the various constructive changes that took place in India, with the emergence of feminist consciousness through Savithribai Phule and Ramabai.

14 Even Hegel did not assert the master–slave bondage to be absolute (Marcuse 1960: 115).

Discrimination against women operates in subtle ways, at both local and global levels. Its complexities are especially related to its decentred character, since a tyrant does not execute it. The global problem of inequality among women that emerges from the economy and the nation, shows the need for greater democratization, rather than its renunciation. For women, despite occupying diverse planetary locations, do not live in isolation from each other. The problem of exploitative conditions and consequences of individual self-determination shows that women lead intersecting lives. Historical sensitivity reveals that the classical liberal Utopia has ostracized women, non-propertied whites, non-white ethnic groups, southern continents and tribes among many others. This is the outcome of its inordinate stress on negative freedom or individual bargaining. Freedom in the context of the global division of labour is understood in the negative sense, as an individual's unhindered capacity for pre-given desires and contracts.[15]

By abstracting the process of contract from its circumstances, negative freedom denies social inter-dependence in several ways. Contract between individuals is possible only when there is property, which in turn is acquired in the social context of exploitation of labour power. The worker who consents to sell his or her labour does so in the absence of property ownership. This transformed class distinctions in the Western world, simultaneously aiding the colonization of Asia, Africa and Latin America. The colonies provided raw materials and cheap labour, worsening the conditions of the non-propertied people and women all over the world. The current process of globalization follows the same trajectory, often casting racial minorities and women

[15] The term negative liberty, derived from Isaiah Berlin, defines freedom as non-interference (1969: 122-31).

into contract and part-time labour.[16] Besides, liberal social relations rely upon a separation of the public sphere from the so-called pre-political and pre-economic private sphere.[17] Such a dichotomy is oblivious to the contribution made by women's unpaid domestic work to the economy and contractarian transactions within public space. Further, most women who work in the economy, suffer from the devaluation of their work, due to their subordinate gendered position. Conversely, their economic condition reinforces their gendered oppression through the sexual division of labour. The electronics, textile and clothing industry in countries like India and Thailand are clear-cut illustrations of this phenomenon; 90 per cent of their workforce is made up of women, most of who work on a contract or part-time basis with negligible health benefits.[18] As feminists constantly remind, women perform double work by labouring both at home and in the public sphere. The predominance of atomic freedom instead of favouring gender equality has, on the contrary, led to the denial of women's work. The conundrum posed for women by public work is poignantly reflected in the fact that many women have not advanced very much despite following de Beauvoir's advice of taking up employment to exercise autonomy (2010: 737). Only privileged women who utilize the services of underprivileged others have benefited by the ideal of

---

16 Legitimate benefits are denied when workers, often women, are termed as temporary or contract (Annuncio 1996).

17 Fraser has lucidly argued against Richard Rorty (1989b, n. 26) and Habermas (Ibid.: 113-43) that feminists need to move beyond the private–public dichotomy to deprivatize housework.

18 Also see Mahadevan (2001). As Mohanty notes repeatedly, Mies's gives an account of women in Narsapur work in the lace-making industry in India for the world market under domestic ideology, rather than contract work (1984: 344-46; 1997: 12-14).

contractarian autonomy. Although women have generated exploitation among themselves by adopting prevailing patriarchal definitions of freedom, one cannot merely juxtapose feminine care as an alternative. In reproblematizing the question of autonomy, one has to take into account the complex terrain of the global intersection between gender and labour, in which care is also enmeshed.

According to classical liberal theory, individuals enter into labour transactions out of their own will. The lord (or the buyer) and the servant (or the seller) are equals; the seller owns labour power, while the buyer owns money-power. They are seen as consensually exchanging their respective property through contracts, wherein each is individuated as the free owner of property prior to socialization. However, neither individual nor property is possible without the relationships of labour. Consequently, the liberal right to property turns out to be an inventory of exclusions. "freedom excludes the coercion that forces certain players in the market to sell their labour; equality excludes the unequal relation between those who sell and those who buy; property also excludes the seller who is unable to own the products of his/her labour" (Marx 1977: 280; Warnke 1987: 115-16).

The presuppositions of coercion and inequality to become owners of property are especially important from the point of view of gender. It is not a coincidence that liberal theorists, ranging from Hobbes to Rawls, maintain a dichotomy between the private and the public sphere that rests upon the sexual division of labour. In the era of classical liberalism, women's domestic work and men's public work made contracts between privileged individuals possible. In contemporary times, the additional task force of women working in the public sphere has enhanced contractarian relations. The individualistic notion of reproductive freedom similarly conceals numerous exclusions. Since individual consent depends on the context of the social circumstances, Mies's Bangladeshi woman does not exercise choice in agreeing to dangerous methods of birth control. Her location in the unequal international relations of labour influences her decision. Instead of treating consent and contract as abstract decisions, one should in a Kantian spirit investigate the conditions that make contracts possible. The latter reveals the pivotal role of social labour in concrete decisions repudiating the professed atomistic logic of liberal freedom.

Yet, one cannot adopt Mies's recommendation of community and nature, since the critique of femininity is an integral part of the feminist project. Care fails to be a critical concept when it tends to strengthen the bemoaned subordinate position of unprivileged women. This is especially so when it is enmeshed in the concept of community as is the case with Mies. Individualist paradigms of freedom and embodied feminine care do not adequately capture the normative alternatives open for the globally intersecting lives of women. Freedom need not be intractably bound to disembodiment and atomic subjectivity; an alternate ethics and politics for women could be opened up by connecting embodiment and "interdependence" characteristic of feminine domestic care with freedom. Such an exploration requires revisiting de Beauvoir's complex and sometimes contradictory thoughts on embodiment, situation and ambiguity, which allow her position to advance over that of Okin's liberal individualism; these thoughts to explore their openings for an "interdependent" model of freedom, especially with respect to integrating the concept of care with that of freedom without compromising either.

Relational Freedom, Embodied Situation and Ambiguity

Much of Mies's critique of de Beauvoir treads a familiar ground to appear convincing at first sight. de Beauvoir does seem to associate freedom with control, as several instances in her writing reveal. At the beginning of "Pyrrhus and Cineas", de Beauvoir (2004: 90) equates the task of working towards projects with images of vanquishing territories. In her *Second Sex*, she suggests that freedom is transcendence or mastery over the body (de Beauvoir 2010: 167-70); she believes that in the case of women such a freedom is particularly important since their weak and onerous bodies — unlike those of men — pull them towards immanence and demoralizes them in the pursuit of their projects (ibid.: 21).[19] Her use of terms like control, vanquish, conquest and mastery has allusions to the masculine in patriarchal "gender regimes".

de Beauvoir turns to consciousness as a primordial fact whose intentional character always directs it towards something other than itself (1972: 16-17). The latter, which she terms as "otherness", includes the physical body of the conscious subject, other human beings, the natural world, the external social world and so forth. Thus, de Beauvoir's human being is split between the poles of consciousness and "otherness" (1972: 725-26; 2010: 769-71; Gatens 1991: 52), where consciousness as the essential force exercises self-determination by negating the contingent other of embodiment, nature and other people (Weir 1996: 16-17). de Beauvoir also uses a language which foregrounds male terms (Kruks 1992: 94-95). Therefore, several feminists have critiqued de Beauvoir for valorizing a masculine way of life in her normative ideal of a liberated woman.[20] According to de Beauvoir:

---

19 For de Beauvoir, the woman's body, weakened, painful and threatening because of the hold that her species has on her through its propagating function, ". . . is not the pure instrument of her grasp on the world but rather an opaque presence . . ." (2010: 672).

20 See Spelman (1991).

> Woman's drama lies in this conflict between the fundamental claim of every subject, which always posits itself as essential, and the demands of a situation that constitutes her as inessential. — 2010: 17

This "drama" is especially because women tend to identify with their inessential recalcitrant bodies — their feminine side — to make them more susceptible to subjugation by sovereign men. Further, according to de Beauvoir, household activities such as cooking instill patience, passivity and mechanical movement through the laws of fire, water and dough (2010: 654). Yet though such activities come close to the technical, they are too basic to teach her the scientific laws of causation.[21] The routine that is observed in the course of domestic work is attributed to magic, so that "woman's mentality perpetuates that of agricultural civilizations that worship the earth's magical qualities . . ." (de Beauvoir 2010: 654). The feminine activities of women do not allow them to master matter in a scientific way, as they are busy with life.[22] Since men do not experience their bodies as burdens, they successfully transcend their "otherness" to become sovereign and make use of womens susceptibility for their own ends. de Beauvoir also indicts women for being complicit in their own oppression for gains of security and comfort in a patriarchal world. Moreover, in her narration of "independent women" she diagnoses women's artistic expression as lacking in an engagement with the human condition *per se*, unlike men. de Beauvoir has also rightly been called into question by

---

21 Besides scientific meaning, de Beauvoir also refers to the technical in early Heidegger's sense of equipmentality (2010: 654). But scientific mastery and Heidegger's equipmentality are not equivalent; the latter is closer to Dewey's instrumentalism.

22 She claims, "A syllogism is not useful in making mayonnaise or calming a child's tears. Masculine reasoning is not relevant to the reality she experiences" (de Beauvoir 2010: 655).

Western feminists such as Moi, who point out that she has failed to "grasp the progressive potential of femininity as a political discourse" (Moi 1998: 86).[23] Thus, she treats the feminine aspect of women's difference from men as an inevitable part of a patriarchal ideology so that feminism is a disavowal of the feminine, as de Beauvoir's valorization of the masculine way of life in her account of the independent woman reveals.[24]

de Beauvoir's critics have attributed the androcentrism of male thinkers to whom she refers as impinging in her own work. Thus, Mies emphasizes Hegel's influence via Sartre on her work, while le Doeuff draws attention to de Beauvoir's self-professed use of Sartrean concepts (le Doeuff 2003: 333).[25] Her disparaging remarks about the female body are attributed to Sartre's analogous views (Kruks 1992: 95). Thus, de Beauvoir professes:

> . . . following Hegel, a fundamental hostility to any other consciousness is found in consciousness itself; the subject posits itself only in opposition; it asserts itself as the essential and sets up the other as inessential, as the object. — 2010: 7

Such a permanent polarization reveals that given the oppositional geography of consciousness, this could take the form of an ascendancy over the other. Freedom exercised by a sovereign subject is separated from the body, other human beings, nature . . . in short, the others. This exclusion generates domination, since solitary freedom is indifferent to the web of relations it controls. Hence, ". . . one needs a problematic other than that of the subject . . ." (le Doeuff 2003: 342), which is disconnected from matters of the body.

---

23 See Gatens (1991: 53-59) and Spelman (1991: 208).

24 See Spelman (1991).

25 See Kruks (1992: 95-96) for de Beauvoir's self-description of deriving her concepts from Sartre.

Thus, prima facie there is good reason to ascribe the logic of domination to de Beauvoir on account of her seeming pejorative attitude to the woman's body, the influence of male philosophers on her work and her valorization of sovereign autonomy of consciousness over the body (Weir 1996: 23-24). Her complex relation to motherhood only buttresses this criticism further (Moi 2005). Moreover, although she critiques femininity in minute detail, she does not give a detailed assessment of masculinity.[26] Since the latter depends upon the former, de Beauvoir does not seem to consistently subject gender roles to criticism. Consequently, she appears to endorse the male model of economic freedom as foundational for women's liberation (de Beauvoir 2010: 680). Political freedom such as the right to vote, in her opinion, does not have meaning without a complimentary "concrete freedom" to work for a livelihood by putting forward goals or projects as a responsible subject (ibid.: 737). de Beauvoir describes the self-esteem of a janitor in achieving a sense of independence through her economic work. In order to avoid the travails of working both in the economy and at home, she believes that concrete economic freedom presupposes a reproductive one of bodily control. This is because "there is one female function that is almost impossible to understand in complete freedom, and that is motherhood . . ." (ibid.: 751). Clearly such a freedom can entrap socially vulnerable women in the "globalization of motherhood".

Yet a closer examination of de Beauvoir reveals that her position is not merely a series of closures with respect to the challenge posed by feminine care or non-Western women. As Gilligan remarks, de Beauvoir's analysis of how "frank and

---

[26] de Beauvoir does fleetingly discuss the correlation between masculinity and femininity (1972: 726-24, 738-39; 2010: 769-82). But she also attributes to women an easy compliance with the demands of masculinity.

fearless"[27] little girls become submissive during adolescence is still pertinent (le Doeuff 2003; Glazer 2004). Gilligan has acknowledged how de Beauvoir has anticipated her own research in this respect. de Beauvoir is also conscious that the term "woman" is not a homogeneous category when she laments that bourgeois women do not feel solidarity with their working-class sisters in holding on to their gendered roles because of the resultant privileges (de Beauvoir 2010: 132). Indeed, in her discussion of motherhood de Beauvoir refers to the diverse ways in which women perform their responsibilities depending on their class location and attitudes (ibid.: 544, 546). This critical insight is precisely what is missing in Ramabai's and Wollstonecraft's notions of motherhood. "Pregnancy and motherhood are experienced in very different ways depending on whether they take place in revolt, resignation, satisfaction or enthusiasm" (ibid.: 546).

As Deutscher observes, de Beauvoir is conscious of women's heterogeneity (2008: 131-58). There are passages where de Beauvoir suggests the interfacing aspects of gender and race, by writing about the white woman's racism against African-Americans in the American South (de Beauvoir 2010: 137-39). She analyses a patriarchal society's requirement of white women's domesticated visibility and a racist society's demand of the African-American's invisibility; this could lead to an analysis of ". . . the contradictory demands on African-American women in this context to be both visible and invisible, sexed and non-sexed" (ibid.: 139). The allegations of Eurocentrism notwithstanding, de Beauvoir's analysis of women's subordination in their embodied situation, is influenced by her knowledge of African-Americans. Thus, "the 'eternal feminine' corresponds to 'the black soul' or 'the Jewish character'" (ibid.: 12). de Beauvoir also remarks that for the

---

27 Gilligan's quote is culled from Glazer (2004).

anti-Semite, Jewishness does not represent inferiority but enmity; hence the domestic ideology of the feminine is closer to the racist ideology faced by Africans. Both are subjugated to paternalism, disciplinary practices, patronizing praise of being childlike and without responsibility by the ideology of the "ruling caste" (ibid.), which is in one case men and the white races in the other. The situation of inferiority is imposed on them through deprivation of opportunities and denigration of their bodies.[28] Moreover, besides her remarkable references to other races and cultures, de Beauvoir is one of the few philosophers to have named colonialism and explored the possibility of resisting it, within her conceptual framework.[29]

Critics such as Mies and le Deouff, who accuse de Beauvoir of copying patriarchal concepts from male thinkers, overlook her own independent thinking, which brings together conceptual categories through critique and appropriation of Hegel via Kojeve, Sartre, Marx, Merleau-Ponty.[30] As Weir notes, de Beauvoir has not given any textual reference from

---

[28] Moi (1998) has pointed to the influence of Franz Fanon on de Beauvoir and Deutscher (2008) to that of Richard Wright.

[29] See for example (de Beauvoir 1962: 95) for her citation of the justification of colonization on the basis of utility. She also analyses the value of "the revolts in India" — perhaps meaning the 1857 mutiny — as laying the foundations of solidarity against British role, rather than as having an immediate impact of overthrowing colonization (Ibid.: 150).

[30] Mies claims that de Beauvoir imposes the gendered categories of man and woman on Hegel's master–slave dialectic via Sartre (1993c: 224). However, against this claim de Beauvoir follows Hegel in treating the relationship between sexes as outside the struggle for recognition through labour in the master–slave dialectic as Lundgren-Gothlin (1998) argues. Indeed, her whole point about women overcoming reproductive work is to enable them to enter the dialectic of recognition through the master–slave relationship.

Hegel's writings for the fundamental hostility of consciousness, although the allusion is clearly to his *Phenomenology of Spirit's* (1977) master–slave passage (Weir 1996: 16). Further, when she directly refers to Hegel in her work on ethics, she does so to disagree with him (de Beauvoir 1962: 70-71). With Hegel she maintains that human identities are the outcome of struggle through which recognition becomes possible. She differs with Hegel in raising the possibility about reciprocal recognition between men and women for which women would have to contest male sovereignty (de Beauvoir 2010: 7). Like Sartre, de Beauvoir distinguishes between the self and the other as ontological categories whose relationship leads to the possibility of an ethical world. Unlike Sartre, she sees the ethical aspect of existentialism and inter-subjectivity as the central feature of her phenomenology of women (ibid.: 17; Kruks 1992: 96-97). Appropriating Marx, she believes that the gender problem can be overcome only through a socialist transformation of the world, despite her critique of Engels's alleged economism. Like Merleau-Ponty, de Beauvoir believes that embodiment is the basic orientation towards the world which makes knowledge, ethics and politics possible. Thus, as le Deouff herself acknowledges, "in sum de Beauvoir's text can only be totalized dialectically" (2003: 334). Hence, rather than dismiss de Beauvoir, one needs to pose some of le Doeuff's questions in a postcolonial context. This might include the question: "how is the choice of this . . . philosophical framework decisive or not for feminist studies?" (ibid.). Its decisiveness lies in the possibility of feminists appropriating ideas that have emerged in male contexts, since ideas do not have absolute meaning; they acquire significance through historically laden practices such as language.[31] Moreover, the philosophical framework

[31] The Introduction makes this point with reference to women's relationship to the history of philosophy.

that de Beauvoir offers is neither homogeneous nor subject-centric. Rather her entry point for sociological and philosophical reflection on women's oppression is their embodiment. She breaks with the male canon in philosophy which begins with thought and also challenges the dualism of mind and body. In her analysis of the woman's body, de Beauvoir makes it clear that she sees it as a situation, rather than merely as an object governed by causes and effects.

Against Mies's claim of disembodied subjectivity, in her *Second Sex* de Beauvoir frames her analysis of the myths of femininity within the embodied situation of being women. Further, her phenomenological account of such a situation is also the basis for her analysis of women's freedom through their "lived experience" from childhood to old age in the second volume of her work. Being in the world is possible through "a body that is both a thing of the world and a point of view . . ." (de Beauvoir 2010: 24); hence the kind of world that one grasps depends on the body and conversely, the way in which one experiences one's body depends on its world so that the two cannot be separated from each other (Kruks 1992: 107).[32] Since women are made aware of their subjectivity by men, de Beauvoir's starting point of analysis is the fact that "'I am a woman'; all other assertions will arise from this basic truth (2010: 5)".[33] de Beauvoir takes the concrete experience of being a human being in a situation, rather than abstract humanity, or an individual, as her point of analysis. Hence,

---

32 Kruks (1992: 107) distinguishes de Beauvoir from Sartre's account of the body as a being for its own self and for others which never meet.

33 de Beauvoir (2010: 5) points out that unlike women, men do not see the need to make their masculinity a point of investigation, since they are equivalent to humanity. Though the emergence of masculinities studies shows the contrary, its motivation through women's studies cannot be overlooked.

"clearly, no woman can claim without bad faith to be situated beyond her sex" (ibid.: 4). The situation of the "sexed body" (Moi 2005: 60) shows that the body is not just an object within the socio-cultural domain, but is this very domain.

In a patriarchal society, women are defined as "sexed beings" (de Beauvoir 2010: 6) as an absolute or the other through deterministic ". . . simple answers: she is a womb; an ovary; she is a female. . . ." (ibid.: 21). A patriarchal society equates the female with "she-animal" (Moi 2005: 60-61) through a range of voracious and threatening behaviours that needs to be tamed.[34] Yet even with respect to biological facts pertaining to women, de Beauvoir cautions against the equation of females in the animal world with women, as the two sexes are not sharply distinguished nor are their functions clearly differentiated in the former. This is especially so in the lower scale of the evolution. Single-celled animals and bacilli do not reproduce through sexuality, while heterogenetic gametes and hermaphroditic species of plants have one individual encompassing both species.[35] de Beauvoir points out that in the higher scale of animal evolution and especially the mammal and human world, there is a sharp division of sexes. She observes that philosophers such as Plato, Aristotle, Aquinas and Hegel have wrongly characterized this difference as one of male activity and female passivity.[36] Offering a more

---

34 Moi (2005: 61) points out that in French there is a distinction between the English female meaning women, girls and animals, and the French *femelle* which refers exclusively to she-animals. But both female and *femelle* have a common meaning in the species that can reproduce by bearing offspring or through eggs. In French the term woman (*femme*) is reduced to *femelle* in a pejorative way.

35 This is derived from de Beauvoir (2010: 21-49).

36 Philosophers have also defined feminine as a deficiency (de Beauvoir 2010: 5).

complementary explanation, she points out that the ovum exists by transcending itself through maintenance which is a process of continuity, rather than static stagnation. The sperm creates by intervening with a separate moment is a temporal continuity. Both processes form a part of the vitality in the embryo as a living, rather than a merely mechanical process. Yet, according to de Beauvoir, with the evolution of the human species there is an increase in individuality, which leads to conflict between the sexes. The male affirms himself through autonomy, while the female loses her individuality to external forces that overwhelm her. In the case of women, they experience their bodies in difficult and complex ways right from birth to puberty and menopause.

> . . . the woman's body does not accept the species' installation in her without a fight; and this fight weakens and endangers her. . . . — de Beauvoir 2010: 40

For instance, women's hormonal difference from men displays lesser muscular strength, respiratory capacity and haemoglobin.

According to de Beauvoir, these biological facts form a significant aspect of the situation and framework through which women grasp the world. Yet, de Beauvoir refuses ". . . the idea that they form a fixed identity for her. They do not suffice to constitute the basis for a sexual hierarchy; they do not explain why woman is the other; they do not condemn her forever to this subjugated role" (ibid.). Biological data, she believes, have to be interrogated in the light of historically rooted concepts from society, economics and psychology. Facts acquire value in accordance with society; thus, for instance the mother's connection to the child will be the source of dignity or indignity depending on social prejudices and norms. Similarly, the lack of muscular strength becomes a derogatory norm in a society that devalues women's work. Thus, de Beauvoir does not accept that the body leads to the position of difference making motherhood a vocation (Kruks 1992: 107). Therefore, according to her, to comprehend the woman's position of alienation, one needs to examine her as a historical species who acts in socio-cultural contexts through her body as a situation. Rather than separate the body from thought following traditional philosophy, de Beauvoir understands the body as cultural and culture as embodied. As Moi and Kruks observe, de Beauvoir avoids both biological determinism of an immutable body and social constructivism of a fictive body. She instead sees the relation between biology and society as dialectical, since the body which is oriented to reproduction is an essential part of her situation though it does not determine her actions (ibid.: 105).

For de Beauvoir, though the woman's enslavement to her species is an important element of her situation, it does not mechanically determine her inferiority; being human, the woman is also a member of the historical species. In her discussion of biological facts, de Beauvoir claims that they are a part of the situation that opens up the world, self and their interrelation by entering the "lived experience" of the human subject (Moi 2005: 63). "The body is both a situation and is placed within other situations . . . a situation is a structural relationship between our projects (our freedom) and the world (which includes our bodies)" (ibid.: 65). It is through interactions with the world that such a "lived experience" becomes a part of the subject's situatedness; thus, freedom and action are a part of lived experience. The embodied situation is taken on by consciousness through action so that it becomes a lived reality. Human actions which create something new or preserve the existing order of things do so through a "synthesis of facticity and freedom" (ibid.). The body is also the entry point to other situations like race, nationality and caste. Women's lived experience is at the intersection of such varied situations which are also bound up with their projects so that there is no one way of experiencing the body, following Moi (ibid.: 66). Thus, de Beauvoir offers the "body-subject" that is open to others as a situated way of comprehending womens oppression and transcending it (Kruks 1992: 105). The body shows how there is a common way of rooting oneself in the world with other people. The overlapping situations within which a woman puts forward her project, are intervened by several other human projects as well. Since a woman is never alone while acting freely in a situation, she has to take the freedom of other human beings into account, as well as the impending hostility that this might invoke. All of this is made possible by the body not as a thing, but as a point of view in the world (ibid.: 107).

For de Beauvoir free actions are embedded in situations,[37] yet instead of being determined by an absolute situation they are possible because of the ambiguity inherent to situations (de Beauvoir 1962: 7-34). Ambiguity implies that situations have several possibilities open because they contain several oppositional elements within them. Moreover, it also means that there is no absolute meaning. Thus, the body as a situation is both an objective fact and a subjective orientation to the world; it has life but will cease to exist some day; it belongs to a separate individual and is yet oriented towards others. To affirm something as ambiguous is to claim that ". . .

---

[37] Holveck (1999) argues that de Beauvoir's notion of freedom (with its stress on responsibility) is joyful and intersubjective. Yet though de Beauvoir is aware of the non-possessive model of freedom (1962: 12-13, 72-73), it is not clear how her consciousness paradigm can achieve it. Holveck observes that there is room for conflict and violence in her account of autonomy; an autonomous person can use violence to dispute the objectivification of subjects. But it is reification and not autonomy that generates violence. Autonomy, however, can contest reification in a "joyful" collective way if one moves beyond consciousness.

its meaning is never fixed, that it must be constantly won . . . it is because man's [sic] condition is ambiguous that he [sic] seeks, through failure and outrageousness, to save his existence" (ibid.: 129). The stereo-typing of the woman in terms of the "eternal feminine" takes place when the ambivalence in her body is denied to determine its meaning forever as say a reproductive organism. Thus, myths about women are constructed when the body is taken in its objective aspect as a set of recalcitrant facts leading to women being perceived as inferior. Hence, the affirmation of ambiguity in an embodied situation is for de Beauvoir the first step towards freedom.

For de Beauvoir, freedom or autonomous will is not immanent in its situation by being determined by an external or an internal force (de Beauvoir 1962: 17-18, 138; 2010: 17).[38] It transcends what is given at present in the facticity of the situation as character or circumstance towards an unpredictable future (ibid. 2010: 17). In her "Pyrrhus and Cineas" de Beauvoir remarks that the human being does not have any readymade ties with a world populated by the "others" of objects and persons, which are indifferent and foreign (de Beauvoir 2004: 92-93).[39] In order to belong with a sense of attachment to objects and persons that are around, the human being should not just exist like an object, but freely engage with it. But de Beauvoir does not construe the free human being to be an isolated agent who is connected to

---

[38] There is a similarity with Kant's concepts of autonomy and heteronomy of the will. But de Beauvoir also differentiates her position from that of Kant in accounting for concrete embodiment (1962: 17, 144), and not simplifying the will into a pure positive force (ibid.: 33-34). de Beauvoir's autonomous will can arrive at a common ground with others, only through a complex confrontation of conflicts with the will of others.

[39] This discussion is derived from de Beauvoir's (2004) "Pyrrhus and Cineas".

objects as possessions on the basis of a contractual relation with them following the liberal tradition. Rather a sense of belonging is attained by accomplishing projects through action; "the only reality that belongs entirely to me is, therefore, my act" (ibid.: 93).

Through participation, the relationships that are forged with things are never immutable, but changing. de Beauvoir upholds that such participation does not comprise merely looking at objects, like photographing a war, but connecting to them so that they are transformed and surpassed. Such an action moves in the direction of the other so ". . . that the difference between me and the other is abolished . . ." (ibid.). Active freedom also releases the object by engaging with it through its project so that other people can relate to it whereby a human being can accomplish ". . . freedom only by perpetual surpassing towards other freedoms; . . ." (de Beauvoir 2010: 17).[40] Thus, according to de Beauvoir, there is an "interrelatedness" to freedom or autonomy, where it is never exercised alone; rather freedom and solidarity imply each other.

The correlation between freedom and solidarity shows that men who force women into the position of the other do so because they renounce their own freedom in being threatened by women or in exploiting them. Women who are pushed into an absolute position of alterity as immanent creatures of feminine bodies, either by a patriarchal society or through their own complicity experience "absolute evil"

---

40 For de Beauvoir (2004), free action is an infinite task, where one proceeds from one project to the other like Pyrrhus's conquests that go on endlessly. She, therefore, opposes Candide's view that one must cultivate one's garden, for there is no fixed garden for the human being who can engage with any number of things without limit.

(ibid.). They have to exercise their autonomy by assuming projects that transcend their situation which forces them into the position of inessentiality. Yet it is because their situation itself is ambivalent in having possibilities of both freedom and bondage that they can exercise such a freedom. Further, since their embodiment brings them into contact with other situations and people, their free actions impact others. de Beauvoir calls for a resolution of hostility between people through reciprocal recognition, made possible by a radical conversion where stereotypes are unlearned and determinism is renounced (de Beauvoir 1962: 13).[41] When men and women undergo such a conversion, they unlearn preconceived notions of the self and others, to acknowledge the ambiguity in situation and their mutual dependence. Radical conversion basically involves not being determined by the situation and being open to the various alternatives that it opens up. It is an acknowledgement of embedded freedom, both in one's self and in the other, where neither is an absolute but is closely linked to the other. It assumes that human beings are without essences and therefore have to make meaning in ambiguous situations. Consequently, radical conversion enables the process of mutual recognition whereby the freedom of all is achieved.

As Moi puts it, the "double claim" (2005: 67) that the body is a situation and is in a situation shows that women will not always be oppressed by their reproductive capacities; nor do they need to deny their reproductive capacities. This opens a way out of the conundrum of the professionalization of motherhood. Just like the relation between sexes, the hierarchy between privileged and underprivileged women is ambivalent

---

41 She distinguishes her position from that of Hegel who wishes to surpass the opposition, while she advocates its conversion to another point of view (1962: 13).

and not absolute. Since it can be changed, those who are regarded as objects — like Jasodā, Jaṭeśvarī — can change their situation. From de Beauvoir's point of view, this requires a conversion where Western feminists unlearn stereotypes about both themselves and their underprivileged counterparts to comprehend their situation as ambiguous.

For de Beauvoir typical male activities of transcendence leading to the subordination of women are also expressions of bad faith (de Beauvoir 2010: 769-76). Similarly in a mode of self-deception, Western feminists think that they have achieved autonomy when in fact it has come at the cost of subordinating women from other parts of the world. They fall into bad faith like the bourgeois woman who ". . . feels no solidarity with working-class women; she feels closer to her husband than to a woman textile worker" (ibid.: 132). Thus, against Mies's indictment, de Beauvoir has the resources for questioning the relation of privilege amongst women by understanding their situation as ambiguous. Further, she offers freedom, rather than some independently given substantive principle or human nature, as the basis of social organization. In her discussion of voluntary motherhood, she is well aware that this is not an individual matter, but has to be accepted by society through ". . . well-organized day nurseries and kindergartens . . ." (ibid.: 752). de Beauvoir points out that in the absence of such institutional support, women end up sacrificing their lives for their children, or then turn to informal modes of support in their families and helpers. This is especially significant in the Indian context, where modernity, pluralistic communities and traditional world-views coexist. Consequently, much of the childcare and care-giving is provided informally by the likes of Jasodā and Jaṭeśvarī. It is in order to avoid subordination of others through one's own freedom that de Beauvoir suggests a balance between freedom and care-giving in her discussion of the indeendent woman (ibid.: 752-53).

Indeed, de Beauvoir is not impervious to the dilemmas posed by the atomic subject, for as the above discussion shows, she offers what Kruks has termed as "a situated subject . . . that is intrinsically intersubjective and embodied, thus always 'interdependent' and permeable rather than walled" (1992: 98).

Thus, the possibility of social equality where the self and other are related in a reciprocal way emerges from such situatedness (de Beauvoir 2010: 5-8, 769-82).[42] Further — unlike Gilligan's articulation of the ethics of care — this bond is not merely restricted to an intimate one of family, nor is it confined to nation like that of Mies. Such a concrete bond makes room for the stranger; ". . . the other consciousness has an opposing reciprocal claim . . . whether one likes it or not individuals and groups have no choice but to recognize the reciprocity of their relation" (ibid.: 7). Thus, it does not have abstract personhood in as its alternative.[43] However, the problem between the sexes — like all other stratifications such as that of Jasodā and her women employers — is that this reciprocity is denied, which de Beauvoir tries to correct. Like Rawls with his difference principle, de Beauvoir remarks that one can justify the control over the other only if it leads to the latter's greater freedom (de Beauvoir 1962: 136-37). Hence, the person saved from death has a right to demand a mode of livelihood from the saviour. Or ". . . the tyranny practised against an invalid can be justified only by his (*sic*) getting better . . ." (ibid.: 137).

de Beauvoir argues that freedom becomes an ethical ideal only when its relation to an ambiguous situation is acknowledged (ibid.: 7-17, 129-55). Yet she differs from Hegel

---

42 As Kruks notes conversely social inequality lacks reciprocity (1992: 100-01).

43 See for instance de Beauvoir 1962: 136, 144.

— belying Mies's claim that she is dependent on Hegel's conceptual categories — in that this failure is not surpassed, it is assumed. Moreover, through such an assumption, freedom becomes materialized in relation to others through a process of struggle in confronting opposition. It is not an isolated formal freedom (ibid.: 13).[44] Nor is it a readymade option; rather freedom has to be won by preserving each individual's specificity in a collective context of all other individuals as well. In the course of demystifying oneself of illusory essential identities, there is recognition that ". . . the freedom of one man (*sic*) almost always concerns that of other individuals" (ibid.: 143). It is not an impersonal abstract subject who is the source of values for de Beauvoir. Rather values are created in the context of a plurality of persons who are accidentally thrown into contact with each other. "An ethics of ambiguity will be one which will refuse to deny a priori that separate existents can, at the same time, be bound to each other, that their individual freedoms can forge laws valid for all" (ibid.: 18).[45]

Speaking about the contemporary relevance of de Beauvoir's work to an Indian newspaper, Malovaney-Chevallier and Borde (2012b), who have recently translated her *Second Sex,* claim that "in the West at least, women control their own biological destinies in childbearing". Yet as has been argued above, this control has come at the cost of non-Western women. Hence, on a cautionary note, their claim in another interview needs to be brought in, "every rights movement is also a question of other people's rights" (Malovaney-Chavallier

---

44. "This freedom is sharply distinguished from the Stoic conversion in that it does not claim to oppose to the sensible universe a formal freedom which is without content." (de Beauvoir 1962: 13.)

45. de Beauvoir is well aware of this tension between the subject and situation in Marxism, Hegel and Kant (ibid.: 18).

and Borde 2012a). Hence, if reproductive freedom is a right its relationship to other people has to be interrogated in de Beauvoir's spirit that freedom is not a given but an achievement. It is for this reason that it cannot be ethically achieved by repressing those such as Jaṭeśvarī and Jasodā. de Beauvoir's account of embodied situation shows that human beings are always thrown into contact with each other. Hence, choices and actions have impact that transcends the self.

Indeed, according to de Beauvoir, bodily vulnerability — which is accented with age, infirmity and death — requires the support of others. Yet, most often, instead of assisting with an individual's freedom, others tend to interfere with it. Men's objectification of women into the eternal feminine or women's objectification of their underprivileged counterparts in their pursuit of independence are cases in point. de Beauvoir believes that even in these contexts of misrecognition or derecognition, a self-identity is acquired. Thus, even damaged identities are based on the fundamental bond between the self and the other. They provide the pretext for critique and transformation as women's situation does. This very process opens the space for others actively assisting one's freedom by reweaving the social dimension in a non-alienated way. To quote de Beauvoir:

> And indeed at every moment others are stealing the whole world away from me . . . by taking the world away from me, others also give it to me, since a thing is given to me only by the movement which snatches it from me. To will that there be being is also to will that there be men by and for whom the world is endowed with human significations. One can reveal the world only on a basis revealed by other men [sic]. No project can be defined except by its interference with other projects. To make being "be" is to communicate with others by means of being. — 1962: 70-71

Yet given the exploitative dimension of reproductive freedom in global contexts, the relevance of de Beauvoir's interdependent model in a postcolonial world needs to be examined in order to explore whether freedom can be integrated with care. Thus, one needs to examine whether re-reading de Beauvoir after Gilligan's ethics of care can have postcolonial significance.

Reproductive Freedom in Global Contexts

de Beauvoir's account of "interdependent" freedom discloses a way out of Mies's false dilemma between abstract individualism and given community. In restoring normative worth to indigenous communities in the name of tradition, Mies inadvertently subscribes to the very same Eurocentrism she denounces. For as Said (1978) has documented, cohesive communitarian images of non-European cultures such as India emerged through the orientalist project of colonizing European nations. Orientalism has played a significant role in contributing to the domestic image of women in India which depicted motherhood as the natural vocation of women.[46] The vestige of such a colonial mindset is reflected in neoliberal policies of institutions such as the World Bank that encourage local community practices led by women, which are depoliticized in the process (Miraftab 2004).[47] Moreover, Mies's concept of a "living relation" with nature and community assumes that women can have separate histories in self-sustaining communities. By replacing de Beauvoir's alleged atomicity of individualism with that of community, Mies dooms intersecting

---

[46] This has been delineated in Chapter 1.

[47] Also see Chapter 1 above for Sangari's similar point. Miraftab (2004: 2) observes that there is a consequent paradox in some women entering decision-making positions in public arenas at the expense of other women losing out on their livelihoods due to neoliberal policies. Also see Ebert (1996) for a critique of positions such as ecofeminism in this context.

histories between women from north and south to exploitative inequalities. Interestingly, the tendency to assume that autonomy or freedom[48] has no bearing on non-Western contexts stems from foundational thinking where it is viewed as belonging to its place of origin in seventeenth-century Europe. Hegel, who is critiqued by Mies, also adheres to this premise when he says:

> A European . . . knows himself as free. Freedom is the substance of his being. — 1985: 76

As argued above,[49] the advent of modernity in India, with its concepts of freedom and equality, occurred during the exploitative period of British colonial rule in the nineteenth century. Yet resistance to colonization and the pioneering women's movement under Savithribai Phule and Ramabai were possible because of these very same ideals of modernity. Hence, quests for cultural self-definitions should be replaced by the ideals governing diverse contexts of women's struggles against patriarchal inequality (Mojab 1998: 27-28).

As discussions of Ramabai and Wollstonecraft reveal, at the time of their inception, women's struggles in India and Britain were committed to freedom through women's entry into the public domain and political participation. However, in India, unlike Britain, there was a greater focus on family reform, rather than suffrage and entry into the workforce. The public sphere itself emerged through a critique of the colonial administration and obsolete social practices (Rajagopal 2009; Bayly 2009); women like Ramabai struggled for women's agency in a masculine public sphere which was concerned about women as objects of reform. In the British context, instead of

---

48 Freedom and autonomy are used interchangeably in this discussion.

49 In Chapter 1.

acknowledging their agency, many feminists construed Indian women as victims needing charity and reform. These contradictory ties between Western feminists and Indian women continued in the postcolonial context with the resurgence of the second wave feminism in the 1960s and 1970s. Under the influence of de Beauvoir and Firestone, Western feminism upheld reproductive freedom as control over the body. In contrast, the Indian feminist movement in the 1970s questioned the family and state for perpetuating violence against women through dowry and rape. In the following decade, Indian feminists brought out unequal interconnecting histories between Indian women and those in the West, by highlighting how reproductive freedom as bodily control comes at the cost of using Indian women as laboratories for experimenting with reproductive technologies. Yet, despite their diversity and hierarchical relation, feminists in the West and in India remained committed to the freedom of women; they also articulated this freedom through a tension with the feminine dimension of care. However, Indian debates on gender have not focused on rethinking the very idea of individual freedom from the point of view of the relational self.

Mies's analysis treats Western societies as homogeneously privileged, by ignoring its heterogeneity of racial minorities or workers. Conversely, she also ignores the benefits of privilege accruing to Indian women — both in India and the West — on the basis of class and caste. Indeed, the north–south[50] split among women, can be seen as another version of

50 ". . . the *North* refers to the pathways of transnational capital and the *South* to the marginalized poor of the world . . ." (Mohanty 2002: 505). This term is used in a metaphorical, rather than in a geographical way following Mohanty who in turn follows Dirlik (ibid.: 5). Thus, this metaphor can be applied to the privilege among women within India, as well. Mainstream feminism in India has ignored the problems faced by women from oppressed castes and tribes.

the tension between feminism and femininity; in their enthusiasm to become feminists, privileged women unintentionally feminize women who are not as privileged as care providers. Following Mojab "... the particulars of Western feminist struggles can turn into universals when taken on by other, non-Western, women's movements, just as Western women can draw universal lessons from the particular experience of women elsewhere" (1998: 28). Rather than debate the metaphysical origins of freedom, feminists need to examine possibilities of reconciling it with care under just social conditions. After all, feminists in variegated historical contexts such as India or the United States struggle towards similar ideals of reproductive choice, parity of pay and health. There is indeed a general agreement among many feminists that freedom and equality should be the basis of their lives despite their differences (ibid.: 25; Weir 1996: 13-14). Yet so that the problem of differences resulting in inequalities of those such as Jaṭeśvarī and Jasodā is addressed, autonomy or freedom has to be treated in a relational mode by drawing out de Beauvoir's theoretical resources.

Women's struggle against patriarchy can, contrary to Mies, only be raised in a modern world where freedom is the foundation of institutions. However, the negative freedom of possessive individualism, characteristic of modern institutions, cannot address the problem of privilege amongst women. As argued above,[51] this is the problem with Okin's attempt to integrate justice and care through the institutions of the liberal state premised on individual freedom. If one does not move beyond it, such a freedom could become a disintegrating force, as the inequalities among women implicit in the concept of reproductive right as bodily control reveals. Inter-subjective freedom, in de Beauvoir's sense, is the precondition for

---

[51] In Chapter 4.

negative freedom as individual choice can be exercised only if the larger framework of relationships and institutions is egalitarian.[52] de Beauvoir's descriptive claim that "... for about a century, the reproductive function has no longer been controlled by biological chance alone but by design" (2010: 537) can be illustrated with reference to the legally permitted practice of commercial surrogacy in India. Unlike many countries which have made commercial surrogacy illegal, it is an expanding commercial venture in India since its legalization in 2002, catering to both non-resident Indians and non-Indians settled in the West.[53] As Bailey (2011: 715-718) has argued, the reason for Western clients choosing Indian surrogacy workers is cheap economics. The clients are from the higher income groups in the West, which include non-resident Indians, while the workers are mostly women from lower income groups from countries such as India. The latter choose to be surrogate mothers because its income is better than the available options; like Jasodā, they use this income for supporting the health or educational needs of family members.[54] The health and futures of these workers are also well looked after in many of the clinics, which retain a personalized relation with them. Yet such benefits are available only through the commercialization of care and for a short span of time. Surrogacy can be viewed

---

[52] This is a reversal of Wellmer's Hegelian view that negative freedom is a precondition for "communal" freedom (1989-90: 250).

[53] Reproductive technologies such as contraception, *in vitro* fertilization, frozen embryos and sperm banks have been debated amongst feminists (Stanworth 1987: 10-11), but surrogacy dramatically illustrates the problem of privilege among women. In a recent leading newspaper's prominent coverage of surrogacy, the American genetic father admitted that surrogacy is inordinately expensive in the US, which prompted him and his wife to turn to India (Deshpande 2010).

[54] Also see the essays in Chavkin and Maher (2010).

as a voluntary contract where those who do not have much money supply services to those who do, for payment. However, as Davis (2011: 222-44) observes, such language of individual consent and contract ignores the factors of class, nation and gender that converge so that only the vulnerable choose surrogacy work.[55] The backdrop of India not being able to provide health and safety to mothers who are economically impoverished frames its reputation as the preferred destination for surrogacy (Bailey 2011: 718-721).[56] Thus, women have access to reproductive health and rights while giving such care-giving work for others such as being surrogates for children of client families other than their own.

Powerful commercial and state interests target economically weak women for birth control and fertility technology. "In a class-and-race divided society, 'pronatalist' and 'antinatalist' policies coincide (e.g. restrictions on abortions and involuntary sterilization), making it necessary for 'reproductive rights' proponents to articulate continuously that 'reproductive freedom means the freedom to have as well as not to have children'" (Petchesky 1980: 682). All of this goes to show that the paradox of the freedom of some as bondage for others, in commercial care can be addressed by locating individual choice in its larger socio-political canvas. In de Beauvoir's terms, choice is situated and embodied, so that the concept of freedom would have to take into account the possibility of one person's freedom leading to another's subordination.

As Petchesky aptly observes Western feminists have been

---

[55] African-American women have been doing surrogacy work taking care of the homes of privileged people as wives and mothers since the nineteenth century (Davis 2011: 138).

[56] For critiques of surrogacy see Qadeer and John (2008); Menon (2012) brings up the vague notions of consent, freedom, gurdian and agency in all of this.

divided along the lines of the materialistic approach which situates autonomous choice in the large context of the circumstances in which it can be exercised and liberalism which views choice as individual and unencumbered (ibid.). Reproductive freedom is defined from the materialist point of view as one in which ". . . the moral imperative itself grows out of the historically and culturally defined position that women find themselves in through motherhood" (ibid.: 676). Much of the Western feminist movement has proceeded along the liberal definition of reproductive freedom as the right to bodily integrity and control by assuming the body to be outside the framework of such material conditions. As Davis observes, its call for a "voluntary motherhood" (2011: 202) in the nineteenth century and birth control in the 1970s is "a prerequisite for the emancipation of women" (ibid.: 202).[57] She argues that, however, the problem with this movement was that it failed to distinguish between "abortion rights" and the "advocacy of abortions" (ibid.: 205). Social conditions such as abject poverty prevented women of colour from supporting the blanket endorsement of abortions. Thus, as Davis notes, though the role of birth control in women's freedom cannot be denied, its historical trajectory was linked only to bourgeois women (ibid.: 208).[58] Hence, to assimilate the material and liberal dimensions of freedom, the notion of reproductive freedom has to be expanded. It would have to include circumstances such as the right to medical information about sterilization and contraception and the right to health care during and after pregnancy (Roberts 1998: 272). One can

[57] Also see Gordon (1982) for an account of the differences between the nineteenth and twentieth-century feminists in the United States on abortion.

[58] Davis (2011: 209) demonstrates how individual right to birth control or abortion became population control for women of colour. Poor Indian women have been in a similar predicament with respect to the individual right to birth control.

especially add the economic right to livelihood and the right to political participation to this list. The choice over one's body has to be situated within such circumstances as society unduly burdens women with the expectation and duties of motherhood, the lack of adequate economic opportunities, health and justice. Thus, reproductive freedom is ". . . the ability to choose whether, when, how, and with whom one will have children".[59] Since social factors play a crucial role in decisions concerning reproduction, choice cannot be viewed as an abstract mental event. As Roberts notes, reproductive freedom is not an abstract decision but is embedded in race and class, to which one can add caste and nation. Her analysis of the predicament of African-American women resonates with Mies's Bangladeshi woman and Devi's Jasodā, all of whom represent the "globalization of motherhood" in diverse contexts.[60] The problem with a liberal contractarian approach to motherhood is that following de Beauvoir, a mother's relationship to her child cannot be dictated through nature or free contract for ". . . this implies an engagement. To have a child is to take on a commitment . . ." (de Beauvoir 2010: 580). Her "interdependent" view of freedom integrated with care incorporates the strengths of th liberal and materialist positions.

In characterizing de Beauvoir's concept of autonomy as an individual self-contained act of consciousness, Mies neglects its moment of transition from self to the oth through overlapping projects. In contrast, autonomy fo de Beauvoir does not comprise of independence frm social relations. Rather for her, the self is an intersection[61] of myriad social relations

---

59 This quotation is taken from Roberts (1998: 9).

60 Davis (2011) has similarly argued in the context of care-providing work done by African-American women.

61 The terms "intersection" and "autonomy" as a process of detachment and reattachment is derived from Wallace (2003) →

so that autonomy detaches the self from one set of social relations — the oppressive — to engage with other freer ones. Individual freedom for de Beauvoir is always exercised in a world where others make their choices, so that it has to be understood in relation to them. Indeed, de Beauvoir is quite aware of the differing meanings that reproductive freedom has in relation to the circumstance of class. In the context of France in the 1940s, where birth control was not permitted by the state, de Beauvoir has described how working-class women had to face dangers for admittance to abortions, unlike bourgeois women's convenient access (ibid.: 540-41). Davis's narrations of the difficulties that women of colour had to get access to abortions (2011: 202-21), resonate with those of de Beauvoir. By ignoring such nuances, Mies reduces de Beauvoir's autonomy to a homogenizing ownership model of the liberal contract tradition such as that of Okin's. This is especially evident in Mies's equation of self-determination with control, overlooking de Beauvoir's explicit claim that the impossibility of appropriating one's surroundings should be viewed as ". . . a triumph, not as a defeat" (1962: 12). Unlike social-contract theorists, de Beauvoir does not advocate calculating a balance among mutually independent desiring subjects as free action. She connects freedom, ambiguity and embodied situation to offer a critique of individual freedom, as well as, an alternative to it.

The lessons from an ethics of care can be integrated with de Beauvoir's "interdependent" model of freedom as both are premised on the relational notion of the self, as well as, its creative orientation. Freedom is autonomous in the sense of being creative, rather than dependent on readymade desires

---

→ who offers a relational account of freedom. Several contemporary feminists have retheorized freedom from a relational perspective, see Campbell (2002) for an overview.

and relationships.[62] In linking autonomy with relationships, de Beauvoir views human beings as inhabiting an interactive web of practices within which they critique and reform existing relationships and initiate new ones through their free actions.[63] Free action for de Beauvoir leads to equality among persons through reciprocal recognition; such an equality linked to the autonomous will is the antithesis of discrimination and not difference (Verma 1995: 443). One could follow through Fraser's insight that when such a reciprocal freedom is linked to care, it takes care-giving and care-receiving as mutually implicated processes. Further, such an interdependence requires that each individual is situated in and constituted through collective contexts. Since such giving and receiving of care is not done under unequal social and political conditions, it cannot be exploited for the freedom of privileged individuals. Thus, for de Beauvoir, rather than individual salvation, women have to work towards collective liberation (2010: 680); this is possible when insights of care and freedom are blended.

Extending de Beauvoir's insight, in order to exercise their reproductive freedom, Western women would have to question the commodification of motherhood and the medical,

---

62 This is analogous to Kant (1983: 7-8, 22-24) who treats freedom as a positive activity of willing, rather than as the unhindered pursuit of desire.

63 Like Kant for (1983: 29-33; 1956: 19-21) de Beauvoir an act is free if it takes the point of view of the other into account. Despite her similarities with Kant, de Beauvoir does not banish the domain of embodied feelings like him. However, Kant locates free activity in the reflections of the subject where the interdependence desired for collectivity is missing. Consequently, as Okin (1989a: 231-35) laments, Kantian freedom exiles feeling, embodiment and women from the province of practical reason in a single stroke. As a feminist, de Beauvoir has reasoned from such a position of exile.

economic, political and social forces on which it rests. Such questioning would be possible only if they listen to Jaṭeśvarī and Jasodā narrate their stories as agents, where they are equal participants in solidarity against an exploitative system.[64] From de Beauvoir's perspective, underprivileged women like Jaṭeśvarī and Jasodā who lack access to reproductive autonomy are encumbered in a situation where medical, social service or governmental agencies govern their lives through profit and paternalism. Returning to a premodern way of life as Mies suggests, would not ameliorate their problem, as their communities have driven them to the global arena in upholding motherhood as a woman's primary duty. The liberal state also exacerbates their problem by abetting commercial and medical forces that control reproduction. de Beauvoir's analysis reveals that privileged women from the West who avail of such labour are also debilitated, since their freedom comes at the cost of others. Thus, de Beauvoir's intersubjective concept of autonomy is critical and open-ended. It is also incomplete because, as Wellmer (1989-90: 250-51) notes, freedom cannot be achieved perfectly. Freedom is not a *telos*, but a process of struggle that questions the dominating status quo to move towards more egalitarian relationships. As a struggle for free collective relationships between human beings who occupy diverse locations, freedom is never won, but is a tenous movement towards change and transformation.

---

64 Through her detailed analyses of the oppression of working-class women in nineteenth-century Europe, she defends socialism as the precondition for feminism (de Beauvoir 2010: 653-80).

Afterword
Towards Global Feminisms

WESTERN feminist theorization does not self-evidently speak to the postcolonial, non-Western context of disenfranchised women, such as Jaṭeśvarī and Jasodā. Thus, non-Western feminism has to interrogate its relevance and explore the possibility of critical dialogue with Western feminism for its own theorizing.[1] The possibility of such a dialogue is one of the central concerns of Western feminism itself. Most of the feminists who have been engaged with in this book acknowledge as much. As Mies (1993a-c), Mohanty (1984) and Okin (1995) have argued, Western feminists tend to use the word "women" in homogenizing ways, oblivious to the differences amongst women on account of race and class. Hierarchical relationships among women are rooted in the exploitation of economically disadvantaged women's care-giving work being exploited by women who are so privileged.

---

1 "Western" and "non-Western" are used to convey privilege among women, rather than hard and fast geographies. Thus, there can be non-Western women within the West, in the sense of social vulnerability. Fraser (1995: 70) acknowledges the privileges of Western women *vis-à-vis* their non-Western others. However, she overlooks that privileged non-Western women settled in the West often employ underprivileged Western and immigrant women as domestic help. In India too, women enjoying class and caste privilege employ those without similar privileges for household chores as testified by Jasodā. Thus, the phenomenon of privileged women is not exclusively Western.

Feminists have often been in such positions of privilege, which is perhaps why domestic work has not been a priority in recent mainstream feminist agendas (Brennan 1999).

This also perhaps explains why pioneering Indian feminism that was influenced by Western ideals, also reflected its limits. Ramabai for the most part confines herself to upper-caste Brahmin women, in keeping with the title of her treatise by the same name. Consequently, the legacy of Indian feminism has been indicted for its neglect of caste. In Britain, despite her critique of slavery, Wollstonecraft remains oblivious to slave women in British colonies. Gilligan, too, does not theorize Western feminism's position of privilege, despite avowing non-Western women in her perspective of relationships of care. But she does acknowledge the convergence between ". . . race and gender, colonialism and masculine narratives. . ." (Gilligan 1993: xxvi). She also underlines the need to remove racial domination through reciprocal relationships that transcend the divide between selfishness and selflessness. Okin similarly recognizes that her theory of justice is open to the accusation of "essentialism" for she speaks on behalf of many who do not share her privileged location (Okin 1995: 274-75). de Beauvoir's feminism has the danger of being restricted to advantaged Western women with its critique of the femininity of self-absorbed fussy conceit of domesticated women (de Beauvoir 2010: 741).[2] The struggle between feminism and femininity is played out in privileged women feminizing the labour of underprivileged women as care. Hence, the extent to which Western feminists such as Okin and de Beauvoir can listen, rather than just speak, to their "others" to interrogate their own hierarchies with non-Western women needs to be examined.

---

2 See de Beauvoir (2010: 740-41).

de Beauvoir, "the mother of second wave feminism,"[3] has been critiqued from diverse perspectives such as Okin's liberalism, Mies's ecofeminism and de Beauvoir scholars such as le Deouf, Moi, Spelman and Deutscher. Okin points out that feminists from the mid-nineteenth century to the 1960s assumed that the category of women "they were liberating would have recourse to servants or . . . 'household help'" (1995: 275). She points out that feminists such as de Beauvoir failed to take the gendered character of such domestic help into account. As Deutscher argues, de Beauvoir is well aware of the existence of other cultures and races, as her notion of double consciousness in *The Second Sex* was influenced by Richard Wright's similar argument regarding race (Deutscher 2008: 131-58). Claims such as "For Arabs and Indians and in many rural populations, a wife is only a female servant appreciated according to the work she provides, and who is replaced without regret if she disappears" (de Beauvoir 2010: 584), reveal de Beauvoir's awareness of cultures besides her own. She also upheld the cause of Algerian women (Malovaney-Chevallier and Borde, 2012a).[4] Yet following Deutscher, she does not bring the racial dimension into contact with gendered identity or oppression. Ambiguity where a human being is both subject and object, self and other, transcendent and immanent, not determined and yet historical, is central to de Beauvoir's analytical categories (Deutscher 2008: 135). Yet as Deutscher observes, she does not seem to take into account the ambiguity of a human being's identity as simultaneously inflected by race, class, culture and gender. de Beauvoir's

---

3 This expression is from Kruks (1992: 94), who in turn quotes Ascher.

4 Algeria was a French colony, which became independent only in 1962, after a prolonged resistance on the part of Algerians. The relationship between de Beauvoir and Algeria, thus, concerns colonization.

statement (2010: 15) "I think certain women are still best suited to elucidate the situation of women", shows that the investigation of women's social inferiority and its overcoming can be raised only by privileged women who have been liberated from the burdens imposed by femininity. She believes that liberated women can provide leadership to younger women because they acquire objectivity in virtue of their detachment from the feminine. Consequently, they understand women's situation through lived experience. Even though such women do not experience the feminine as immanent, their rootedness in it allows them to know it very closely, unlike men.

All of this goes to show that Western feminism has assumed a position of authority with reference to non-Western women. Though Okin excludes contemporary Western feminists such as herself from neglecting the predicament of non-Western women, she ascribes a leadership position to Western feminists like de Beauvoir. According to her, privileged Western women have an ethical responsibility to dialogue with women from other cultures, given that women share more or less the same situation globally. She argues that the public–private dichotomy and the use of male pronouns as generic have placed an undue burden on women who for the most part do domestic care-giving work. Okin (1995: 280) believes that this predicament of unrecognized labour gets worse in poorer countries. In an attempt to remedy such indifference, she suggests that Western feminists make themselves pertinent by listening to women from other cultures. Okin also cautions that they do so critically, as women from non-Western cultures could have internalized the cruelties meted out to them. She suggests that Western feminists help women from cultures besides their own as progressive outsiders (ibid.: 293). Interestingly, de Beauvoir scholars such as le Doeuff, Moi, Spelman and Deutscher, despite diagnosing essentialism as a problem in de Beauvoir, do not provide recommendations for global feminism.

Okin's sensitivity to non-Western cultures notwithstanding, she herself homogenizes women into a binary that is characteristic of the Western feminism represented by de Beauvoir that she criticizes. Western women in her scheme have greater potential for individual freedom without cultural-barriers, while their non-Western counterparts are victims of superstitious cultures and underdeveloped economies. This replicates de Beauvoir's claim that "in Latin and Eastern countries woman was oppressed by customs more than by laws" (2010: 148). Okin similarly notes, ". . . *committed* outsiders . . . as a part of their constructive criticism, is to try to encourage those within the culture to think about some of its oppressive, or at least questionable, practices from various points of view, including that of the least advantaged" (1995: 293). Thus, Western women are given the superior ethical and political task of saving perceived women victims of so-called developing countries from cultural burdens that range from economic dependence to sex-selected abortion of female foetuses.[5] However, women both in the West and outside do not form a homogeneous category, but are fractured along the lines of race, class and caste. de Beauvoir (2010: 8) has made this observation in the late 1940s, in her *The Second Sex*.

Okin does not interrogate the basic structural problem of an unequal relationship between Western feminists and their others. This becomes clear in the faith that she reposes in the

---

[5] Nussbaum (1999) also upholds a similar position; see Kapur (2012), Mahadevan (2001) for a critique of Nussbaum's imperialism. Mohanty (1984: 338) has critiqued some of the left feminist authors of the Zed Press who have adopted such a patronizing tone. However, she does not discuss the problematic position of patronage in the liberal feminist attitude towards women from cultures other than theirs.

World Bank for gender equality (Okin 2003). She critiques the World Bank for its indifference to gender and poverty with the structural adjustment programmes that it imposed on so-called developing nations, from the 1980s to the mid-1990s. These programmes were premised on the neglect of the family and labour put in by poor women in tasks such as childcare and farming for their "elasticity" (ibid.: 285) to save costs. She notes that in the wake of the neglect of development and analyses such as those of Sen and Nussbahm, the World Bank has changed to adopt a more constructive approach towards the poor in terms of the inherent value of development (ibid.: 313-16). She urges it to complement development by including the matrix of gender to address the needs of women from poorer countries. Okin's critical and yet hopeful attitude to the World Bank echoes her approach to the state as a partner in gender justice.[6] She is aware of the acute need to remedy the condition of poor women; however, this is possible only through patronage from the state and institutions such as the World Bank. Okin fails to examine how the state, far from being neutral body, is controlled by exploitative corporate interests. The World Bank itself is governed by the interests of powerful Western countries, especially the United States, its largest donor, since its inception in 1944. The institutionalization of care and justice through the liberal state and the World Bank would therefore be a limited process, subject to the norms of profit, rather than as per Okin's vision. Paradoxically, the very nations that contribute to structural inequality are in charge of alleviating poverty in the so-called under developed parts of the planet through the World Bank.[7]

---

[6] See Chapter 4.

[7] Recently, the Nigerian Finance Minister Ngozi Okonjo-Iweala could not win the World Bank Presidency even though she was backed by African and South American countries. This was because the countries with the largest stakes in the World →

Though the dialogue between Western feminists and non-Western women is necessary, this dialogue cannot assume the legitimacy of the Western feminist location. Rather, such dialogue would have to probe into the Western feminist's position of privilege that is predicated on the vulnerability of women from underprivileged backgrounds. Following Spivak, for Western feminism to be critical,

> . . . there has to be a simultaneous other focus: not merely who am I? but who is the other woman? How am I naming her? How does she name me? . . . — 1987: 150

The problem of privilege among women cannot be remedied merely through cultural reform, as Western feminists such as Okin suggest. Rather, it requires a critical intervention in tune with the democratic outlook of Western feminism. The latter questioned the very notion of a singular human subject as grounded on male freedom that presupposes feminine care-work. Since Western feminists have been similarly privileged with respect to women from poorer nations, they need to apply their critique of patriarchy to themselves. Self-criticism on the part of Western feminism and non-Western feminism's activist criticism can allow for greater egalitarian intersections between them.

To address the adversarial relation between Western women and those such as Jasodā and Jaṭeśvarī,[8] the patriarchal and imperialist overtones underlying terms like "woman",

---

→ Bank, the US, Japan and Western Europe supported the Jim Yong Kim (Joel and Adib 2012). The World Bank, which has always been under American governance, failed to elect a woman from Africa (from where only three countries have seats in the World Bank).

[8] This relationship is also played out within countries like India between privileged and underprivileged women. Jasodā's relationship with her women employers demonstrates as much.

"autonomy" and "reproductive freedom" would have to be impugned (Spivak 1993: 121-40).[9] The idea that feminine care-work is naturally fit for women governs the unpaid labour of feminists in the domestic sphere, ". . . prevailing social attitudes continue to associate the eternal feminine condition with images of brooms and dustpans, mops and pails, aprons and stoves, pots and pans" (Davis 2011: 224). This in turn requires the dismantling of the private–public dichotomy, as the works of Gilligan and Okin suggest; such a dichotomy sanctions the exploitation of women from vulnerable social strata with its naturalization of care and individualization of consent. Following Davis, who offers a more consistent analysis of the role of such work, feminists have to question the liberal capitalist framework itself. As Davis argues in an Engelsian tone, it is with the rise of private property under liberal capitalism that women became isolated in their domestic sphere; this is the outcome of the production process physically shifting from the home to the factory (ibid.: 227). The capitalist economy does not view domestic work as a commodity that can be rewarded with profit. Rather, as Davis notes, it separates domestic labour from wage labour structurally, labelling the former as inferior. Yet, the liberal economy presupposes reproductive domestic labour as a pre-condition for so-called productive factory work. However, women's consensual paid work on the public sphere has assumed rather than challenged, the naturalization of care by integrating such feminine tasks into the economy. The latter as Davis observes is one of the most "closely guarded secrets of advanced capitalist societies" (ibid.: 223). This is precisely why one cannot follow Claassen (2011) to treat care as a capability to be human,

---

[9] Spivak (1993: 125-130) admits that the lessons of deconstruction are drawn by negotiating with Nietzsche's and Heidegger's patriarchal anti-humanist tradition of philosophy.

that is paid for as a commodity in the market.[10] Although the market approach rids care-giving of the bureaucracy that Okin's proposal introduces, it does not necessarily defeminize care. There are burgeoning, mostly female, teams of cleaners, domestic helps, nannies, cooks, nurses, sweepers and errand personnel performing care-work, which may have led to the "obsolescence of the housewife" (Davis 2011: 243). But care-work is neither remunerated sufficiently, nor formalized adequately as public labour. Given its feminine, monotonous, repetitive and unprofitable character, care-work is not taken seriously enough by the liberal capitalist economy to commodify it in the formal economy. Further, Claassen's proposal would also make care out of reach for women from impoverished background, given the logic of the market. It is only economically privileged individuals, such as Jasodā's employers in Devi's story, who can purchase care labour through contract. Much of public care-work benefits privileged women; women who provide care-work at the socio-economic level undertake responsibility for their own housework, like Jaṭeśvarī and Jasodā, as they are in no position to employ domestic labour. Clearly if the masses of women who do not wield power are to enjoy a modicum of freedom, they need access to institutions that provide them with subsidized support for housework. This in turn requires that the individualistic ideals and public–private dichotomy in liberal institutions be dismantled through the socialization of care-work whereby those who provide and receive care can

---

[10] Claassen evokes Nussbaum's capabilities approach, in her attempt to resolve the dilemma between care as an informal feminine work and as masculine organized work (2011). However, she does not explain how the concept of care as a commodity in the market would defeminize it. Consequently, this dilemma is not resolved since the liberal assumptions of contract are left intact. See Mahadevan (2001) for a critique of Nussbaum's capabilities in the Indian context.

do so in reciprocal and egalitarian ways. Following Fraser, the rotation of care-giving and care-taking in non-profit public institutions will lead to dissolving the dichotomy between care as formal work and informal affect (Fraser 1994: 613). The divide between paid work and social service will be blurred when workers are also assumed to be care providers for which they get time and compensation. Moreover, informal care-work can also be given institutional state support outside the home, for those who are not fortunate to have immediate friends and family. Such institutions can be looked after by people who are in a position to give care — both men and women — in a "democratic and self-managed" (ibid.: 613) way. Undeniably, this calls for restructuring institutions on the ideal of the interdependent model of freedom, rather than individual autonomy. It also calls for thinking beyond the market forces of capitalism whose sole aim is profit.

de Beauvoir and Davis differ from Okin in maintaining that for denaturalizing care-work, women will have to question the liberal capitalist economy that is oriented towards profit. This entails naming care as social labour, rather than a feminine natural attribute. Further, rather than restrict this labour to women from socially vulnerable strata, there should be a reciprocal distribution of care among both the privileged and the vulnerable. Such a participation would prevent it from being a drudgery for a few and would also make facilities like day-care available to all women. Nevertheless, such renaming and critique, which is the first step to the transformation of institutions, is possible only through solidarities between women across what Mohanty (2002) calls transnational networks of struggle against capitalism.

Mohanty enumerates three models of feminist interaction between women who are advantaged and those who are not; these include the feminist as a tourist, an explorer and as someone in solidarity with the other's struggles (ibid.: 518-

24). The tourist model treats women from the global south as homogeneous victims through stereotypes such as dowry deaths, while the explorer model focuses on more subtle cultural details of women from non-Western cultures. However, neither paradigm examines the intersection between the lives of women with privilege and women without. Mohanty rightly suggests the solidarity model as being able to see the lives of women from north and south as interconnected, both materially and symbolically, but in different ways, with common features and differences that crisscross.[11] Mohanty's attempt to connect women's lives through solidarity has parallels with de Beauvoir, for whom "the other's freedom alone is capable of necessitating my being" (de Beauvoir 2004: 129). It is only when one is faced with free human beings that one participates in projects that define one's presence that one communicates. As Gilligan (1993: xvi) remarks, the voice is embodied in cultural and psychological ways. Hence, by speaking ". . . an intensely

---

11 Yet her naming of the Indian non-governmental organization SEWA (Self Employed Women's Association) as an instance of such solidarity is problematic in the context of her critique of paternalism (Mohanty 1997: 25-27). SEWA's primary aim is to teach self-employment to poorer women, rather than function as a critical body. As a co-operative, it functions within the available socio-economic opportunities, rather than address or question structural inequalities. The support it provides to poor women in India — such as Jaṭeśvarī or Jasodā — has to be contextualized against the inability of the state to provide welfare. SEWA draws support from existing economic, social and political institutions. This is so even at the global level. It is, therefore, not surprising that Hillary Clinton has named Ela Bhatt, the SEWA leader as one of her "heroines" (PTI 2012). Clinton's appreciation is precisely that despite being rich, Bhatt has spent her life taking care of the poor. Coming from a position of privilege, Bhatt's care-giving is well acknowledged, while those whom she cares for are nameless poor women.

relational act . . ." (ibid.: xvi) human beings connect to each other. Speaking is inextricably tied to listening to others and also being heard. Thus, in de Beauvoir's spirit, interactive communication is a part of freedom and action. Since actions create situations for others, agents have to be responsible for them (de Beauvoir 2004: 126). Yet as Gilligan (1993: xviii) observes, feminist women who have found their voices — after a long history of silence — are problematizing their differences as well. They are doing so by actively contesting the prevalent meanings of words such as reproductive freedom through repudiation and reconstruction (Fraser 1986). Hence, as de Beauvoir notes, "language is an appeal to the other's freedom . . ." (2010: 133), but such an appeal presupposes prior engagement with the other, either as allies or adversaries (ibid.: 135). The latter would depend on whether the agent's project synchronized or contradicted them.

At the outset, as Spivak attests, there is a seeming absurdity of high theoretical pursuits in the context of India's colonial legacy and pressing practical concerns (1987: 122-23). Academic feminism speaks from a position of privilege. Yet it has an inevitable relation to the political practice of a feminist movement for social change. Thus, an academic feminism that engages with an international division of labour among women and the corporatization of motherhood is never outside the system it criticizes. Theory opens the space for academic feminists to criticize their own privileges in the course of accepting, repudiating and reconstructing notions such as reproductive freedom. Women such as Jaṭeśvarī, Jasodā or Mies's Bangladeshi woman, upon whom the privileges of academic feminism rest without naming them, are reminders of the impossibility of finding a constant referent for the term "woman" following Spivak.[12] The academic feminist, who is

---

12 An indigenous conceptual paradigm such as that of Indian

→

entrenched in structures of exploitation, tries to subvert them internally by expanding the term "woman" to those such as Jaṭeśvarī and Jasodā who have been deprived of it (ibid.: 139-40). Further, this act of naming is one of listening to their voices to learn from them and dialogue with them. Consequently, it is a movement away from patronizing concern for the under-privileged to self-criticism of the privileges that one enjoys on account of others.[13] Following de Beauvoir, such an act of naming is free or autonomous in the sense of being an ongoing process that is attempted in and through its distortions. Such naming is also a critique of prevailing inequalities to work towards greater democratization and pluralism. Communication between women through their interwoven hierarchical contexts is also an act of solidarity in the search for a more egalitarian world.

Feminists who addressed their invisibility or visibility through the domestic feminine in traditional moral philosophy did not merely insert the word "woman" into its corpus. As Gilligan's and Okin's writings reveal, they challenged notions of the individual subject to offer a relational model. Reading de Beauvoir's work subsequently, her "interdependent" account of freedom compatible with the relational self, goes beyond

→ philosophy is often suggested as an alternative to the dominance of Western theory (Kapur 2012: 265). But indigenousness does not carry a spontaneous normativity with it. It too requires the privileged perspective of academics to be articulated and, as argued in the Introduction, is rife with patriarchal overtones. Hence, the turn to the indigenous would have to take the critical dimension into account.

13 Butler (1998: 285-86) pursues this line of thinking in responding to the criticism of her vocabulary being anti-humanistic. She defines her task as one of working the legacy of humanism against itself. By utilizing the humanistic term "subject", Butler wishes to expose the tensions and limits implicit in this word (ibid.: 279-82).

the liberal notion of freedom as control. Similarly, while addressing the existing unequal global relations among women, one cannot merely add underprivileged women from the south into existing feminist theory. Rather one needs to interrogate the prevailing hierarchies in the social division of labour. If one follows Hartmann in defining patriarchy "as a set of social relations which has a material base" (1997: 103), social labour matters as an analytical category.[14] In the global context, both underprivileged Western and non-Western "other" women are labouring agents who provide the "material base" of patriarchy through the conduits of domestic sphere and the market. Women who emulate the male conception of autonomy perpetuate these relations of domination among themselves.

Thus, Gilligan's and de Beauvoir's relational self leads to an "interdependent" paradigm of freedom which questions positions of privilege among women by adopting perspectives of solidarity with each other. Such a freedom opens the space for critiquing coercive forces of economics, bureaucracy and politics to denaturalize and desacralize terms such as "care" and "consent". Both Jaṭeśvarī and Jasodā were named as divine mothers who voluntarily took care of society to conceal the exploitation of their labour. By relating care-giving to labour, which benefits privileged women and their individualist

---

14 This is not intended as a deterministic claim about economic base and superstructure. The complex relation between Marxism and feminism hinted in Chapter 4 is worthy of a separate discussion. In any case, given feminist arguments about the neglect of gender in class, and the significance of Marxism in the context of labour, one could envisage a complementary relation between the two following Fraser (1998). This is especially because, "The identity of every social order is simultaneously gendered, raced and classed" (ibid.: 3), as well as caste-based in the Indian context.

notions of freedom, the concept of reproductive freedom is reconstructed. Hence, in a spirit of questioning, rather than mere control over the body, the latter as the right to choose motherhood in embodied and intersubjective situations of solidarity among women, needs to be articulated.

The relation between freedom and solidarity, following de Beauvoir, avoids celebrating an oppressive feminine identity in the name of women and provides the resources for critiquing women's subordination.[15] Collective contexts of identity formation do not treat men as primary beings who create identities of women by a founding act. The oppressive practices of femininity reflect the interests of privileged men within the horizon of economics and history. According to de Beauvoir (2010: 781), men would have to unlearn their privileges and conveniences by willing the freedom of women, as women dismantle the oppressive features of their feminine identity. Analogously, so that women can evenly avail of reproductive freedom, those who enjoy the privileges of the "globalization of motherhood" have to unlearn them; those who provide such services will have to renounce their quick benefits, in the struggle for a just social order. Further, "to emancipate woman is to refuse to enclose her in the relations she sustains with man, but not to deny them; while she posits herself for herself, she will none the less continue to exist for him *as well* . . ." (ibid.: 782). Unlearning privilege and easy returns do not undermine differences, for just as the differences between men and women matter for de Beauvoir (2010: 782), the differences between women are also valued in the course of overcoming their relation of privilege.

---

15 Ryle (1986: 61-62) analogously sees the issue of mechanism's threat to volition to be linked with the metaphysical tripartite distinction between the faculties of knowing, feeling and willing. He rightly suggests that by abandoning metaphysics, one also abandons the view that volition is a mysterious inner essence.

However, de Beauvoir's relational paradigm of freedom can work in a non-individualist way, if it also addresses women as a heterogeneous collectivity, socialized under the matrices of class, race, caste and nationality, rather than merely as concrete individuals. Despite her acceptance of human plurality as the starting point for a freedom that implies solidarity, de Beauvoir claims that her ethics of ambiguity starts with the premise of separate selves and the possibility of relating them together. In her *Ethics of Ambiguity* she asks, "How could men, originally separated, get together" (1962: 18). In her *The Second Sex*, she critiques Engels for associating private property as the foundation of gender inequality, since this overlooks its more fundamental cause in the inherent hostility of consciousness.[16] According to her, the male subject has the tendency to posit himself as autonomous in the sense of sovereignty, singularity and separateness. de Beauvoir points out that human consciousness is structured to be hostile towards another consciousness, its other, and also dominate it. Else ". . . the discovery of the bronze tool could not have brought about women's oppression" (de Beauvoir 2010: 67). Yet her understanding of women's oppression as rooted in the structure of consciousness belies her simultaneous analysis of situation and embodiment as central to such oppression. Moreover, by maintaining that Engels roots women's oppression in an ". . . abstraction *Homo economicus*" (ibid.: 65), she fails to notice his concrete, historical analysis of gender oppression in the model of private ownership. Indeed, rooting women's oppression in the structure of consciousness makes it ahistorical and abstract. de Beauvoir (ibid.: 782) conversely underlines the need for both men and women becoming sovereign subjects after a long struggle of conflictual relations with each other. This contradicts her claim that socialism is a necessary condition for removing the oppression of women. Thus, despite conceding to collective

16 This is derived from de Beauvoir (2010: 63-69).

contexts and impact of ethical choice, de Beauvoir accords absolute value to the concrete individual (1962: 156). But her dichotomy between an abstract collectivity and a concrete (non-intimate) individuality misses the possibility of theorizing the concrete collective other.[17]

Gilligan's ethics of care is also premised on such a choice, with the exception that its concrete individual is affirmed in the framework of intimate relationships. It offers a way of thinking about collectivities in concrete contexts; however, the problem is that it restricts itself to the intimate sphere of family and personal relations. In contrast, Fraser's concept of the concrete collective other envisages the possibility of also relating to non-personal relationships. This matters because by caring for strangers, such as Jaṭeśvarī and Jasodā, whom Western feminists have never met, they can unlearn their privileges and affirm non-dominating freedoms through engagement with free projects. This is what de Beauvoir (2004: 94) herself means when she claims that a French national can feel for the Chinese by establishing a bond with them through action. Further, her own insight in *The Second Sex* is that individual identities are acquired in collective contexts.[18] Thus, it is because of the inferior value attached to women's biologies by a sexist society that women are pushed into a compromising feminine status. Jaṭeśvarī and Jasodā are not just concrete individuals, but concrete members of disenfranchised collectivities. de Beauvoir's relational freedom can enable global feminism to critique the narrow concept of reproductive freedom predominantly adopted by Western feminism. But for this it should situate individual women in larger concrete collectivities, which intersect with each other through

---

17 See Chapter 3 above for this point.

18 See Chapter 3 above for a discussion of the relation between individualization and socialization.

hierarchies of economy and nation — intersections that also enmesh with the values of care and freedom.

In naming and listening to women such as Jaṭeśvarī, Jasodā and surrogate workers in a spirit of self-criticism, one does not as an academic feminist, eradicate the tension between femininity and feminism. The lives and writings of Ramabai and Wollstonecraft show that it is precisely such a tension that led to the articulation of feminist thought. Gilligan, Okin and de Beauvoir reveal that this tension underlines their rich theoretical debates between difference and equality. The crisscrossing lives of women from the north and south demonstrate a global shift in the concept of care, where feminine labour is associated with underprivileged women and feminism with the privileged. Yet as the discussion above reveals, this shift too has led to an enormous debate about hierarchy amongst women and its overcoming through solidarity. Hence, feminist thought does not necessarily renounce the feminine. Even de Beauvoir (2010: 739-40) upholds that women who renounce their femininity would be forsaking their humanity. This is because women do not voluntarily undertake feminine practices, but are socialized into them. Hence, as feminists they need to work towards liberating interpretations of the feminine such as that of Gilligan's critical concept of care or Okin's affective justice and de Beauvoir's relational autonomy. Therefore, a reconciliation of freedom and care would have to heed the tension between the feminine and the feminist perspectives through hierarchies and privileges among women's intersecting global histories. Else it will miss out on the solidarity amongst women, as the instance of Ramabai's failure to get the support of British women for transforming the situation of Indian women reveals. In linking together freedom with solidarity, women from diverse backgrounds, who constitute a concrete collectivity, would have to strive towards democratic futures. Yet such solidarity will be possible only if women who enjoy privileges of exploitative care labour renounce them.

Returning to de Beauvoir's *The Second Sex*, a feminism that integrates care and freedom in its tension with diverse femininities ". . . has never been an autonomous movement. . . . Never did women form a separate caste . . ." (2010: 15).[19] Yet, it problematizes women's difference and their relation to other political movements, such as socialism. Women, both privileged and otherwise, as well as men recognize their interdependence through their involvement in a network of relations, such as labour and language, which are entangled with elements of subordination and freedom. Since social relations are not absolute (Benhabib 1999: 345), social subjects should be seen as actors whose identities cannot be exhaustively determined by their social location. The process of socialization enables actors to reconstruct social relations in dominating, as well as egalitarian ways,[20] whereby caring for others and being cared for by others are acknowledged as aspects of human life lived in concrete collective contexts.

---

[19] Later on in 1971, de Beauvoir felt the need for a separate women's movement (Moi 1998: 87). However, this need not imply an identity politics. Indeed, as women's movements all over the world have demonstrated, their strategic independence enables them to critique mainstream political movements. For the want of space, the complex relationship between the feminist and socialist movements will have to be explored in another work.

[20] As Ryle (1986: 77) and Benhabib (1999: 349) proclaim, the rules of grammar do not exhaust the innumerable ways in which sentences can be composed.

Bibliography

Adorno Theodor and Horkheimer Max, 1979, *Dialectic of Enlightenment*, London: Verso.

Agnes, Flavia, 2008 (1990), "Women's Movements in a Secular Framework: Redefining the Agendas", in *Women's Studies in India: A Reader*, ed. Mary John, pp. 501-08, New Delhi: Penguin Books India.

Altekar, A.S., 2001 (1999), (1938), "The Position of Women in Hindu Civilization: Retrospect and Prospect", in *Women in Early Indian Societies*, ed. Kumkum Roy, pp. 49-81, New Delhi: Manohar.

Annuncio, Charubala, 1996, "Flouting Norms", *Outlook*, 7 August 48-49.

Anthias, Floya and Yuval-Davis, Nira, 1994, "Women and the Nation-State", in *Nationalism*, ed. John Hutchinson and Anthony D. Smith, pp. 312-16, Oxford: Oxford University Press.

Ardnt, Bettina, 2003, "Baby's Home, but not Daddy", *The Sydney Morning Herald*, 14 November, available from http://www.smh.com.au/articles/2003/11/13/1068674311777.html. accessed on 6 June 2011.

Auerbach Judy, Linda Blum, Vicki Smith, Christine Williams, 1985, "On Gilligan's in a Different Voice", *Feminist Studies*, **11**(1): 149-61.

Austin, J.L., 1962, *How to Do Things with Words*, Oxford: Clarendon Press.

Bailey, Alison, 2011, "Reconceiving Surrogacy: Towards a Reproductive Justice Account of Indian Surrogacy", *Hypatia*, **26**(4): 715-41.

Banerjee, Nirmala, 1989, "Working Women in Colonial Bengal: Modernization and Marginalization", in *Recasting Women*, ed. Kumkum Sangari and Sudesh Vaid, pp. 269-301, New Delhi: Kali for Women.

———, 1999, "Analysing Women's Work Under Patriarchy", in *From Myths to Markets: Essays on Gender*, ed. Kumkum Sangari and Uma Chakravarti, pp. 321-37, New Delhi: Manohar.

Bartky, Sandra Lee, 1990, *Femininity and Domination: Studies in the Phenomenology of Oppression*, New York and London: Routledge.

Bayly, C.A., 2009, "The Indian Ecumene: An Indigenous Public Sphere", in *The Indian Public Sphere: Readings in Media History*, ed. Arvind Rajagopal, pp. 49-64, New Delhi: Oxford University Press.

Belsare Vaijayanti, 2003, "The Doctrine of Purusartha: A Gender Perspective", in *Feminism in Search of an Identity: The Indian Context*, ed. Meena Kelkar and Deepti Gangavane, pp. 164-77, Jaipur and New Delhi: Rawat Publications.

Benhabib, Seyla, 1986, "The Generalized and the Concrete Other: The Kohlberg–Gilligan Controversy and Feminist Theory", *Praxis International*, **5**(4): 402-24.

———, 1992, *Situating the Self*, Cambridge: Polity Press.

______, 1999, "Sexual Difference and Collective Identities: The New Global Constellation", *Signs: Journal of Women in Culture and Society*, **24**(2): 335-60.

Berlin, Isaiah, 1969, *Four Essays on Liberty*, Oxford: Oxford University Press.

Bhelke, S.E. and Gokhale P.P. (eds.), 2002, *Studies in Indian Moral Philosophy: Problems, Concepts and Perspectives*, Pune: Indian Philosophical Quarterly.

Blum, Lawrence, 1998, "Gilligan and Kohlberg: Implications for Moral Theory", *Ethics*, **98**(3): 472-91.

Brennan, Samantha, 1999, "Recent Work in Feminist Ethics", *Ethics*, **109**: 858-93.

Brown, Wendy, 1995, *States of Injury: Power and Freedom in Later Modernity*, Princeton: Princeton University Press.

Burton, Antoinette, 1995, "Colonial Encounters in Late Victorian England: Pandita Ramabai at Cheltenham and Wantage, 1883-86", *Feminist Review*, **49**: 29-49.

Butler, Judith, 1993, *Bodies that Matter*, New York and London: Routledge.

———, 1995a, "Contingent Foundations", in *Feminist Contentions: A Philosophical Exchange*, by Seyla Benhabib, Judith Butler,

Drucilla Cornell and Nancy Fraser, pp. 35-58, New York: Routledge.

———, 1995b, "For a Careful Reading", in *Feminist Contentions: A Philosophical Exchange,* by Seyla Benhabib, Judith Butler, Drucilla Cornell and Nancy Fraser, pp. 127-44, New York: Routledge.

———, 1997, *Excitable Speech: A Politics of the Performative,* London: Routledge.

______, 1998, "How Bodies Come to Matter: An Interview with Judith Butler", Interview by Irene Costera Meijer and Baukje Prins, *Signs: Journal of Women in Culture and Society,* **23**(2): 275-86.

———, 2007 (1990), *Gender Trouble,* New York and London: Routledge.

Cameron, Deborah, 1992 (1985), *Feminism and Linguistic Theory* Hampshire and London: Macmillan Press.

Campbell, Sue, 2002, "Relational Autonomy: Feminist Perspectives on Autonomy, Agency, and the Social Self", *Hypatia,* **17**(2): 165-68.

Chakravarti, Uma, 1989, "Whatever Happened to the Vedic Dasi? Orientalism, Nationalism, and a Script for the Past", in *Recasting Women,* ed. Kukum Sangari and Sudesh Vaid, pp. 27-87, New Delhi: Kali for Women.

———, 2006 (1998), *Rewriting History: The Life and Times of Pandita Ramabai,* New Delhi: Zubaan.

———, 2001 (1999), "Beyond the Atlekarian Paradigm: Towards a New Understanding of Gender Relations in Early Indian History", in *Women in Early Indian Societies,* ed. Kumkum Roy, pp. 72-81, New Delhi: Manohar.

———, 2002, "Through Another Lens: Men, Women and Caste", in *Translating Caste,* ed. Tapan Basu, pp. 198-218, New Delhi: Katha.

———, 2003, *Gendering Caste: Through a Feminist Lens,* Calcutta: Stree.

Chakravarti, Uma and Kumkum Roy, 1991, "Therigatha: Songs of the Nuns, 6th Century BC", in *Women Writing in India: 600 BC to the Present Volume I: 600 BC to the Early 20th Century,* ed. Susie Tharu and K. Lalitha, pp. 65-70, New York: The Feminist Press at City University of New York.

Chakravarti, Uma and Preeti Gill, 2001, *Shadow Lives: Writings on Widowhood,* New Delhi: Kali for Women.

Chaudhry, Lakshmi, 2006 (March 12) " Men growing up to be Boys: madison Avenue cultivates a Peter Pan Version of Masculinity" *In these times* http: //www.inthesetimes.com/article/2526 accessed on January 9, 2009.

Chattopadhyaya, Debiprasad, 1973 (1959), *Lokāyata: A Study in Ancient Indian Materialism*, New Delhi: People's Publishing House.

Chavkin Wendy and Maree Maher Jane (eds.), 2010, *The Globalization of Motherhood: Deconstruction and Reconstruction of Biology and Care*, Ozon and New York: Routledge.

Chhatre, Lata, 2003, "Empowerment of Women: The Buddhist Perspective", in *Feminismin Search of an Identity: The Indian Context*, ed. Meena Kelkar and Deepti Gangavane, pp. 121-38, New Delhi and Jaipur: Rawat Publications.

Chodorow, Nancy, 1994, "Gender, Relation and Difference in Psychoanalytic Perspective", in *The Polity Reader in Gender Studies*, pp. 41-49, Cambridge: Polity Press.

Chodorow, Nancy and Susan Contratto, 1982, "The Fantasy of the Perfect Mother", in *Rethinking the Family: Some Feminist Questions*, ed. Barrie Thorne and Marilyn Yalom, pp. 54-75, New York and London: Longman.

Claassen, Rutger, 2011, "The Commodification of Care", *Hypatia*, **26**(1): 43-64.

Connell, R.W., 1994, "Gender Regimes and the Gender Order", in *The Polity Reader in Gender Studies*, pp. 29-49, Cambridge: Polity Press.

Cornwall, Andrea, 2000, "Missing Men? Reflections on Men, Masculinities and Gender in GAD", *IDS Bulletin*, **3**(2). http://www.brad.ac.uk/acad/dppc/gender/mandmweb/acornwalltext.html accessed on 7 February 2009.

Davis, Angela, 2011 (1981), *Women Race and Class*, New Delhi: Navayana.

Deakin, Michael A.B., 1994, "Hypatia and Her Mathematics", *The American Mathematical Quaterly*, **101**(3): 234-43. www.maa.org/pubs/Calc_articles/ma055.pdf. accessed on 6 June 2009.

———, 1995, *The Primary Sources for the Life and Work of Hypatia of Alexandria*, http://polyamory.org/~howard/Hypatia/primary-sources.html. accessed on 6 June 2009.

de Beauvoir, Simone, 1962, *The Ethics of Ambiguity*, New York: Citadel Press.

———, 1972 (1949), *The Second Sex,* tr. H.M. Parshley, Middlesex: Penguin.

———, 2004, "Pyrrhus and Cineas", in her *Philosophical Writings,* ed. Margaret A. Simons, pp. 77-149, Urbana and Chicago: University of Illinois Press.

———, 2010, *The Second Sex,* tr. Constance Borde and Sheila Malovany-Chevallier, London: Vintage.

de Saussure, Ferdinand, 1966 (1959), *Course in General Linguistics,* New York: McGraw Hill.

Descartes, Rene, 1951a (1641), "The Meditations Concerning First Philosophy", in his *Philosophical Essays,* ed. Laurence J. Lafleur, pp. 61-143, Indianapolis: Bobbs-Merrill Educational Publishing.

———, 1951b (1628), "Rules for the Direction of Mind", in his *Philosophical Essays,* ed. Laurence J. Lafleur, pp. 147-236, Indianapolis: Bobbs-Merrill Educational Publishing.

Delhi University Forum for Democracy, 2001, *Women in Early India,* New Delhi: Progressive Printers.

Desai, Rajani, et al. (eds.), 2000, *On the Woman's Question,* Mumbai: Research Unit for Political Economy.

———, 2001, *Controversies on the Woman's Question and Women and Globalisation,* Mumbai: Research Unit for Political Economy.

Deshpande, G.P., 2009, *The World of Ideas in Modern Marathi,* New Delhi: Tulika Books.

Deshpande, Swati 2010, "Made in 2007, born in 2010" *Times of India* (Feb 2): 4.

Deutscher, Penelope, 2008, *The Philosophy of Simone de Beauvoir,* Cambridge, New York: Cambridge University Press.

Devi, Mahasweta, 1987, "The Breast-Giver", in *In Other Worlds: Essays in Cultural Politics* by Gayatri Chakravarthy Spivak, pp. 222-40, New York and London: Methuen.

———, 2004a, "Ma, from Dusk to Dawn", in *In the Name of the Mother,* pp. 1-32, Calcutta, New Delhi: Seagull Books.

———, 2004b, *In the Name of the Mother,* Calcutta, New Delhi: Seagull Books.

Doniger, Wendy and Brian K. Smith (eds.), 1991, *The Laws of Manu,* New Delhi: Penguin.

Ebert, Teresa L., 1996, "After Transnationalism and Localism: Toward a Red Feminism", *Against the Current,* **65**: 27-31.

Eckert Penelope and Sally McConnell-Ginet, 2003, *Language and Gender*, Cambridge: Cambridge University Press.

Engels, Friedrich, 1970 (1884), "The Origin of the Family, Private Property and the State", in *Karl Marx and Frederick Engels: Selected Works* in 3 vols., vol. 3, pp. 204-334, Moscow: Progress Publishers.

Evans, Mary, 1987, "Engels: Materialism and Morality", in *Engels Revisted: New Feminist Essays*, ed. Janet Sayers, Mary Evans and Nanneke Redclift, pp. 81-97, London and New York: Tavistock Publications.

Ferguson, Moira, 2001, "Mary Wollstonecraft and the Problematic of Slavery", in *Feminism: Critical Concepts in Literary and Cultural Studies,* ed. Mary Evans, vol. 1, pp. 371-92, London and New York: Routledge.

Finke, Laurie, 1992, *Feminist Theory, Women's Writing,* Ithaca and London: Cornell University Press.

Firestone, Shulamith, 1997, "The Dialectic of Sex", in *The Second Wave: A Reader in Feminist Theory,* ed. Linda Nicholson, pp. 19-26, New York and London: Routledge.

Fraser, Nancy, 1986, "Toward a Discourse Ethic of Solidarity", *Praxis International,* **5**(4): 425-29.

———, 1989a, "Talking About Needs: Interpretive Contests as Political Conflicts in Welfare-State Societies", *Ethics,* **99**: 291-313.

———, 1989b, *Unruly Practices: Power, Discourse and Gender in Contemporary Social Theory,* Minneapolis: University of Minnesota Press.

———, 1994, "After the Family Wage: Gender Equity and the Welfare State", *Political Theory,* **22**(4): 591-618.

———, 1995, "False Antitheses", in *Feminist Contentions: A Philosophical Exchange,* ed. Seyla Benhabib, Judith Butler, Drucilla Cornell and Nancy Fraser, pp. 59-74, New York: Routledge.

Fraser, Nancy and Linda Gordon, 1997, "Dependency Demystified: Inscriptions of Power in a Keyword of the Welfare State", in *Contemporary Political Philosophy: An Anthology,* ed. Robert E. Goodin and Philip Petit, pp. 618-33, Oxford: Blackwell Publishers.

———, 1998, "A Future for Marxism", *New Politics,* **6**(4) (new series), whole no. 24, available from siwyg://94/http://www.wilpaterson.edu/~newpol/issue24/fraser.24.htm; internet. accessed on 8 June 2009.

Friedan, Betty, 1984 (1963), *The Feminine Mystique,* New York: Dell Publication.

———, 1998 (1981), *The Second Stage,* Cambridge, MA: Harvard University Press.

Friedman, Marilyn, 2000, "Feminism in Ethics: Conceptions of Autnomy" in *The Cambridge Companion to Feminism in Philosophy*, ed. Miranda Fricker and Jennifer Hornsby, 205-224. Cambridge: Cambridge University Press.

Gangavane, Deepti, 2004, "Kant on Femininity", *Indian Philosophical Quarterly,* **31**(1-4): 359-76.

Gatens, Moira, 1991, *Feminism and Philosophy: Perspectives on Difference and Equality,* Cambridge: Polity Press.

Giles, Mary E., 1982, "The Feminist Mystic", in *The Feminist Mystic and Other Essays on Women and Spirituality,* ed. Mary E. Giles, pp. 6-38, New York: Crossroad.

Gilligan, Carol, 1982, *In a Different Voice: Psychological Theory and Women's Development*, Cambridge, MA: Harvard University Press.

———, 1984, "The Conquistor and the Dark Continent: Reflections on the Psychology of Love", *Deadalus,* **113**(3): 75-95.

———, 1986, "Reply", *Signs: Journal of Women in Culture and Society,* **11**(2): 324-33.

———, 1988, "Remapping the Moral Domain: Images of Self in Relationship", in *Mapping the Moral Domain,* ed. Carol Gilligan and Janie Victoria Ward et al., pp. 3-19, Harvard: Harvard University Press.

———, 1991, "Teaching Shakespeare's Sister: Notes from the Underground of Female Adolescence", *Women's Studies Quarterly,* **19**(1/2): 31-51.

———, 1993, "Letter to Readers", in her *In a Different Voice: Psychological Theory and Women's Development*, pp. i-xxvii, Cambridge, MA: Harvard University Press.

———, 1995, "Hearing the Difference: Theorizing Connection", *Hypatia,* **10**(2): 120-27.

———, 2000, "An Interview with Carol Gilligan Restoring Lost

Voices", Interview by Mark F. Golberg, *The Phi Delta Kappan*, **81**(9): 701-02, 704.

Gilligan, Carol and David A.J. Richards, 2009 (2008), *The Deepening Darkness: Patriarchy, Resistance and Democracy's Future*, Cambridge: Cambridge University Press.

Glazer, Sarah, 2004, "Lost in Translation", *New York Times*, 2 August.

Goddard, Angela and Patterson Lindsey Mean, 2000, *Language and Gender*, London and New York: Routledge.

Gordon, Linda, 1982, "Why Nineteenth Century Feminists Did Not Support 'Birth-Control' and Twentieth Century Feminists Do: Feminism, Reproduction and the Family", in *Rethinking the Family: Some Feminist Questions*, ed. Barrie Thorne and Marilyn Yalom, pp. 40-53, New York and London: Longman.

Greig, Alan, Michael Kimmel and James Lang, 2000, "Men, Masculinities and Development: Broadening Our Work Towards Gender Equality", *Gender in Development Monograph Series*, #10. Available at www.health.columbia.edu/pdfs/men_masculinities.pdf accessed on 18 January 2009.

Grimshaw, Jean, 1986, *Feminist Philosophers: Women's Perspectives on Philosophical Traditions*, Sussex: Wheatsheaf Books.

———, 1988, "Autonomy and Identity in Feminist Thinking", in *Feminist Perspectives in Philosophy*, ed. Morwenna Griffiths and Margaret Whitford, pp. 90-108, Hampshire and London: Houndsmill, Basingstoke.

Haack, Susan, 1999, "Knowledge and Propaganda: Reflections of an Old Feminist", in *The Theory of Knowledge: Classical and Contemporary Readings*, ed. Louis P. Pojman, pp. 616-24, Belmont: Wadsworth Publishing Company.

Habermas, Jürgen, 1974 (1971), *Theory and Practice*, Boston: Beacon Press.

———, 1987, *The Philosophical Discourse of Modernity*, Cambridge MA.: MIT Press.

———, 1989-90, "Justice and Solidarity: On the Discussion Concerning" Stage 6, *The Philosophical Forum*, **XXI**(1-2), Fall–Winter: 32-52.

———, 1990, *Moral Consciousness and Communicative Action*, Cambridge, MA: MIT Press.

———, 1993, *Justification and Application: Remarks on Discourse Ethics*, Cambridge, MA: MIT Press.

———, 1996, "Modernity: An Unfinished Project", in *Habermas and the Unfinished Project of Modernity*, ed. Maurizio Passerin D' Entreves and Seyla Benhabib, pp. 38-55, Cambridge: Polity Press.

Hartmann, Heidi, 1997, "The Unhappy Marriage of Marxism and Feminism: Towards a More Progressive Union", in *The Second Wave: A Reader in Feminist Theory*, ed. Linda Nicholson, pp. 97-102, New York and London: Routledge.

Hegel, G.W.F., 1977 (1807), *Phenomenology of Spirit*, Oxford: Clarendon Press.

———, 1985, *Introduction to the Lectures on the History Philosophy*, Oxford: Clarendon Press.

Held, Virginia, 1998, "Feminist Reconceptualizations in Ethics", in *Philosophy in a Feminist Voice: Critique and Reconstructions*, ed. Janet A. Kourany, pp. 92-115, Princeton: Princeton University Press.

Hermit, 2003, *Hypatia Virian Saint*, vol. 1(1). http://www.churchofvirus.org/zine/1.1/hermit2.pdf. accessed on 7 August 2009.

Holveck, Eleanore, 1999, "The Blood of Others: A Novel Approach to the Ethics of Ambiguity", *Hypatia*, **14**(4): 3-17.

hooks, bell, 1994, *Teaching to Transgress: Education as the Practice of Freedom*, New York and London: Routledge.

Horner, I.B., 2001 (1930), "Women Under Primitive Buddhism: Laywomen and Almswomen", in *Women in Early Indian Societies*, ed. Kumkum Roy, pp. 82-109, New Delhi: Manohar.

Hornsby, Jennifer, 2000, "Feminism in Philosophy of Language: Communicative Speech Acts", in *The Cambridge Companion to Feminism in Philosophy*, ed. M Fricker and J. Hornsby, pp. 87-106, Cambridge: Cambridge University Press.

Hubbard, Elbert, 1928 (1908), "Hypatia", in *Little Journeys to the Homes of the Great*, v (X), East Aurora, New York: The Roycrofters. available from http://www.newcv.org/nl/newslog.php/_v308/_show_article/_a000308-000216-htm. accessed on 18 July 2009.

Hume, David, 1983 (1898), *An Enquiry Concerning the Principles of Morals*, Indianapolis: Hackett.

Humphries, Jane, 1987, "The Origin of the Family: Born out of Scarcity and not Wealth", in *Engels Revisited: New Feminist Essays*, ed.

Janet Sayers, Mary Evans and Nanneke Redclift, pp. 11-36, London and New York: Tavistock Publications.

International Centre for Research on Women (ICRW) 2002, *Men, Masculinity and Domestic Violence in India: Summary Report of Four Studies* ICRW+USAID: Washington ww.icrw.org/docs/Dv_India_Report4_52002.pdf

Irigaray, Luce, 1985a, *Speculum of the Other Woman*, Ithaca: Cornell University Press.

———, 1985b, *This Sex Which Is not One,* Ithaca: Cornell University Press.

———, 1994 (1989), *Thinking the Difference: For a Peaceful Revolution,* New York: Routledge.

———, 2004, "Towards a Sharing of Speech", in her *Key Writings,* pp. 77-94, London: Continuum.

Jacob, Smita, 2009, "Tribes of Neverland", *Tehelka,* 12 September http://archive.tehelka.com/story_main42.asp?filename=cr120909tribes_of.asp accessed on 10 May 2012.

Jacobsen P. Joyce, 2006, "Men's Issues in Development", in *The Other Half of Gender,* ed. Ian Bannon and Maria C. Correia, pp. 1-28, Washington DC: The World Bank.

Jaggar, M. Alison and R. Susan Bordo, 1992, *Gender/Body/knowledge: Feminist Reconstruction of Being and Knowledge,* New Brunswick: Rutgers University Press.

Jaggar, Alison M., 2000, "Feminist Ethics", in *The Blackwell Guide to Ethical Theory,* ed. Hugh LaFollette, pp. 348-74, Massachusetts and Oxford: Blackwell.

Jay, Martin, 1994, *Downcast Eyes: The Denigration of Vision in Twentieth-Century French Thought,* Berkeley: University of California Press.

Jensen, An-Magritt, 2005, "Fatherhood and Childhood: Between Demography and Ideology", Paper presented at Our Demographic Future: A Challenge. On the Need for Demographic Analyses. The 15th Nordic Demographic Symposium, 28-30 April, Aalborg Denmark, available from www.dst.dk/upload/session14-1fatherhood_and_childhood-anmagritt.pdf. accessed on 6 May 2010.

Jhamb, Bhumika, Yamini Mishra, Navanita Sinha, 2013, "The Paradox of Gender Responsive Budgeting", *Economic and Political Weekly,* **48**(20): 35-38.

Joel, Blaze and Taha Adib 2012, "World Media Criticize Bank Policies", *The Dartmouth,* available from http://thedartmouth.com/2012/4/18/news/bank accessed on 4 May 2013.

John, Mary E., 2005, "Feminist Perspectives on Family and Marriage: A Historical View", *Economic and Political Weekly,* **40**(8): 712-15.

Joshi, Tarkateerta Laxmanshastri, 2004, *Spiritual Materialism: A Case for Atheism,* Mumbai: Lokvangmaya Griha.

Justice, Faith, 2002, *My Hunt for Hypatia, Lady Philosopher of Alexandria: 355 AD – 415 AD,* www.coachlightpress.com/bygone/hypatia.shtml accessed on 6 May 2012.

Kamtekar, Rachna, 2002, "Distinction Without a Difference? Race and Genos in Plato", in *Philosophers on Race: Critical Essays,* ed. Julie K. Ward and Tommy L. Lott, pp. 1-13, Oxford: Blackwell.

Kakkath, Seetha, 2009, "Social Support for Hunter-gatherers: Care or Curse?", *Economic and Political Weekly,* **44**(36): 70-73.

Kant, Immanuel, 1956 (1788), *Critique of Practical Reason,* tr. Lewis White Beck, New York and London: Macmillan/Collier Macmillan.

———, 1965 (1781a, 1787b), *Critique of Pure Reason,* tr. Norman Kemp Smith, New York: St. Martin's Press.

———, 1983 (1785), "Grounding for the Metaphysics of Morals", in his *Ethical Philosophy,* tr. James W. Ellington, pp. 1-69, Indianapolis: Hackett.

———, 1985 (1797), *The Metaphysical Elements of Justice,* tr. John Ladd, New York: Macmillan.

———, 1996 (1798a/1800b), *Anthropology from a Pragmatic Point of View,* tr. Victor Lyle Dowdell, Carbondale and Edwardsville: Southern Illinois University Press.

Kapur, Ratna, 2012, "Emancipatory Feminist Theory in Postcolonial India: Unmasking the Ruse of Liberal Internationalism", in *Indian Political Thought: A Reader,* ed. Aakash Singh and Silika Mohapatra, pp. 257-68, London and New York: Routledge.

Kaur, Ravinder, 2009, "The Making of the New Family", *Times of India,* Crest, 19 December.

Kelkar, Meena, 2003, "Man–Woman Relationship in Indian Philosophy", *Feminism in Search of an Identity: The Indian*

Context, ed. Meena Kelkar and Deepti Gangavane, pp. 101-20, New Delhi and Jaipur: Rawat Publications.

Kelkar, Meena and Deepti Gangavane (eds.), 2003, *Feminism in Search of an Identity: The Indian Context*, New Delhi and Jaipur: Rawat Publications.

Kirk, G.S. and J.E. Raven (eds.), 1957, *The Pre-Socratic Philosophers: A Critical History with a Selection of Texts*, Cambridge: Cambridge University Press.

Kittay, Eva Feder, 2001, "A Feminist Public Ethic of Care Meets the New Communitarian Family Policy", *Ethics*, **111**: 523-47.

Kneller, Jane, 1993, "Discipline and Silence: Women and Imagination in Kant's Theory of Taste", in *Aesthetics in Feminist Perspective*, ed. Hilde Hein and Carolyn Korsmeyer, pp. 179-92, Bloomington and Indianapolis: Indiana University Press.

Kohlberg, Lawrence, 1966, "Moral Education in Schools: A Development View", *The School Review*, **74**(1): 1-30.

———, 1971, "From Is to Ought: How to Commit the Naturalistic Fallacy and Get Away with It in the Study of Moral Development", in *Cognitive Development and Epistemology*, ed. Theodore Mischel, pp. 151-235, New York and London: Academic Press.

———, 1973, "The Claim to Moral Adequacy of a Highest Stage of Moral Judgment", *Journal of Philosophy*, **70**(18): 630-46.

———, 1982, "A Reply to Owen Flanagan and Some Comments on the Puka-Goodpaster Exchange", *Ethics*, **92**: 513-28.

——— and Carol Gilligan, 1971, "The Adolescent as Philosopher: The Discovery of Self in a Post-Conventional World", *Deadalus*, **100**(4): 1051-86.

Kohlberg, Lawrence and Charles Levine et al., 1984, "Synopses and Detailed Replies to Critics", in his *Psychology of Moral Development: Essays on Moral Development*, vol. 2, San Francisco: Harper and Row.

Kolbert, Kathryn, 1988, "Developing a Reproductive Rights Agenda", in *Reproductive Laws for the 1990s: A Briefing Handbook*, ed. Nadine Taub and Sherill Cohen, Clifton, NJ: Humana Press.

Korsmeyer, W. Carolyn, 1988 (1975), "Reason and Morals in the Early Feminist Movement: Mary Wollstonecraft", in *A Vindication of Rights of Woman: An Authoritative Text, Backgrounds, The Wollstonecraft Debate, Criticisms*, ed. Carol H.

Poston, pp. 285-97, New York and London: W.W. Norton and Co.

Kosambi, Meera, 1995 (1993), *At the Intersection of Gender Reform and Religious Belief: Pandita Ramabai's Contribution and the Age of Consent Controversy*, Mumbai: Research Centre for Women's Studies, S.N.D.T. University.

———, 2000, *Pandita Ramabai Through Her Own Words: Selected Works*, New Delhi: Oxford University Press.

Kruks, Sonia, 1992, "Gender and Subjectivity: Simone de Beauvoir and Contemporary Feminism", *Signs: Journal of Women in Culture and Society*, **18**(1): 89-110.

———, 1998, "Beauvoir: The Weight of Situation", in *Simone de Beauvoir: A Critical Reader*, ed. Elizabeth Fallaize, pp. 43-71, London and New York: Routledge.

le Doeuff, Michelle, 2003, "From Existentialism to the Second Sex", in *French Feminism*, ed. Danielle Haare et al., pp. 333-43, New Delhi: Sage Publications.

Lenin, V.I., 1965, *On the Emancipation of Women*, Moscow: Progress Publishers.

Leonard, Debali Mookerjea, 2010, "To be *Pure* or not to be: Gandhi, Women, and the Partition of India", *Feminist Review*, **94:** 38-54.

Leslie, Julia I., 1995 (1989), *Tryambakayajvan the Perfect Wife (Stridharmapaddhati)*, tr. from the Sanskrit with an Introduction by I. Julia Leslie, London: Penguin Books.

Locke, John, 1997 (1690), *An Essay Concerning Human Understanding*, London: Penguin Books.

Lundgren-Gothlin, Eva, 1998, "The Master-Slave Dialectic in The Second Sex", in *Simone de Beauvoir: A Critical Reader*, ed. Elizabeth Fallaize, pp. 93-108, London and New York: Routledge.

Luxemburg, Rosa, 1971, "Women's Suffrage and Class Struggle", in *Selected Political Writings*, ed. Dick Howard, pp. 216-22, London: Monthly Review Press.

MacIntyre, Alasdair, 2007 (1981), *After Virtue: A Study in Moral Theory*, Indiana: University of Notre Dame Press.

Mahadevan, Kanchana, 2001, "Capabilities and Universality in Feminist Politics", *Journal of Indian Council of Philosophical Research*, **XVIII**(4): 75-106.

———, 2002, "Colonial Modernity: A Critique", *Indian Literature*,

Sahitya Akademi's Bi-Monthly Journal (May-June), **XLVI**(3): 193-211.

———, 2007, "Wounding Words and Speech Acts", *Atenea*, **27**(2): 9-32.

———, 2008, "Rorty, Haack and Feminist Epistemology", *Journal of Indian Council of Philosophical Research*, **XXV**(2): 27-49.

———, 2010, "Philosphizing with a Material/Maternal Touch", in *Indigenous Philosphizing: Indian Horizons*, ed. Saju Chackalackal, pp. 161-72, Bangalore: Dharmaram Publications.

———, 2013, "Care Ethics", in *Understanding Ethics*, ed. Vibha Chaturvedi and Pragati Sahni, pp. 199-209, New Delhi: Macmillan.

Malovany-Chevallier and Constance Borde, 2012a, "We Need to Transcend Our Sex and Station in Life to Evolve", interview by Yamini Deendayalan and Bhamati Sivapalan, *Tehelka*, 12 January.

———, 2012b, "Renewed Interest in de Beauvoir's 'The Second Sex'", interview, *IANS*, 19 January.

Mani, Braj Ranjan and Pamela Sardar (eds.), *A Forgotten Liberator: The Life and Times of Savitribai Phule*, New Delhi: Mountain Peak.

Marcuse, Herbert, 1960, *Reason and Revolution*, Boston: Beacon Press.

Martin-Kershaw, Nancy, 2000, "Mirabai in the Academy and the Politics of Identity", in *Faces of the Feminine in Ancient, Medieval, and Modern India*, ed. Mandakranta Bose, pp. 162-82, New Delhi/Oxford: Oxford University Press.

Marx, Karl and Friedrich Engels, 1959 (1848), "Manifesto of the Communist Party", in *Basic Writings on Politics and Philosophy*, ed. Lewis S. Feuer, pp. 1-46, New York: Anchor Books.

Marx, Karl, 1977 (1867), *Capital: A Critique of Political Economy*, tr. Ben Fowkes, New York: Vintage.

Menon, Nivedita, 2012, "The Regulation of Surrogacy in India — Questions and Concerns": SAMA http://kafila.org/2012/10/the-regulation-of-surrogacy-in-india-questions-and-concerns-nivedita-menon accessed on 13 May 2013.

Meyers, Diana, 2000/1999, "Feminist Perspectives on the Self", *Stanford Encyclopedia of Philosophy*. http://plato.stanford.edu/entries/feminism-self, accessed on 20 January 2002.

Midgley, Clare, 2007, *Feminism and Empire: Women Activists in Imperial Britain (1790-1865)*, Oxon and New York: Routledge.

Mies, Maria, 1993a, "New Reproductive Technologies: Sexist and Racist Implications", in *Ecofeminism*, ed. Maria Mies and Vandana Shiva, pp. 174-97, London: Zed Books.

———, 1993b, "From the Individual to the Dividual: The Supermarket of Reproductive Alternatives", in *Ecofeminism*, ed. Maria Mies and Vandana Shiva, pp. 198-217, New Delhi: Kali for Women.

———, 1993c, "Self-determination: The End of Utopia", in *Ecofeminism*, ed. Maria Mies and Vandana Shiva, pp. 218-30, New Delhi: Kali for Women.

Mill, John Stuart, 1996 (1869), *The Subjugation of Women*, Hertfordshire: Wordsworth.

Miller, Nancy, 1995, "Changing the Subject: Authorship, Writing and the Reader", in *Authorship from Plato to the Postmodern*, ed. Sean Burke, pp. 193-211, Edinburgh: Edinburgh University Press.

Miraftab, Faranak, 2004, "Invited and Invented Spaces of Participation: Neoliberal Citizenship and Feminists' Expanded Notion of Politics", *Wagadu*, **1**: 1-7.

Mohanty, Chandra Talpade, 1984, "Under Western Eyes: Feminist Scholarship and Colonial Discourse", *Boundary* 2, **12**(3): 333-53.

———, 1997, "Women Workers and Capitalist Scripts: Ideologies of Domination, Common Interests, and the Politics of Solidarity", in *Feminist Genealogies, Colonial Legacies, Democratic Futures*, ed. M. Jacquie Alexander and Chandra Talpade Mohanty, pp. 3-29, New York: Routledge.

———, 2002, "Under Western Eyes", Revisited: Feminist Solidarity Through Anticapitalist Struggles, *Signs: Journal of Women in Culture and Society*, **28**(2): 499-535.

Moi, Toril, 1985, *Sexual/Textual Politics: Feminist Literary Theory*, London and New York: Methuen.

———, 1997, "Feminist, Female, Feminine", in *The Feminist Reader: Essays in Gender and the Politics of Literary Criticism*, ed. Catherine Belsy and Jane Moore, pp. 104-16, London: Macmillan.

———, 1998, "Independent Women and Narratives of Liberation", in *Simone de Beauvoir: A Critical Reader*, ed. Elizabeth Fallaize, pp. 72-91, London and New York: Routledge.

———, 2002, "While We Wait: The English Translation of The Second Sex", *Signs: Journal of Women in Culture and Society,* **27**(4): 1005-35.

———, 2005, *Sex, Gender and the Body,* Oxford: Oxford University Press.

Moitra, Shefali, 2002, *Feminist Thought: Androcentrism, Communication and Objectivity,* New Delhi: Munshiram Manoharlal.

Mojab, Shahrzad, 1998, "'Muslim' Women and 'Western' Feminists: The Debate on Particulars and Universals", *Monthly Review,* **50**(7): 19-30.

Morgen, Thaïs E, 1994, *Men Writing the Feminine: Literature, Theory and the Question of Genders,* Albany: State University of New York Press.

Myers, Mitzi, 1988 (1975), "Reform or Ruin: A Revolution in Female Manners", in *A Vindication of Rights of Woman: An Authoritative Text, Backgrounds, The Wollstonecraft Debate, Criticisms,* ed. Carol H. Poston, pp. 328-43, New York and London: W.W. Norton and Co.

Narayan, Uma, 1995, "Colonialism and Its Others: Considerations on Rights and Care Discourses", *Hypatia,* **10**(2): 133-40.

———, 1997, "Contesting Cultures: 'Westernization', Respect for Cultures, and Third-World Feminism", in *The Second Wave: A Reader in Feminist Theory,* pp. 396-414, New York and London: Routledge.

Nashrulla, Tasneem, 2008, "Where Is Your Daddy?", *Sunday Hindustan Times,* 14 December.

Natarajan, Kanchana, 2013, *Transgressing Boundaries,* New Delhi: Zubaan Books.

Nicholson, Linda, 1997, "The Myth of the Traditional Family", in *Feminism and Families,* ed. Hilde Lindemann Nelson, pp. 27-42, New York and London: Routledge.

Nikhilananda, Swami, 1957, *The Upanishads: A Third Selection Aitareya and Brihadaranyaka,* London: Phoenix House.

Noronha, Ernesto and R.N. Sharma, 1999, "Displaced Workers and Withering of Welfare State", *Economic and Political Weekly,* **34**(23): 1454-60.

Nussbaum, Martha, 1998, "Public Policy and International Feminism", *Ethics,* **108**: 762-96.

———, 1999, "The Professor of Parody", *The New Republic Online* http://www.tnr.com/index.mhtml accessed on 7 May 2012.

Olavarría, José, 2006, "Men's Gender Relations, Identity, and Work-Family Balance in Latin America", in *The Other Half of Gender*, ed. Ian Bannon and Maria C. Correia, pp. 29-42, Washington DC: The World Bank.

Okin, Moller Susan, 1979, *Women in Western Political Thought*, Princeton: Princeton University Press.

———, 1987, "Justice and Gender", *Philosophy and Public Affairs*, **16**(1): 42-72.

———, 1989a, "Reason and Feeling in Thinking About Ethics", *Ethics*, **99**: 229-49.

———, 1989b, *Justice, Gender and the Family*, New York: Basic Books.

———, 1991, "Philosopher Queens and Private Wives: Plato on Women and the Family", in *Feminist Interpretations and Political Theory*, ed. Mary Lyndon Shanley and Carole Pateman, pp. 11-31, Oxford: Polity Press.

———, 1994, "Political Liberalism, Justice and Gender", *Ethics*, **105**(1): 23-43.

———, 1995, "Inequalities Between the Sexes in Different Cultural Contexts", in *Women Culture, and Development: A Study of Human Capabilities*, ed. Martha C. Nussbaum and Jonathan Glover, pp. 275-97, Oxford: Clarendon Press.

———, 1997, "Families and Feminist Theory: Some Past and Present Issues", in *Feminism and Families*, ed. Hilde Lindemann Nelson, pp. 13-26, New York and London: Routledge.

———, 2003, "Poverty, Well-being and Gender: What Counts? Who's Heard?", *Philosophy and Public Affairs*, **31**(3): 280-316.

Pal, Parthapratim and Tina Dutta, 2012, "Politics Overpowering Welfare", *Economic and Political Weekly*, **47**(7): 26-30.

Panda, Pradeep Kumar, 1997, "Female Headship, Poverty and Child Welfare: A Study of Orissa", *Economic and Political Weekly*, **32**(43): WS73-82.

Patel, Sujata, 1988, "The Construction and Reconstruction of Women in Gandhi", *Economic and Political Weekly*, **23**(8): 377-87.

Pedicini, Jameela, 2011, "The Two Indian Welfare Systems: State and Corporate Responses", *Barnett Papers in Social Research*, http://www.spi.ox.ac.uk/fileadmin/documents/pdf/J_Pedicini_final__2_.pdf accessed on 2 May 2013.

Plato, 1987a (1961), "Charmides", in *The Collected Dialogues of Plato,* ed. Edith Hamilton and Huntington Cairns, pp. 99-122, New Jersey: Princeton University Press.

———, 1987b (1961), "Protagoras", in *The Collected Dialogues of Plato* ed. Edith Hamilton and Huntington Cairns, pp. 308-52, New Jersey: Princeton University Press.

———, 1987c (1961), "Cratylus", in *The Collected Dialogues of Plato* ed. Edith Hamilton and Huntington Cairns, pp. 421-74, New Jersey: Princeton University Press.

———, 1987d (1961), "Republic", in *The Collected Dialogues of Plato* ed. Edith Hamilton and Huntington Cairns, pp. 575-844, New Jersey: Princeton University Press.

———, 1987e (1961), "Timaeus", in *The Collected Dialogues of Plato,* ed. Edith Hamilton and Huntington Cairns, pp. 1151-1211, New Jersey: Princeton University Press.

Petchesky, R.P., 1980, "Reproductive Freedom: Beyond 'A Woman's Right to Choose'", *Signs: Journal of Women in Culture and Society,* **5**(66): 1-85.

Pinnick, Cassandra L., 1994, "Feminist Epistemology: Implications for Philosophy of Science", *Philosophy of Science,* **61**(4): 646-57.

Poonacha, Veena, 1995, *Gender Within the Human Rights Discourse,* Mumbai: RCWS.

PTI, 2005, "NE Conflict-led to Raise in Female-headed Households", *The Financial Express,* 29 January.

———, 2012, "Ela Bhatt One of My Heroines: Hillary", *Times of India,* 23 June.

Puka, William, 2010, "Moral Development", *The Internet Encyclopedia of Philosophy,* available from http://www.iep.utm.edu accessed on 8 May 2012.

Qadeer, Imrana and Mary John, 2008, "Surrogacy Politics", available from http://kafila.org/2008/12/25/surrrogacy-politics-imrana-quadeer-mary-e-john accessed on 10 May 2012.

Rai, S. Amit, 2002, *Rule of Sympathy: Sentiment, Race and Power: 1750-1850,* New York: Palgrave.

Rajagopal, Arvind, 2009, "Introduction: The Public Sphere in Indian Structure and Transformation", in his edited *The Indian Public Sphere: Readings in Media History,* pp. 1-28, New Delhi: Oxford University Press.

Rawls, John, 1971, *A Theory of Justice*, Cambridge, MA: Harvard University Press.

Roberts, Dorothy E., 1998, "The Future of Reproductive Choice for Poor Women and Women of Color", in *The Politics of Women's Bodies: Sexuality, Appearance and Behavior*, ed. Rose Weitz, pp. 270-77, Oxford and New York: Oxford University Press.

Roy, Kumkum, 2001 (1999), "Introduction" to *Women in Early Indian Societies*, ed. Kumkum Roy, pp. 1-45, New Delhi: Manohar.

Rubin, Gayle, 1997, "The Traffic in Women: Notes on the 'Political Economy' of Sex", in *The Second Wave: A Reader in Feminist Theory*, ed. Linda Nicholson, pp. 27-62, New York and London: Routledge.

Ryle, Gilbert, 1986, *The Concept of Mind*, Middlesex: Penguin.

Said, Edward, 1978, *Orientalism*, London: Routledge.

Sainath, P., 2004, "How the Better Half Dies", *The Hindu*, 1 August.

Sangari, Kumkum, 1990a, "Mirabai and the Spiritual Economy of Bhakti", *Economic and Political Weekly*, **25**(27): 1464-75.

———, 1990b, "Mirabai and the Spiritual Economy of Bhakti", *Economic and Political Weekly*, **25**(28): 1537-52.

———, 1993, "The 'Amenities of Domestic Life': Questions on Labor", *Social Scientist*, **21**(9-11): 3-46.

———, 1994 (1991), "Relating Histories: Definitions of Literacy, Literature Gender in Nineteenth Century Calcutta and England", in *Rethinking English: Essays in Literature, Language, History*, ed. Svati Joshi, pp. 32-123, Oxford: Oxford University Press.

———, 1995, "Politics of Diversity: Religious Communities and Multiple Patriarchies", *Economic and Political Weekly*, **30**(52): 3381-89.

———, 1999, *Politics of the Possible*, New Delhi: Tulika.

Sarma, D.S., 1961, *The Upanishads: An Anthology*, Bombay: Bharatiya Vidya Bhavan.

Saul, Jennifer, 2010, "Feminist Philosophy of Language", *The Stanford Encyclopedia of Philosophy*, http://plato.stanford.edu/entries/feminism language/. accessed on May 3, 2011.

Sen, Samita, 1999, *Women and Labour in Late Colonial India: The Bengal Jute Industry*, Cambridge: Cambridge University Press.

Sequeira, Rosy, 2012a, "Sita Followed Ram Why Can't You? HC Advises Woman in Divorce Battle", *Times of India,* 9 May, p. 1.

———, 2012b, "HC Says More Women Are Filing for Divorces", *Times of India,* 9 May, p. 7.

———, 2012c, "Marriage More Important Than Comp Training", *Times of India,* 9 May, p. 7.

Singh, Rahul, 2008 (Dec, 21) "Like to Cook? Got a Lover? The Army is not for You." *The Hindustan Times*, p. 16.

Sinha, Chitra, 2007, "Images of Motherhood: The Hindu Code Bill Discourses" *Economic and Political Weekly* **XLII**(43): 49-57.

Sinha, Kounteya, 2011, "India not the Best Place for Mums", *Sunday Times of India* (Mumbai), 8 May, p. 9.

Shramjivikanchi Ekta Samiti, 1994, *Beware of the Sweet Nothings of the Maharashtra Government's Women's Policy!,* Mumbai: Shramjivikanchi Ekta Samiti.

Spelman, V. Elizabeth, 1991, "Simone de Beauvoir and Women: Just Who Does She Think 'We' Is?", in *Feminist Interpretations and Political Theory,* ed. Mary Lyndon Shanley and Carole Pateman, pp. 201-16, Cambridge: Polity Press.

Spivak, Gayatri Chakravorty, 1987, *In Other Worlds: Essays in Cultural Politics,* New York and London: Methuen.

———, 1993, *Outside in the Teaching Machine,* New York: Routledge.

Stanworth, Michelle, 1987, "Reproductive Technologies and the Deconstruction of Motherhood", in *Reproductive Technologies: Gender, Motherhood and Medicine,* ed. Michelle Stanworth, pp. 10-35, Cambridge: Polity Press.

Taylor, Barbara, 2003, *Mary Wollstonecraft and the Feminist Imagination,* Cambridge: Cambridge University Press.

Teresa, Saint 1957 (1588), *The Life of Saint Teresa of Avila by Herself,* tr. with an introduction by J.M. Cohen, Harmondsworth, Middlesex: Penguin Books.

Tharu, Susie and K. Lalita (eds.), 1991, *Women Writing in India: 600 BC to the Present* (vol. 1), New York: The Feminist Press.

Thorne, Barrie, 1982, "Feminist Rethinking of the Family: An Overview", in *Rethinking the Family: Some Feminist Questions,* ed. Barrie Thorne and Marilyn Yalom, pp. 1-24, New York and London: Longman.

Tong, Rosemarie, 1989, *Feminist Thought: A Comprehensive Introduction,* Boulder, CO: Westview Press.

Vanita, Ruth, 2003, "The Self Is not Gendered: Sulabha's Debate with King Janaka", *NWSA Journal*, **15**(2): 76-93.

Verma, Roop Rekha, 1995, "Femininity, Equality, and Personhood", in *Women Culture, and Development: A Study of Human Capabilities*, ed. Martha C. Nussbaum and Jonathan Glover, pp. 433-43, Oxford: Clarendon Press.

Verma, Chapla, 2000, "'The Wildering Gloom': Women's Place in Buddhist History", in *Faces of the Feminine in Ancient, Medieval, and Modern India*, ed. Mandakranta Bose, pp. 69-86, New Delhi/Oxford: Oxford University Press.

Vijayan, P.K., 2002, "Outline for an Exploration of Hindutva Masculinities", in *Translating Desire: The Politics of Gender and Culture in India*, ed. Brinda Bose, New Delhi: Katha.

Viswanathan, Gauri, 2007 (1998), "Silencing Heresy", in *Women and Social Reform in Maharashtra*, vol. I, ed. Sumit Sarkar and Tanika Sarkar, pp. 249-97, Ranikhet: Permanent Black.

Wallace, Kathleen, 2003, "Autonomous 'I' of an Intersectional Self", *The Journal of Speculative Philosophy*, **17**(3): 176-91.

Warnke, Georgia, 1987, *Gadamer: Hermeneutics, Tradition and Reason*, Stanford: Stanford University Press.

Warren, Karen (ed.), 2009, *An Unconventional History of Western Philosophy: Conversations Between Men and Women Philosophers*, Lanham, Boulder: Rowman and Littlefield.

Waugh, Patricia, 1992, "Stalemates? Feminists, Postmodernists and Unfinished Issues in Modern Aesthetics?", in *The Politics of Pleasure: Aesthetics and Cultural Theory*, ed. Stephen Regan, pp. 177-201, Buckingham: Open University Press.

Weir, Allison, 1996, *Sacrificial Logics: Feminist Theory and the Critique of Identity*, London: Routledge.

Weitz, Rose, 1998, "A History of Women's Bodies", in her edited *The Politics of Women's Bodies: Sexuality, Appearance and Behavior*, pp. 3-11, Oxford: Oxford University Press.

Wellmer, Albrecht, 1989-90, "Models of Freedom in the Modern World", *The Philosophical Forum*, **21**(1-2): 227-52.

Winfield, Richard, 1991, *Freedom and Modernity*, Albany: SUNY.

———, 2001, "Postcolonialism and Right", in his *Autonomy and Normativity: Investigations of Truth, Right and Beauty*, pp. 161-75, Aldershot: Ashgate.

Wittgenstein, Ludwig, 1958, *Philosophical Investigations*, New York: Macmillan.

Wollstonecraft, Mary, 1790, *A Vindication of the Rights of Men*, http://files.libertyfund.org/files/991/Wollstonecraft_0532_EBk_v6.0.pdf accessed on 6 May 2012.

———, 1988/1975 (1792), "A Vindication of the Rights of Woman" in *A Vindication of Rights of Woman: An Authoritative Text, Backgrounds, The Wollstonecraft Debate, Criticisms*, ed. Carol H. Poston, pp. 1-194, New York and London: W.W. Norton and Co.

Zack, Naomi, 1997, "'The Family' and Radical Family Theory", in *Feminism and Families*, ed. Hilde Lindemann Nelson, pp. 43-51, New York and London: Routledge.

Zaretsky, Eli, 1982, "The Place of the Family in the Origins of the Welfare State", in *Rethinking the Family: Some Feminist Questions*, ed. Barrie Thorne and Marilyn Yalom, pp. 188-224, New York and London: Longman.

Žižek, Slavoj, 1993, "From Courtly Love to the Crying Game", *New Left Review*, **202**: 95-108.

Index

Abolition of Sati, 49
abortions, blanket endorsement of, 218
absolute evil, 206
academic
  feminism, 234
  philosophy, centre of, 29
accusation of essentialism, 224
acquiescence of the female population, 50
act(s) of solidarity, 58, 235
activity of philosophy, xiii, 23
adequacy of moral judgement, 108
Adorno, Theodor, 167
African-American
  mother, 139
  women, 197, 217, 219
Afro–Asian philosophies, 2
Agarkar, Gopal Ganesh, 48-49
Age of Consent Bill, 54
Age of Consummation of Marriage, 49
Agnes, Flavia, 40
Akkal, Avudai, 72
alleged Western emphasis on rights, 29
ambiguity, 182, 192, 204, 207, 220, 225
  of a human being's identity, 225
ambiguous, 204, 208
  situation(s), 181, 207, 209
ambivalence, 87, 137, 205
ambivalent, 207, 208
American genetic father, 216
analogy between family loyalty and patriotism, 73
analytic, xviii
  ethics, 114
androcentrism, 23, 26
Anglo-American feminism, 28
Annuncio, Charubala, 190
anti-intellectual femininity, 47
antithesis of discrimination, 221
Arendt, Hannah, 5
arid intellectualization, 152
Aristotle(lian), 1, 94, 108, 144, 156, 201
  denigration of the household, 156
  tradition, 125
  Christian world-view, 113
Arthur, J. Thomson, 25
Arya Mahila Samaj, 54
association of ideas, 79, 100
assumptions of self-sufficiency, 90
atomic, 175, 188, 190, 192, 209
atomicity, 212
  of individualism, 212
atomistic, 192

atomists, 2
attitude, 227
Auerbach, Judy, 107, 120, 123, 137, 140
Austin, J.L., 12
autobiographical, xiv
autobiography, 96
autonomous, 35, 110, 114-16, 119, 139, 178, 205, 218, 220, 235, 238, 241
autonomy, xv-xvii, xxi, 7, 21, 47, 60, 86, 107, 115, 118-20, 122, 124, 130, 137, 139-40, 178-80, 182-83, 185, 187-91, 196, 202, 204-08, 213, 215, 219, 221-22, 230, 232
    dialectical mixture of, 120
    intersubjective concept of, 222
Ayer, A.J., 1

Bahinabai, 71
Bailey, Alison, 216-17
Banerjee, Nirmala, 38-39
Bartky, Sandra Lee, 124-25, 133, 136
basic premise of liberalism, 172
basis of
    feminist moral philosophy, 19
    political principles of justice, 157
Belsare, Vaijayanti Arun, 29
Benhabib, Seyla, 11, 27, 111-13, 121-22, 127, 129-30, 133, 139-40, 241
Berlin, Isaiah, 189
Bhatt, Ela, 233
Bhave, Vinoba, 63
Bhelke, S.E., 4
bias against women in Western tradition, 112
Blair, Tony, 170
Blake, William, 75-76
body, 2-7, 9, 18, 20, 29, 68, 78, 79, 95, 98, 125, 130, 183, 186, 193, 195, 200-02, 204-05, 207, 218-19, 237
    as a situation, xxii
    subjective subjugation of, 95
Borde, Constance, xv, 210
bourgeois
    feminism, 184
    Western, xvii
    motherhood, unavailability of, 161
brahma-māyā, 7
Brennan, Samantha, 224
Bṛhadāraṇyka Upaniṣad, 66
British
    domestic ideology of motherhood, 44
    empire, xvi, xx, 44-45, 77, 82, 90
Brown, Wendy, 164, 166, 171, 175, 178-79
Buddhism's positive image of women, 64
Burke's
    conservative outlook, 75
    notion of the family, 82
Burton, Antoinette, 59
Butler, Judith, 12, 17, 235

Campbell, Sue, 220
care, xiv-xvii, xix-xxii, 5, 8, 11, 14-15, 18-19, 21, 33, 47, 57, 60, 62, 64, 73, 82, 86, 89, 102, 105-07, 113-14, 117-20, 122-26, 128-32, 134-37, 139-42, 145,

153-55, 158-59, 167, 172, 175-76, 178-82, 185, 187-88, 191-92, 196, 208, 212, 214-16, 221, 223-24, 226, 228-31, 233, 236, 240-41
as a critical concept, 182
as a feminine virtue, 123
as a virtue, 118
colonial roots of, 168
commercialization of, 216
critical concept of, 240
equation of, 130, 136
ethical insight of, xxi
ethics of, xxi, 106, 120, 140
function of, 125
meaning of, 139
naturalization of, 230
non-violent approach of, 139
notion of, 137
perspective, xxi, 142, 154
principle of, 127
recipients of, 175
reciprocal distribution of, 232
relationship of, 132
theorization of, 106
care-based approach, 122
care-giving, 11, 124, 132, 175, 187, 221, 231, 233, 236
activities, 145
work, 217
family as a centre of, 140
Carpenter, Mary, 58
Cartesianism, 97
categorical imperative, 110
Chakravarti, Uma, 33, 35-36, 42-45, 48-50, 52, 54, 64-66, 83, 163, 186
Chaudhry, Lakshmi, 171
Chavkin, W., 185, 216
Chhatre, Lata, 65
Chicago, Judy, 93
child marriage,
abolition of, 45
consummation of, 48
Chodorow, Nancy, 5, 141, 154, 172
Christian patriarchal order, 72
Cioux, Helene, 19
civil society, 36, 44, 170, 179
civilization, 43, 45, 53, 76-77, 105, 132, 141, 160
classical liberalism, era of, 191
Clinton, Hillary, 233
collective feminist act, 72
colonial, xiv, xvi-xix, 24, 30, 33-34, 36-40, 42-44, 46-48, 51-52, 56-57, 60, 73, 85-86, 90, 105-06, 123, 126, 131-32, 142, 163, 168, 171, 178, 181-82, 186, 212-13, 234
education policies for Indian women, 86
model of dominance, 47
rule, contradictory character of, 40
colonialism, 224
commercial surrogacy, 182
practice of, 216
communitarian
otherness, 188
caring, 187
companionate wives, 48
concept of
a living relation, 212
a linear development, 138
autonomy, 180

care, 140, 192
freedom, 184, 217
gender, 22, 25
reproductive freedom, 237
the concrete collective other, 239

conflict between
care and freedom, 178
femininity and feminism, 79
self-reliance and nurture, 178

Connell, R.W., 5

conservative
patriarchy, 90
understanding of motherhood, 141

Constitution of India, 173

Contratto, Susan, 141

conventional, 109-10

conversion, 208

Conway, Ann, 97

Copernican revolution, 10

corporate globalization, 171

critical, xvi, xviii, xix, 14, 26, 30, 35, 63, 76, 79, 85, 87, 126, 141, 163-65, 178, 182, 192, 197, 222-23, 228-29, 235, 240
dialogue, possibility of, 223

critique, 73, 89, 100, 143

critique of
civilization, 77
domesticity, 91
individual freedom, 220
mainstream ethics, 107
Nussbaum's
capabilities, 231
imperialism, 227
patriarchy, 229
prevailing inequalities, 235
social hierarchy, 83
the femininity, 101, 224
Western
ethical theory, 141
feminism, 181

cultural marginalization, 165

cultures, awareness of, 225

darśana, 3

Davis, Angela, xxii, 91, 139, 217-18, 220, 230, 232

Dayanand, Swami Saraswati, 45, 186

Deakin, A.B. Michael, 92

de Beauvoir, Simone, xiii-xv, xvii, xxi- xxii, 5, 8-10, 12, 14-15, 17-21, 74, 95, 97, 133, 176, 179-83, 186-90, 192-94, 196-98, 200-201, 203-05, 207-09, 211-12, 215, 217, 219-22, 224-26, 232-33, 235, 237-39, 241

Dêd, Lal, 71

deliberative democracy, 130

Descartes, Rene, 1-3, 79, 89

Deshpande, G.P., 63, 216

Deutscher, Penelope, xv, 197-98, 225-26

developmental psychology, 118, 138

Devi, Mahasweta, 161, 167, 179, 185-86, 219, 231

Dewey, John, 194

dharma, 41, 112

dialogue partners, welfare of, 129

difference(s), 79, 106, 139, 145, 154, 175, 195, 202, 206, 221 152, 215, 223, 240

principle, 148-49, 151, 154, 209
different voice, 105, 120, 139, 142
discrimination against women, 189
problem of, 45
disembodied, 7-8
distinct women centric philosophical terminology, 9
diverse
conceptions of reason, 114
sexual preferences, 184
social strata, 71
dogma of Eurocentrism, 27
domestic
care, 187
feminine, 90
femininity, 86, 118, 162
manners, 80
relationships, 133
women, rights of, 163
domesticity, 5
ideology of, 36
rejection of, 94
Doniger, Wendy, 41
double-aspect identity, notion of, 134
double claim, 207
dual systems theory, 177
Dutta, Tina, 173

early feminist movement, 83
earthly love, metaphor of, 95
Ebert, L. Teresa, 212
Eckert, Penelope, 13
ecofeminism, 212, 225
eco-feminist, xxi
effeminate Indian men, 45
egalitarian relationships, 222
embodied, 2, 11, 13, 67, 95, 192, 200, 203, 209, 211, 217, 233
care-giving, providers of, 180
situation, 192, 220
embodiment, xiii, 2, 8, 23, 28, 65, 96, 100, 130, 182, 192, 193, 199, 200, 205, 207, 221, 238
emergence of
feminist consciousness, 188
mainstream Indian feminine identity, xx
the women's movement in the West, 163
Emilus's rational education, 77
Engels, Friedrich, 17, 99, 160, 176-77, 199, 238
Engelsian tone, 230
English
middle-class women, 46
radical, 75
enlightened West, knowledge mission of, 43
Enlightenment, 183-84
entangled space, 34
equal respect, principle of, 135
era of classical liberalism, 191
Erikson, Erik, 112
essentialism, accusation of, 224
established reproductive rights, 183
eternal feminine, 197, 205, 211, 230
condition, 230
ethic(s) of
ambiguity, 210, 238
care, xx, 28, 105-06, 129, 152, 178, 181, 209, 212, 220, 239

disembodiment, 4
Eurocentric, 180, 188
dogma of, 27
Western feminist norm, 180
Eurocentrism, 27, 188, 197, 212
European
modernity, 36, 44
woman, middle-class, 45
Evans, Mary, 176
exclusion of women, 25
in language, 25
exile, 221
experience(s) of
exclusion, 99
mysticism, 95
oppression, 99
of upper-caste women, 86
exploitation of women in the public sphere, 86
exploitative care labour, privileges of, 241
extremes of total self-sacrifice or rigid individual, 136
fairness, logic of, 119
family, xiii, xxi, 8, 9, 37, 39, 40, 46, 50, 70, 73, 82, 87, 106, 109, 113-14, 116, 123, 131-33, 136, 140-45, 147, 149-54, 156-60, 162-63, 165, 169-72, 176-79, 209, 213-14, 216, 228, 239
domestic value of, 87
historicization of, 178
involvement, antithesis of, 171
notions of, 87
relationships, 136
Fanon, Franz, 198
fear of legal punishment, 110
female(s), 9, 13, 15, 17-18, 20, 25-27, 35, 47, 50, 54-56, 61-62, 77-80, 84, 86-88, 90, 92, 99-100, 137, 154-55, 164, 170, 185, 201, 231
ancestry, 62, 92
desire, imperial construction of, 47
education, 61
experience, 99
foetuses, sex-selected abortion of, 227
manners,
patriarchal dimension of, 77
reform of, 77
moral autonomy, power of, 47
parenting, formative influence of, 154
passivity, 201
population, acquiescence of, 50
readership, 86
sensibility, uncatalogued, 137
subjectivity, denial of, 79
world, 35
headed households, 170
feminine, xiii-xvii, xix-xxii, 5-7, 9-10, 14-21, 25-27, 29, 34-35, 37, 42, 51, 55-56, 59-60, 63-66, 71, 77-79, 82, 84-85, 88-92, 94, 97, 99, 101-02, 105-07, 112-14, 117, 123, 125, 127, 130, 135-36, 141, 158, 163, 175, 181-82, 185, 191-92, 194-96, 198, 201, 206, 214, 226, 229-32, 235, 237, 239-40
activities of women, 194
as immanent, 226
aspect of nurture, 106
behaviour, path of, 20

care, xvi-xvii, 19
  patriarchal notions of, 21
  perspective of, 182
  private domain of, 185
  theoretical concept of, xxi
care and feminist freedom, debate between, xxi
care-giving, 175
care-work, 229
charm, 82
critic of, 182
cultural
  behaviour of, 99
  expectations of, 124
  traits, xxi
development, 106
dimension(s), xxi, 63
domestic
  care, 192
  ideology of, 198
domesticated, 42
grievance, bitter sense of, 84
ideal, 19
identity, 20, 35
  oppressive features of, 237
liberating interpretations of, 240
notion of, 79
nurture, 18
perspective of, 89
  care, xx, 18
reasoning, 8
seclusion, bonds of, 56
sphere of care, 113
traits, 10
virtue(s), xiv, 126
virtue of
  care, xix
  care, idealization of, 60
  nurture, 105
feminine/feminist perspectives, conflict of, 105
feminine/masculine binary, 20
femininity, xiv, xvi, xx, 5, 10, 14-16, 18-19, 33-35, 47, 50-51, 59, 61-62, 74, 79, 86, 88, 95-96, 99, 100-101, 105, 118, 124-25, 132, 143, 156, 162-63, 166, 181, 192, 195-96, 200, 215, 224, 226, 237, 240
  myths of, 200
  situation of, 95
  social standards of, 16
  specific forms of, 166
feminism, xiv, xviii, xxi-xxii, 8, 11-12, 16-19, 26, 28-30, 33-35, 50, 52, 58, 60-61, 63, 66, 79, 86, 96, 98-101, 105, 124, 128, 135, 143, 175, 181, 185, 215, 222-26, 229, 234, 236, 240-41
  Anglo-American, 28
  black/lesbian, 28
  in colonial India, 30
  led extraordinary lives, 98
  defence of, 17
  philosophical treatments of, xviii
  pioneering, xiv
  practice of, 33
  public dimension of, 86
  third world, 28
feminism's internal debate, perspective of, xvii
feminist(s), xiii-xiv, xvi-xxi, 1-2, 4-5, 7, 8-10, 14-15, 17-18, 20, 22, 28-29, 34, 39, 51-53, 57-63, 65, 69, 70-73, 81, 83, 86-87, 89, 90, 92, 94, 96-101, 105-07, 113, 122, 125, 129-30, 132,

134, 136-37, 141, 143, 145, 147, 150-52, 162, 164, 168, 177, 180, 182-83, 186-88, 190, 192-93, 195, 199, 214-15, 218, 221, 223-25, 227, 229-30, 232, 234, 236, 240-41
activism, 61
in India, 34
alternative to feminine domesticity, 90
and feminine ethics, distinction between a, 136
and socialist movement, complex relationship between, 241
approaches to care, xvi, 136
appropriation(s), 21
characteristic of, 93
challenge, xix
consciousness, xiv, 71, 84, 134
in India, 34
pioneers of, 84
context, 147
critique(s), 10, 105
of British imperialism, 73
of domesticity, 62, 92
engagement with academic philosophy, 26
ethics, 129, 136
first generation of, 163
feminine, xvi
gains, 152
heritage, 94
ideals, xiv, 62
ideas, 186
interaction, three models of, 232
interest, growth of, xviii
intervention
in philosophy, 9
theoretical, 27
language philosophers, 15
minded, 137
moment of disentangling, 18
moral
philosophers, 130
philosophy, xix, 20
movement(s), 132, 162
oriented sense, 69
path, 63
philosophers, xiii, 1, 14
cognition of, xviii
philosophical
texts, xxii
vocabulary, xiii
philosophy, xiii-xiv, xvii-xviii, xx, 14-16, 21-25, 27, 29, 74, 99
theoretical terrain of, xvii
philosophy's theoretical task, 22
point of view, 151
position, xix
scholars, 65
text, foundational, 78
themes, xviii
theorization, fulcrum of, 99
theorizing, 98
theory, 27, 101
epochal history of, xix
thinker, xix
understanding of motherhood, 141
Ferguson, Moira, 85
Finke, Laurie, 79, 92
Firestone, Shulamith, 177
framework of
institutional structures, 162
intimate relationships, 239
justice as fairness, 149

Fraser, Nancy, 132-33, 135, 166, 168, 175, 181, 190, 221, 223, 232, 236, 239
freedom, xiii, xv, xvii, xx-xxii, 4, 14-15, 18, 28, 36, 42, 48, 56, 72, 75, 87, 106, 116, 124-26, 135, 140, 148-49, 158, 171, 173, 178-85, 187-93, 196, 200, 203, 205-06, 208-09, 211-13, 215, 217-22, 227, 229, 231, 234-35, 237-38, 240-41
  central concept of, xvii
  liberal conception of, 179
  material dimensions of, 218
  non-individualist notion of, xxi
  non-possessive model of, 204
  notion of, 204
  patriarchal definitions of, 191
  pursuit of, 124
Freeman, Alice, 62
French Revolution, 75-76, 82, 101
Freud, Sigmund, 107
Friedan, Betty, 179
fulcrum of feminist theorization, 99

Gandhi, M.K., 112
Gangavane, Deepti, xix, 3, 5, 7, 10
Gārgī, 50, 63, 66, 68, 71
Gatens, Moira, xiii, 8, 21, 44, 77, 79-80, 87, 89, 193, 195
Geddes, Patrick, 25
gender
  biased language, 145
  egalitarianism, 61
  equal implications, 145
  equality, 190, 228
    arguments for, xvi
  idealist understanding of, 17
  inequality, 150, 153
    foundation of, 238
  justice, 153, 228
  lynchpin of, 156
  matrix of, 228
  neutral, xiii, 1, 9, 11, 13, 29, 85, 107, 169
    concepts, xiii
    education, 85
  neutrality, 23, 100, 107
  order, 6
  parity in education, 52
  pure identities of, 29
  regime(s), 5-6, 16, 24, 35, 147, 193
    hierarchical dimension of, 24
  related questions, 23
  social inequality of, 96
  specific *gurudhamas*, 65
  structured character of contemporary society, 147
gendered
  divide, 39
  embodiment, 23
  hierarchy, 65
  history, contexts of, 1
  identities, reproduction of, 156
  identity, 101
  point of view, 101
genderless
  customs, 155
  institutions, 155
generalized other, 127
genteel
  curiosity, 46
  women, company of, 77
Gilbert, Sandra, 98

Giles, E. Mary, 94-95
Gill, Preeti, 42, 66
Gilligan, Carol, xiii-xvii, xxi, 5, 9, 18-19, 106-07, 111-23, 125, 127-31, 133-42, 154, 158, 172, 175, 180-81, 196, 212, 224, 230, 233, 235, 239-40
Glazer, Sarah, 197
global
- division of labour, 184, 189
- feminism(s), xxii, 227, 239
- intersection between gender and labour, 191

globalization of motherhood, 185, 187, 196, 219, 237
Goddard, Angela, 13
Godwin, William, 74-75
Gokhale, P.P., 4
Golden Rule, 110
Goldwin, William, 75-76
good life, 113, 126-27, 129, 135
Gordon, Linda, 168, 175, 218
greater egalitarian intersections, 229
Greig, Alan, 168
Grimshaw, Jean, 5
growth of feminist interest, xviii
Gubar, Susan, 98
gurudhammas, 64

Haack, Susan, 1, 9, 17
Habermas, Jürgen, 22-23, 25, 35, 41-42, 50, 126-29, 134-35, 137-38, 190
Hartmann, Heidi, 176-77, 236
Hayes, Mary, 75
health of Indian women, 57
Hegel, G.W.F., 7, 188, 195, 198, 201, 207, 209, 213
- master–slave dialectic, 198

Heidegger, Martin, 1, 194, 230
Held, Virginia, 114, 122, 130, 133, 136
hermeneutic, xviii
Hermit, 92
heterogeneity of racial minorities, 214
hidden female nature, 27
hierarchical relationships among women, 223
Hindu Code Bill, 163
Hindu
- identity, 42
- Indian womanhood, 34
- law, 42
- metaphysics, ambit of, 68
- patriarchal
  - order, 72
  - practices, 44
- tradition, 69

history of
- patriarchal practices, 42
- philosophy, 13, 71, 100
- spirituality, 71
- tradition, liberalism of, 72

Hobbes, Thomas, 113, 115, 131, 133, 138, 191
hooks, bell, 98, 100
homogeneous Indian femininity, 33
Horkheimer, Max, 167
Horner, I.B., 37
Hornsby, Jennifer, 15
household(s), 39, 49, 55-56, 106,

114, 144, 156-58, 160, 166, 170
housewife, obsolescence of, 231
Hubbard, Elbert, 92-93
human
  being's identity, ambiguity of, 225
  differences, appreciation of, 151
  identity, analysis of, 26
  relationships, context of, 119
Hume, David, 131
Humphries, Jane, 176-77
Hypatia, xx, 92-94, 96-98
  and St. Teresa, legacy of, 96

ICWR, 169
ideal femininity, constitution of an, 34
ideal role-taking, 110, 112
Indian
  and Western women, divide between, 51
  culture as inimical to women, 62
  ethics, proponents of, 29
  femininity, forging of, 50
  feminism, xvii-xviii, 224
    legacy of, 224
  feminist(s), 28
    movement, 214
  middle-class women, 46
  nationalists, 90
  scholarship on
    feminism, xviii
    gender, xviii
  society, reorganization of, 37
  women
    as epitomes of chastity, 44
    health of, 57
    new domestic, 49
individual, 7
  freedom, implications of, 187
  Kohlbergian separateness of, 133
  self-determination, 189
individualism
  of existentialism, 128
  atomicity of, 212
individualist notion of
  freedom, 180
  self-determination, 182, 236
individuality, sharp boundaries of, 134
individualized concrete other, 135
inegalitarianism, forms of, 85
inequality,
  emerging structures of, 40
  existing structures of, 40
informal feminine work, 231
injustice in the family, 143
insights of
  care, 221
  freedom, 221
institutional care, notion of, 62
institutionalization of care-giving, 167
integration of care, xxi, 139
interdependence, xxi, 7, 106, 172, 176, 189, 192, 221, 241
interdependency, 132
interdependent, 192, 209, 219-20, 232, 235
  view of freedom, 212, 219
interdisciplinarity, xx
interdisciplinary, xiv, 22-23

International Monetary Fund (IMF), 37
interpersonal relationships, psychology of, 118
interrelatedness, 206
intersectionality, xiv, xx
intersubjective, 204, 209, 215, 222, 237
  freedom, 215
inter-subjectively, 135
inter-subjectivity, 199
interwoven hierarchical contexts, 235
Irigaray, Luce, 1-2, 5, 7-8, 11, 15, 19, 24, 26, 64, 92
is–ought, 108

Jacob, 174
Jacobson, 169
Jaggar, M. Alison, 7, 113, 136
Jasodā, 186, 208, 215-16, 219, 222-23, 229, 231, 234, 236, 239
Joel, Blaze, 229
John, E. Mary, 163-64, 217
Jones, William, 43
Joshi, Tarkateerta Laxmanshastri, 3
justice, xiii, xvi-xvii, xxi, 3-4, 18, 21, 82, 110, 112-13, 121, 126, 128-29, 135-37, 140, 142-46, 148-49, 151-52, 155-56, 158, 165, 178-79, 215, 219, 224, 228, 240
  domain of, 143
  ethics of, 136
  family as
    a domain of, 145
    an institution of, 141
  notion of, 18
  theory of, 144
Justice, Faith, 93
justification of interdependency, 132

Kabīr, 71
Kālī, goddess, 68
Kamal, Ram Sen, 43
Kametkar, Rachna, 3
Kant, Immanuel, 4, 7, 10-12, 98, 107, 101, 111-12, 128, 133, 138, 146, 152, 205, 221
Kantian spirit, 192
Kapur, Ratna, xviii, 235
karma, 56
  law of, 70
Kauṭilya, 1
Kauśika, 69, 71
Kelkar, Meena, xix, 3, 5, 7
Kerber, Linda, 139
King Janaka, 67-68
Kirk, G.S., 2
Kittay, Eva Feder, 123-24, 128, 140
Kneller, Jane, 10
Kohlberg, Lawrence, 7, 107-16, 127-29, 133-38, 142, 144
  foundational data, 111
  rights-based approach, 134
Korsmeyer, W. Carolyn, 73, 78-80
  progressive ideals, 91
Kosambi, Meera, 5, 47-48, 51-55, 57, 61, 73
Kristeva, Julia, 28
Kruks, Sonia, 193, 195, 199-200,

203-04, 209, 225

Lakshmibai, 50
labour, division of, 37
Lalita, K., 27, 34, 51, 62, 70, 185
language, 11-15, 24-26, 29
  force of, 11

legal punishment, fear of, 110
Lenin, V.I., 177
Leslie, I. Julia, 19, 50
liberal
  feminist attitude, 227
  freedom, atomistic logic of, 192
  individualism, assumption of, 160
  theory, pitfalls of, 142
liberated woman, normative ideal of, 193
lived experience(s), xiv-xv, 10-11, 91, 97, 101-02, 200, 203, 226
  dimension of, 10
  domain of, xv
  perspective of, xiv
local feminisms, xvii
Locke, John, 1-2, 78-80, 89, 100, 131
  notion of association of ideas, 100
logic of fairness, 119
Lord Kṛṣṇa, 186
Lundgren-Gothlin, Eva, 198
Luxemburg, Rosa, 177

Macaulay, Catherine, 81
MacIntyre, Alasdair, 125, 128
Mahābhārata, 67, 69
Maher, J.M., 185, 216
Mahila Seva Mandal, 62
mainstream
  feminism, 214
  feminist agendas, 224
Maitreyī, 63, 66, 71
male philosophical concepts, categories of, 9
manners, 77-78, 80, 82-83, 85, 88, 90, 132
Manu, laws of, 19, 41, 55-56, 110
Manu's Dharmaśāstras, 55
Manusmṛti, 41-42
Married Women's Property Act, 83
martial–mercantile character, 37
Marx, Karl, 160, 176-77, 191, 198
Marxism, 23
  significance of, 236
Marxist treatises on gender, 177
masculine emphasis on
  entitlement, 106
  impartiality, 106
masculinities, 170
masculinity, 10, 19, 34, 171, 196, 200
  and femininity, correlation between, 196
mass
  male migration, 170
  participation, 38
McConnell-Ginet, 13
Mean, Patterson Lindsey, 13
men,
  effeminization of, 77
  equal participation of, 155
Menon, Nivedita, 217

Merleau-Ponty, Maurice, 198
metrosexual, 171
 lifestyle, 171
 image of, 171
le Michelle, Doeuff, 195, 197, 199, 226
Midgley, Clare, 48, 86
Mies, Maria, xvii, xxi-xxii, 18, 180-84, 187-90, 192, 195, 198, 200, 208-10, 212, 214-15, 219, 222-23, 225, 234
Mill, James, 43, 44
Mill, John Stuart, 17, 44, 99, 143, 158
Miller, Nancy, 101
mind's eye, 2
Mīrābāī, 63, 69-71, 97-98
Miraftab, Faranak, 212
Mitchell, Juliet, 91
modern, 41, 50
 feminism, 63
  key themes of, 86
 natural law, 42
 patriarchy, 50
 world, political characteristics of, 35
modernity, xx, 24, 33-36, 39, 41, 44, 50-51, 59, 63, 75-76, 164, 208, 213
Mohanty, Chandra Talpade, xxii, 27, 190, 214, 223, 227, 232
Moi, Toril, xiv-xv, 10, 12, 14-17, 19-21, 25, 28, 99, 101-02, 195, 198, 201, 204, 207, 225-26, 241
Moitra, Shefali, xix
Mojab, Shahrzad, 213, 215
moral
 authority at home, 77
 education of children, 158
 interests of the women, 131
 intuition, universally shared, 138
 judgement, adequacy of, 108
 predicament, 115
 theorizing, 112
 thinking, basis of, 121
 reasoning
  of women, 118
  account of, 123
  philosophical justification of, 114
  significant differences in, 111
morality,
 definition of, 113
 practice of, 157
More, Hannah, 47, 73
motherhood, xvii, 20, 44-45, 60, 87-88, 90, 105-06, 141, 157, 161, 163, 178, 184-86, 196-97, 203, 207-08, 212, 218-19, 221, 234, 237
 by hire, 185
 choice of, 184
 commodification of, 222
 corporatization of, 234
 defence of, 88
 notion(s) of, 90, 197
 nurturing, 163
 professionalization of, 207
 republican, 87
 symbol of sacrificing, 186
 voluntary, 218
 women's right to choose, 184
Ms Magazine, 137
Muktabai, 63
Müller, Max, 43, 55

multiple patriarchies, 35, 50
Myers, Diana, 87
myth(s), 19, 181, 200, 205

Narayan, Uma, 131, 132
Nashrulla, Tasneem, 170
National Commission for Women in India, 169
National Tribal Policy (NTP), 174
Natarajan, Kanchana, 66, 72
nation, 45-46, 51, 53, 57, 60, 88-89, 105, 109, 209, 217
nationalism, xvi-xvii, 34, 49, 82, 132, 187
nationalist(s), 43, 45, 48, 51, 54, 56, 58
natural law, 41
naturalistic, 137
  fallacy, 108
negative freedom, 48, 189
  of possessive individualism, 215
Nehru, Prime Minister, 174
Ngozi Okonjo-Iweala, 228
Nicholson, Linda, 176
Nietzsche, Friedrich Wilhelm, 230
Nikhilananda, Swami, 66
non-European cult, cohesive communitarian images of, 212
non-feminist nationalist contemporaries, 51
non-interference, 115, 116
non-Western
  cultures, 86, 227, 233
  feminism, xxii
normative, xviii, 4, 16, 19, 22, 25-27, 30, 35, 39, 47, 50, 76, 87, 106-07, 125, 144, 181, 187, 192-93, 212
  feminist perspective, 27
  role, 169
norms, non-discriminatory choice of, 148
notion of
  a passive citizen, 10
  self, 121
nurture, xx-xxi, 16-17, 33, 47, 52, 77, 80, 105-06, 119, 158, 161-62, 171, 178, 186, 188
  path of, 171
Nussbaum, Martha, xviii, 227-28, 231

Okin, Moller Susan, xiii-xv, xvii, xxi, 5, 8, 9, 18, 21, 87, 113, 141-44, 146-47, 149-54, 156-58, 160, 162, 165, 170-72, 175, 178-84, 192, 215, 220-21, 223-28, 230, 232, 235, 240
oppression of
  women, 25
  working-class women, 222
other(s), 19, 22, 27-28, 45, 56, 68, 100, 120-21, 123, 129, 133, 137, 149, 154, 157, 176, 181, 188, 193, 195, 199, 201, 205-11, 219, 222, 224-25, 227, 229, 233-34, 236, 239, 241
  notion of recognizing, 127
  perspective of, 157
  woman, 187
  women, 187-88
otherness, 28-29, 188, 193-94

Paine, Thomas, 75-76
Pal, Parthapratim, 173
Panda, Pradeep Kumar, 170
parliamentary compulsion, 13
Parshley, H.M., xv
Pateman, Carol, 124
patriarchal, xiii, xvii, 5, 7, 11-12, 14-16, 18-21, 24, 26-27, 39-40, 42, 44-47, 49, 62, 64, 69, 72, 77, 79, 90, 99, 101, 106-07, 113-14, 120, 122-23, 125-26, 131, 141, 144, 149, 151, 159, 164, 168, 186, 191, 193-95, 197-98, 201, 206, 213, 229-30, 235
  feminine, xv
  ideal, reaffirmation of, 49
patriarchy, 5, 16, 21, 35, 44, 50, 52, 79, 90, 130, 236
patriotism, 73
Pauline doctrine, 93
Pendicini, Jameela, 173
personal
  and philosophical, xiv, 10, 102
  care-giving relationships, 159
perspectives of
  femininity, 100
  feminism, 100
  solidarity, 236
Petchesky, R.P., 217
phenomenological, xxii, 200
phenomenology, 199
  of oppression, 136
philosophical concepts, xiii, xv
Phule, Jotirao, 48-49, 63
  critical of Hinduism, 63
Phule, Savithribai, 53, 62-63, 188, 213
Piaget, Jean, 107
Pinnick, L. Cassadtra, 9
pioneering feminism, xiv
Plato('s), 1-4, 6-8, 9, 84, 94, 156, 201
  epistemological categories, 9
  moral categories, 9
Platonic, 114
poles of
  femininity, 90
  feminism, 90
political
  character of sympathy, 48
  practice of a feminist movement, 234
possibility of theorizing the concept woman, xiv
postcolonial, xiv, xvi-xix, xxi, 102, 105-07, 123, 142, 171, 180-82, 185-86, 199, 212, 214, 223
postconventional, 110, 128-29, 138
practical, 47
prakṛti, 67
precolonial, 186
preconventional, 109
preexisting British patriarchal attitudes, 46
prefeminist, 57, 81
  feminine dimension, 105
  phase(s), xvii, 125
pre-Socratean philosophers, 94
preferred destination for surrogacy, 217
premodern, 36-38, 40-41, 50, 63, 64, 72, 74, 123, 222
  women's intellectual history, 74

Price, Richard, 75, 82
Priestly, J.B., 76
primary care-giving, 117
private–public dichotomy, oppressiveness of, 154
private sphere(s), 35, 40, 46-47, 49, 79, 113-14, 124, 143, 158-60, 165, 190
privileged women, phenomenon of, 223
professional
  motherhood, 186
  woman, 84
progressive potential of femininity, 195
propagation of communitarian care, 187
psychoanalytic(al)
  feminism, 143
  feminists, 143
  sociological frames, 139
psychology of separateness, 115
public
  space(s), 62, 70, 84, 93
  sphere, 40, 49, 54, 71, 77, 81, 84, 86, 92, 94, 105, 124, 145, 151, 156, 158-59, 178, 190, 191, 213
    exploitation of women in, 86
puruṣa, 67
puruṣa–prakṛti, 7
puruṣārtha(s), 29

Qadeer, Imrana, 217

radical, 207
Rai, S. Amit, 131
Rāma, 6
Ramabai, xiv-xvii, xx, 8, 18, 30, 34, 51-63, 69, 72-74, 77, 83-86, 88-89, 91-92, 97-98, 100-101, 105-06, 124-26, 135, 141, 158, 178, 181, 188, 197, 213, 224, 240
Rāmāyaṇa, 6
Ranade, Ramabai, 48, 54
rational, 3, 14, 78, 80, 88-89, 110, 147, 150, 153
rationality, 148
Raven, J.E., 2
Rawls, John, xiii, xxi, 7, 18, 112, 114-15, 142, 144, 146-48, 150-54, 191, 209
Rawlsian liberalism, 153
reason, xiii, 3-4, 7-8, 78-81, 88, 100, 114
reconstructive, 30
relation between
  feminine and feminist perspective, 21
  feminism and philosophy, 8
  globalization and gender, 187
  Marxism and feminism, 236
relational, 121, 133, 178, 214, 220, 235, 238
  autonomy, 240
  freedom, 192, 239
  self, 180
relationality, 175
relationship(s), xiii, 2, 7-8, 18, 105, 112, 116, 118-19, 121-22, 127-28, 132-33, 135, 154, 191, 206, 216, 221-24, 239
  between feminist aspirations and feminine care, xix
  of care, perspective of, 224

reproductive
- choice, ideals of, 215
- freedom, 186, 191, 211, 214, 218, 220-21, 230, 234, 237, 239
  - exploitative dimension of, 211
  - narrow concept of, 239
  - notion of, 191
- rights, 182-83, 217
- technologies, 184, 214, 216

Republic, 4, 8
resisting colonial power, task of, 36
responsibility, narrower sphere of, 116
revolution, female manners, 80
revolutionary democracy, 75
Ṛgveda, 66
Richards, A.J. David, 130
rights, xiii, 23, 29, 74, 81, 83, 97, 107, 111, 117, 119-21, 128, 134, 142, 144, 152, 166, 169, 182, 210
- of women, defence of, 74

Roberts, E. Dorothy, 219
Roe vs Wade, 117, 140
Rorty, Richard, 1, 190
rotation of
- care-giving, 232
- care-taking, 232

Rousseau, Jean Jacques, xiii, 76-79, 87, 89
Roy, Kumkum, 45, 48, 50, 52, 54, 64-65, 83
Roy, Raja Rammohun, 45
Rubin, Gayle, 17, 176
rubric of nurture, 162
Ruddick, Sara, 130
"ruling caste", ideology of, 198
Ryle, Gilbert, 237, 241

Said, Edward, 43, 212
sāmānya dharma, 41
Sainath, P., 170
Śākta philosophy, 7
Sangari, Kumkum, 34-35, 37, 39-40, 43-44, 46-47, 51, 71
Sarma, D.S., 66
Sartre, Jean-Paul, xiii, xv, 10, 195, 198, 200
Sartre's analogous views, 195
Sartrean concepts, 195
satī, 45
- practice of, 55

Sītā, 6, 50, 112
Saul, Jennifer, 15
de Saussure, Ferdinand, 12, 14
Sāvitrī, 50
Sawarkar, 63
second wave, xiv, 27
- feminism, 143, 214
- mother of, 225

sectarianism of the Anglican Church, 56
self-determination, Mies's equation of 220
Self Employed Women's Association, 233
self, non-atomistic notion of, 128
Sen, Samita, 228
Seneca Falls agreement, 80
SEWA, 233
sex(es)
- difference(s), 145, 153, 155
- egalitarian relation between, 22
- equality of, 49

- linguistic patterns of, 15
- sexual, 37
  - division of labour, 5, 91, 147, 151, 154, 169, 190-91
  - hierarchy, 202
- sexuality, sublimation of, 95
- sexually oppressed women, 54
- Shah, A.B., 51
- Sharada Sadan, 58, 62
- Sheila, Malovany-Chevallier, xv, 210
- Shelly, Mary, 75
- Shinde, Tarabai, 63
- Showalter, Elaine, 27
- Shramjivikanchi Ekta Samiti, 40
- Simpson, Mark, 171
- Singh, Rahul, 170
- Sinha, Kounteya, 162
- situated, 217, 221
- situation, 95, 192, 200, 202-05, 207-08, 211, 222, 226
- Smith, K. Brian, 41
- social
  - concern, morality of, 142
  - contract, 110, 113
    - theories, 113
    - theorists, 220
  - division of labour, 236
  - equality, possibility of, 209
  - mobility, possibility of, 37
- solidarity, xxii, 51, 58, 61, 86, 129, 134-35, 178, 197, 198, 206, 208, 232-33, 235-38, 240
  - act of, 235
- Sophia's affective education, 77
- space for women, 67
- specialized publics, 167
- speculative logic, violence of, 28
- Spelman, V. Elizabeth, 195, 225-26
- spiritual egalitarianism, 70
- Spivak, Gayatri Chakravorty, xxii, 28, 184-85, 187, 229-30, 234
- Srivastava, V.K., 174
- Stanworth, Michelle, 216
- state, xxi, 10, 46, 81, 143, 153-54, 159-60, 162-64, 166-67, 170, 172-73, 176, 179-80, 182-83, 214-15, 222, 228, 233
- stereotypical notions of women's hysteria, 80
- *Strī Dharma Nīti*, 52-53, 57
- *strīdharma*, 42-43, 49
  - *paddhati*, 50
  - traditional conception of, 49
- *strī-svabhāva*, 49
- structural inequality, 228
- struggle
  - against patriarchy, 215
  - between feminism and femininity, 224
  - for women's self-reliance, 141
  - with male patriarchy, 79
- subject, 6, 11-12, 15, 18, 20, 26
- subordination and freedom, elements of, 241
- Sulabhā('s), 67-69, 71-72
  - logical victory, 68
- surrogacy, 182, 185, 187, 216
- *sva-dharma*, 41
- sympathy, 47-48, 86, 113, 129, 131, 135

- *tabula rasa*, 80

Tantra philosophy, 7
Taylor, Barbara, 74, 77-78, 82-84, 87-88, 143
tension between
 feminine and feminist dimension, 89
 feminine and feminist moments, xix
 feminine and feminist perspective, 240
 femininity and feminism, 33, 96, 143, 215
Teresa, St., xx, 92, 94, 96-98
Tharu, Susie, 27, 34, 51, 62, 70, 185
theorizing the concrete collective other, 239
*therigāthā*s, 64
thinking, non-Kohlbergian way of, 117
Thorne, Barrie, 141
Tilak, Lokmanya, 48, 52
tradition(s), xx, 7-8, 19, 22, 24, 27, 29, 33-36, 40-41, 50-51, 59, 63, 66-67, 72, 115, 128, 162, 212
traditional, 37, 112, 164
 femininity, oppressive dimension of, 113
 hierarchies of gender, 37
 Indian world-view, 41
 social hierarchies, 36
 world-views, 208
transcendence, typical male activities of, 208
truth, elementary silence of, 20
upper-caste woman, plight of, 56
utilitarian, 110
validating ground of feminist theory, 98
values
 of care, 240
 personal dimension of, 110
Vanita, Ruth, 67, 69, 71
Vedic
 dāsī, 45
 tradition, 66
Verma, Chapla, 64,
Verma, Roop Rekha, xviii, 19, 221
victims of
 inhuman practices, 47
 superstitious cultures, 227
Victorian
 feminists, 45
 norms of respectable dress, 131
Vidyalankar, 43
village economies, overhauling of, 38
violent absolutism, paradox of, 112
virtue ethics, 129
vision, 1-4, 6
Viswanathan, Gauri, 52
Vivekananda, Swami, 1, 45

Wallace, Kathleen, 219
Warnke, Georgia, 191
Warren, Karen, 97
weak constitutional guarantee, 173
Weir, Allison, 193, 199, 215
Wellmer, Albrecht, 222
Wellmer's Hegelian view, reversal of, 216

Western
- academic world, 30
- colonial men, 133
- ethical theories, 7
- ethics, 107
- feminism, xiv, xvi-xvii, 61, 84, 105, 132, 181, 214, 223-24, 226-27, 229, 239
  - canvas of, 181
  - characteristic of, 227
  - conceptual schemes of, xvii
- feminist(s), xiv, xxii, 27-28, 34, 208, 217, 223-24, 226-27, 229, 239
  - location, legitimacy of, 229
  - movement, 183, 218
  - movement, insights of, 62
  - perspective of reform, 164
  - theorization, 223
  - theory, 27
  - thought, xxii
- intellectual life, margins of, 84
- theory, dominance of, 235

white women's burden, 45

Widow Remarriage Act, 49

widow remarriage, legalization of, 60

willed ignorance, 46

Winfield, Richard, 36

Wittgenstein, Ludwig, 11-12

Wollstonecraft, Mary, xiii-xvii, xx, 5, 8, 18, 21, 34, 72-89, 91-92, 94, 96-98, 100-101, 105-06, 124-26, 132-33, 141, 143, 158, 178, 181, 197, 213, 224, 240

womanhood
- as a punishment for past *karma*, 56
- mythological paradigms of, 53
- universal models of, 91

women('s)
- agency of, 69
- aspirations of, 63
- cause, champion of, 52
- centric vocabulary, xiii
- development, elusive mystery of, 117
- difference, theoretical aspect of, 106
- different voice of, 105
- differentiating virtue of, 105
- distinctive mark of, 19
- education in India, 58
- education of, 45
- emancipation of, 218
- emancipation, sign of, 72
- equal participation of, 155
- equality, 106
- essentialization of, 43
- exclusion, 100
- greater incarceration of, 37
- headed households, 158, 168, 170
- heterogeneity, 197
- in Hinduism, subordinate position of, 51
- in the Anglican clergy, 59
- lived experience, 101
- lives, 18-19, 28
  - patriarchal aspects of, 126
- moral
  - development, 115
  - strength, 119
- movement, 164
  - in India, trajectory of, 162
- natural vocation of, 212

oppression, 24, 100
phenomenology of, 199
philosophical
  history, xx, 71
  sensitivity to, 17
philosophers, 19
  legacy of, xx
philosophy, traceable sources of, 64
protest against injustices of, 49
rights,
  materiality of, 74
  movement, 83, 97
saints of
  ancient India, 34
  medieval India, 34
space for, 67
traditional
  exclusion, 112
  roles of, 49
two roles, 52
Upaniṣad's complex attitude to, 66
upper-caste Indian, 61
violence against, 164
vulnerability of, 229

Wordsworth, William, 75
World Bank, 37, 212, 228
Wright, Richard, 198, 225
Yājñavalkya, 66, 68
Yong, Jim Kim, 229
Zack, Naomi, 159-60
Žižek, Slavoj, 19-20